Listening to the Word

FRED B. CRADDOCK

photo by Red Holsclaw

STUDIES IN HONOR OF
FRED B. CRADDOCK

GAIL R. O'DAY & THOMAS G. LONG
EDITORS

ABINGDON PRESS
Nashville

LISTENING TO THE WORD:
STUDIES IN HONOR OF FRED B. CRADDOCK

Copyright © 1993 by Abingdon Press

This book is printed on recycled, acid-free paper.

Library of Congress Cataloging-in-Publication Data

Listening to the word: studies in honor of Fred B. Craddock / Thomas
G. Long and Gail R. O'Day, editors.
    p. cm.
   Includes bibliographical references.
   ISBN 0-687-37062-0 (acid-free paper)
   1. Preaching. 2. Word of God (Theology) 3. Listening—Religious
aspects—Christianity. 4. Craddock, Fred B. I. Craddock, Fred B.
II. Long, Thomas G., 1946–   . III. O'Day, Gail R., 1954–
BV4211.2.L543   1993
251—dc20   92-38030
                                        CIP

93 94 95 96 97 98 99 00 01 02　—　10 9 8 7 6 5 4 3 2 1

MANUFACTURED IN THE UNITED STATES OF AMERICA

CONTENTS

89008

III. TURNING TO THE LISTENER

SELECTED BIBLIOGRAPHY OF FRED B. CRADDOCK

BOOKS

The Pre-Existence of Christ. Nashville: Abingdon Press, 1968.

As One Without Authority. Enid, Oklahoma: Phillips University Press, 1971. Reprint. Nashville: Abingdon Press, 1979.

Pentecost 3. Pentecost. Series B, with Leander Keck. Philadelphia: Fortress Press, 1976.

Overhearing the Gospel, Beecher Lectures for 1978. Nashville: Abingdon Press, 1978.

The Gospels. Nashville: Abingdon Press, 1981.

Epiphany 2. Proclamation, Series B, with Ernest W. Saunders. Philadelphia, Fortress Press, 1981.

John. In Knox Preaching Guides, John H. Hayes, ed. Atlanta: John Knox Press, 1982.

Preaching the New Common Lectionary (9 volumes) with John H. Hayes, Carl R. Holladay, and Gene M. Tucker. Nashville: Abingdon Press 1984–87.

Interpretation, Philippians: A Bible Commentary for Teaching and Preaching. James L. Mays, Patrick D. Miller, Paul J. Achtemeier, eds. Atlanta: John Knox Press, 1985.

Preaching. Nashville: Abingdon Press, 1985.

Interpretation, Luke: A Bible Commentary for Teaching and Preaching. James L. Mays, Patrick D. Miller, Paul J. Achtemeier, eds. Atlanta: John Knox Press, 1990.

ARTICLES AND CHAPTERS IN BOOKS

"All Things in Him," *New Testament Studies* 7 (October 1965): 78-80.

"The Poverty of Christ," *Interpretation* 22 (April 1968): 158-70.

"Recent New Testament Interpretation and Preaching," *Princeton Seminary Bulletin* 66 (October 1973): 76-82.

"The Gift of the Holy Spirit and the Nature of Man," *Encounter* 35 (Winter 1974): 23-26.

"Occasion-Text-Sermon: A Case Study," *Interpretation* 35 (January 1981): 59-71.

"The Commentary in the Service of the Sermon," *Interpretation* 36 (October 1982): 386-89.

"The Sermon and the Use of Scripture," *Theology Today* 42 (April 1985): 7-14.

"Preaching the Book of Revelation," *Interpretation* 40 (July 1986), 270-282.

"The Gospels as Literature," *Encounter* 49, no. 1: 19-35.

"Christian Unity and the New Testament: A Conversation Between Luke and John," *Mid-Stream* 37 (January 1988): 1-12.

"Worship Among Disciples: Literature and Practice," *The Disciples Theological Digest* 3, 1988: 5-22.

"The Gospel of Luke" in *Harper's One-Volume Commentary*, pp. 1010-43. New York: Harper & Row, 1988.

"Preaching and Aging," *Journal of Religion and Aging* 6, nos. 2-3: 153-62.

"Preaching to Corinthians," *Interpretation* 44 (April 1990): 158-68.

Listening to the Word

INTRODUCTION

The twelve essays in this book reflect the shape and direction of Fred B. Craddock's work. Beginning with his ground-breaking study, *As One Without Authority,* Craddock's work has concerned the double dimensions of *textuality* and *orality* in preaching. Craddock's work has emphasized the rhetorical dimension of biblical texts and the oral dimension of how the preacher communicates those texts in a sermon.

Focus on the rhetorical dimension of the biblical text includes attention to the literary details of the text and to the inseparable union of form and content. Craddock's work has shown how attention to textual detail is an essential part of sermon preparation. Attention to the rhetoric of the text provides the preacher with direction as he or she shapes the rhetoric of the sermon. A hallmark of Craddock's work has been the conviction that the rhetoric of the biblical text and the sermon should complement each other.

Focus on the oral dimension of communicating the biblical text includes attention to the preacher's ability to use the spoken word to create an imagistic world. Craddock's work has stressed the preacher's use of language and images to create a world in and through the sermon in which the listener is invited to dwell for a while. Craddock's focus on the oral dimension of preaching also includes attention to the listener's role in completing the meaning of the sermon.

This book is structured to reflect the dual concerns of rhetoric and orality. In part 1, "Turning to the Text," the focus is on the rhetorical dimension of the biblical text. Gail O'Day examines how the Bible can provide both warrants and metaphors for preaching instead of providing simply sermon ideas and content. Her essay highlights the interface between the language of Scripture and the language the contemporary church uses for its proclamation. Gene Tucker suggests that genre competence—awareness of the genre of a text, its type of literature, mood, tone, and perspective—is essential when preaching the Old Testament. Eugene Boring explores the ways in which the structure of the Gospel of Matthew facilitates the communication of what the First Evangelist has to say about righteousness. To that end, Boring studies Matthew's compositional techniques in the Gospel as a whole and the Sermon on the Mount in particular. Leander Keck undertakes a close reading of the rhetoric of Romans 5:1-11 in order to show how a full understanding of Paul's theology depends on careful observation of textual details. All four essays share a common interest in how biblical texts communicate the Word.

Part 2, "Turning to the Sermon," focuses on the bridge between textual work and the sermon, more particularly on the theological character of preaching itself. Eugene Lowry provides an overview of the "revolution" of sermonic shape initiated by Craddock's *As One Without Authority*. Lowry's central concern is assessing the current state of "narrative preaching." Richard Lischer calls for a reexamination of the relationship of tradition and experience in preaching. He suggests that the preacher should understand the language and imagery of the sermon as reflecting the world of the living church, and the purpose of such language as formative of community identity rather than primarily persuasive. Paul Scott Wilson contributes an essay about imagination in preaching in which he identifies some of the specific functions of imagination in the sermon. David Bartlett explores how the biblical text can shape the form of the sermon as well as its content and rhetorical purpose. Each essay in part 2 thus addresses how the preacher listens to the Word in the crafting of the sermon.

Part 3, "Turning to the Listener," focuses on the ways in which the sermon evokes the listener's active participation in the preaching moment. Thomas Long reviews the theological developments that led to listener-oriented preaching and assesses the strengths and weaknesses of this orientation. He proposes that listener-oriented preaching become more tightly wedded with ecclesiology. David Buttrick asks the question, Who is listening? As an answer to this question, he examines how communication theories can enhance the preacher's understanding of his or her listeners. Barbara Brown Taylor describes the importance of preaching "body language," of using vivid metaphors and images in sermons that can serve as a bridge between human experience and the transcendent reality of God. Henry Mitchell explores the ways in which the listener experiences the Word and strategies the preacher can employ to enhance that experience. Each essay in part 3 understands the listener's participation to be essential for the proclamation of the Word.

The title of this book, *Listening to the Word,* was chosen to convey the full breadth of Craddock's concerns. The preacher must listen to the Word in the biblical text in order to preach faithfully, but the preacher must also listen to the way words are at work and at play in the life of the congregation and the world in order to communicate the Word effectively. Similarly, the congregation listens to the Word in the sermon as well as to the "wordfullness" of their faith and life experiences. Listening has both textual and oral dimensions for Craddock, because the Word dwells in Scripture and "among us" (John 1:14).

Gail R. O'Day
Thomas G. Long

PART I
TURNING TO THE TEXT

CHAPTER ONE

TOWARD A BIBLICAL THEOLOGY OF PREACHING

Gail R. O'Day

THE LANGUAGE OF THE GOSPEL

In *As One Without Authority,* Fred Craddock drew attention to "the theology implicit in the method of communication."[1] The Bible, he wrote,

> is rich in forms of expression; poetry, saga, historical narrative, proverb, hymn, diary, biography, parable, personal correspondence, drama, myth, dialogue, and gospel, whereas most sermons, which seek to communicate the messages of that treasury of materials, are all essentially the same form. Why should . . . the multitude of needs in the congregation be brought together in one unvarying mold, and that copied from Greek rhetoricians of centuries ago? An unnecessary monotony results, but more profoundly, there is an inner conflict between the content of a sermon and its form.[2]

The issue Craddock raises, however, runs deeper than a call to reassess the forms and modes of contemporary preaching. It touches on the critical question of what language the church will speak in its proclamation of the gospel and how that language shapes the church's identity. Indeed, Craddock questions whether the use of "forms of Greek logical discourse did not of itself radically affect the nature of the message, the type of audience to which it would appeal, and eventually the constituency of the church."[3]

As One Without Authority anticipated the concerns of subsequent theologians. For example, George Lindbeck, in *The Nature of Doctrine*, directly addresses the church's crisis of language and identity.[4] He maintains that the challenge for the church is to learn (relearn) the language of our faith. "Just as an individual becomes human by learning a language, so he or she becomes a new creature through learning and interiorizing the language that speaks of Christ."[5] Instead of continuing to interpret the gospel story through the language and categories of the world, the church must now interpret the world through the language and categories of the gospel. We must become competent speakers of our own language again.[6]

The challenge to the church to know and speak its own language rests acutely on the preacher, because the preacher's work depends on language. The preacher has nothing but words for proclamation, and so which words and whose words are spoken is critical. Is the preacher's primary language the language of the gospel? Preachers readily turn to Scripture for the subject of sermons, but that is not enough. The Bible offers much more than the subject matter for preaching. Preachers also need to turn to Scripture for the decisive, shaping language of sermons. That does not mean simply that the words of Scripture should pepper one's sermons, but that the preacher embrace the entire *language world* of Scripture. That is, faithful sermons are molded by the language of our faith and tradition, so that reality is redescribed for us by Scripture. To preach the gospel, we must know and be shaped by the primary language of our faith. We must enter into the language of Scripture, listen to what and how that language speaks about God and our relationship to God. We must listen to how the Bible itself proclaims the gospel and allow our preaching to be reshaped by the Bible's preaching. Wendell Berry has written "Poetry can be written only because it has been written."[7] The truth of that seeming tautology applies to preaching also: The gospel can be preached only because it has been preached. That is, we can preach the gospel because we have heard it preached before. And the first place we heard it preached is in Scripture itself.

What I am proposing, then, is the beginning of a biblical theology of preaching. I want preachers to think about the Bible not as a source to be mined for its content, but as a model that can provide both warrants and metaphors for what preachers do. If we turn to the Bible as a model for preaching and not simply as a source, we will find ways to reinvigorate our preaching with the primary language of our faith.

I want to illustrate the interface between the primary language of faith and the proclamation of the church by focusing on one example from Scripture. The example I have chosen is the salvation oracle, a form characterized by its hope-filled words: "Fear not." The salvation oracle has its beginnings in Israel's core liturgy. It moved most powerfully into the community's proclamation in the exilic preaching of Second Isaiah. The proclamation of the early church in turn was shaped by this language learned from Israel's liturgy. The language of those who boldly proclaim "fear not" can reteach the church the primary language of faith and provide a generative paradigm for the theological and pastoral work of preaching.

A WORD OF HOPE SPOKEN IN THE FACE OF FEAR

The presence of the salvation oracle in Israel's liturgy testifies to the power of God's spoken word to offer hope in the face of fear. Israel's earliest experience of its God was of one who attends to the people's cries. The events of the Exodus begin this way: "I have heard their cry . . . I know their sufferings . . . I have come down to deliver them" (Exod. 3:7-8). This experience of God had a decisive influence on the development and shape of Israel's liturgy.[8] Our primary access to that liturgy is through the psalms. It usually comes as a surprise to contemporary Christians (especially if one judges by the selections of psalms in hymnals and lectionary readings) that a large number of the prayers and songs in the psalter are laments—individual and communal prayers of desperate longing, heart-wrenching brokenness, pained injustice. The laments confront God with startling candor, placing full-bodied pleas and petitions for help

19

and deliverance before God. These candid psalms of complaint and desperation have a regular home in Israel's liturgy. Israel knew that its worship had to allow for the honest articulation of pain and fear. Pain and fear must be handed over to God in disciplined, liberated speech if they are ever to be transformed.

What is most astonishing about the lament psalms is that the liturgy worked: The transformation of pain and fear did indeed take place. Psalms that begin as *plea* end as *praise*.[9] The lament psalms not only contain words of lament, petition, and complaint, but also words that reflect change, transformation, and hope. Reality does indeed seem to change for the petitioner from the beginning of the psalm to the end.

Psalm 13, for example, opens with a bitter, pained cry:

> How long, O LORD? Will you forget me forever?
>   How long will you hide your face from me?
> How long must I bear pain in my soul,
>   and have sorrow in my heart all day long?
> How long shall my enemy be exalted over me?
>
> Consider and answer me, O LORD my God!
>   Give light to my eyes, or I will sleep the sleep of death.
>   (Ps. 13:1-3)

The psalmist knows himself to be in constant pain and sorrow, threatened by enemies, absent from God's presence, standing on the verge of death. Yet, somehow, Psalm 13 does not end with such despairing, grief-filled words. Much to our surprise, the mood of this psalm changes to full-bodied praise:

> But I trusted in your steadfast love;
>   my heart shall rejoice in your salvation.
> I will sing to the LORD,
>   because he has dealt bountifully with me.
>   (Ps. 13:5-6)

The psalmist moves from complaint about a God who has abandoned him to praises of a God who has dealt bountifully with him. The psalmist does not praise a God who *will deal* bountifully with him, but a God who already *has dealt* bountifully with him. God's bountiful, gracious acts are as real to the psalmist in verse 6 as God's silence and seeming abandonment were in verses 1-3. What makes such a turnabout possible?

The most widely accepted explanation for this turnabout is that, within the context of the liturgy, the answer to the petitioner's plea has been given. At the moment in the liturgy when the complaint and plea have been placed before God, the priest, the leader of the liturgy, addresses the petitioner with a "salvation oracle."[10] This "salvation oracle," as it is called, assures the petitioner that his or her plea has been heard by God and that God's presence and help are sure. The leader of the liturgy speaks the words *fear not*, words that communicate the reassuring power of God's promise for life and deliverance.

The dynamic movement in Israel's liturgy, from the desperate plea of the petitioner to the world-transforming answer of God, is succinctly captured in a text from Lamentations:

> I called on your name, O LORD,
>   from the depths of the pit;
> you heard my plea, "Do not close your ear
>   to my cry for help, but give me relief!"
> You came near when I called on you;
>   you said, "Do not fear!"
>   (Lam. 3:55-57)

Into the midst of the pain and fear of the petitioner, a word of God enters to banish fear and to open the petitioner to new, courageous possibilities of life. The salvation oracle as such is not enough to explain the change from plea to praise in the lament psalms. That is, there is nothing magical about the speech form *per se*, but it is "the word which in these oracles came from God to the one petitioning and lamenting" that makes the change possible.[11] We all live in fear, waiting to be addressed in our need, and as Brueggemann has observed, "when we are decisively addressed by one with power and credibility, it does indeed change our world."[12] The word embodies the reality of God's fear-banishing presence and promise.

Three elements come together to create the cadences and language world of the salvation oracle in Israel's liturgy:

21

(1) Israel's core liturgy depends on the central dynamic of *speaking and being answered.* The language of the liturgy asserts that Israel can entrust its life to God in pained and demanding speech and that God will respond. Israel is not abandoned in its pain but is met by God's hope-filled presence.

(2) The response to Israel's spoken pain is also speech. Israel's speech is met with a decisive spoken word of God that *transforms despair to hope* and makes new life possible. The liturgy enacts the transforming power of God's word.

(3) Integral to these two affirmations about address and response is Israel's unshakable *refusal to take the world in fear.* The very fact of this liturgy in Israel's life evidences Israel's refusal to accept fear as the governing word in the world. Israel's liturgy insists that there is always another word more powerful than the language of fear. Israel's liturgy was a moment when the life-changing, grace-filled, fear-banishing word of God could be spoken and embraced.

PREACHING GOD'S PROMISES IN EXILE

The language of Israel's liturgy was not static. It did not remain frozen in the Book of Worship, locked inside the priest's study, but moved with the people of Israel into fresh situations of pain and need. The exile of 587 B.C.E. was one such situation of need. Through the preaching of Second Isaiah (Isaiah 40–55), the language of the liturgy was again given a chance to have its say.

The wonder of Second Isaiah's preaching to the exiles is that he found a way in the midst of grief, despair, and fear to preach a word of hope. There was no arguing about the data: Israel was indeed in exile and its life was irrevocably changed. The land; the people; the social, political, and religious institutions were all lost. Lost, too, was the courage to hope in God's promised future.

Israel in exile was convinced that it had no future: How could this community be expected to believe in the future when everywhere they turned there were more reasons for despair? They were literally trapped (so they thought), held by

22

circumstances seemingly beyond their control. This community knew themselves to have no other option than to accept their anguished fate. They would make the best of their life in exile in order to survive their daily existence in Babylonian captivity, because they knew that survival was the best they could hope for. Such a technique of accommodation and resignation, however, meant the end of hope, promise, and the joyous possibility of fullness of life. It was in such a despairing community, among such a grief-filled people, that Second Isaiah lived.

The preacher of Second Isaiah read the data differently from his fellow sufferers. He held firmly to the language of the liturgy that knows God as one who hears and delivers. He did not discount the pain and suffering of exiled Israel, but he knew that another way was possible for Israel because another way had been promised. Second Isaiah looked at his Babylonian captors and at the Babylonian customs to which his people were slowly but surely capitulating and was uncowed. Instead of hopelessness and resignation, Second Isaiah knew it was possible to speak of homecoming and the end of exile. The challenge for this poet and preacher was to enable other exiles to share in his vision, to reteach the language and cadences of hope.[13]

Second Isaiah used the salvation oracle from Israel's liturgy to reteach his fellow exiles their own language. Second Isaiah's theological genius and pastoral creativity were to appropriate the words *do not fear* from the liturgy of the temple and make them the stuff of proclamation. In the liturgy, the words of the oracle were not simply an urging for the petitioner to be fearless, a reminder that the petitioner should merely get tough and show what he or she is made of. Rather, in the moment when the salvation oracle is spoken, with the articulation of God's word of "fear not," *fear is removed.*[14] A real change is wrought by virtue of God's assuring word, evoking God's assuring presence. It is the moment of speaking that permits the petitioner to engage in a life of new possibilities.

Second Isaiah remembered this language of the liturgy and believed that the salvation oracle was an authentic embodiment of God's dealing with God's people. He believed that the spoken word of God's assurance could indeed banish fear and open up the present to the inbreaking of the future. In the proclamation of Second Isaiah, the cultic moment of decisive speaking is transformed into the *preaching moment of decisive speaking.*[15]

Second Isaiah has a "text," then, for his preaching to his community: the fear-banishing words from Israel's liturgy. With that text he preaches the good news. That text allows and empowers Second Isaiah to speak the language of faith into a situation of distress and need. I shall look briefly at one use of the salvation oracle in Second Isaiah's preaching, Isaiah 41:8-13 (cf. 41:14-16; 43:1-4, 5-7; and 44:1-5).

Isaiah 41:8-13 opens with words of direct address (vv. 8-9):[16]

> But you, Israel, my servant,
>   Jacob, whom I have chosen,
>   the offspring of Abraham, my friend;
> you whom I took from the ends of the earth;
>   and called from its farthest corners,
> saying to you, "You are my servant,
>   I have chosen you and not cast you off."

Fearful, heartbroken Israel stands before God, and God's words of address acknowledge Israel's presence. Israel understands itself in terms of judgment, exile, and despair; but God knows different names for Israel: my servant, my chosen one, the offspring of Abraham, my friend. Even if Israel has forgotten its name, God remembers who Israel really is and insists on that identity.

After the opening address, Second Isaiah's preaching pronounces the word of salvation: "Fear not." These words are spoken twice, at the beginning and end of the unit (vv. 10, 13) and are the words around which the community is to rally and out of which they are to act. The words *fear not* simultaneously recognize the reality of the community's situation and deny that situation ultimate power. On the one hand, behind the words *fear not* one can hear echoes of the community's fear of being abandoned by God, of being victims of enemy captors, of being powerless. The words *fear not* will be without force and meaning unless they arise out of and meet a situation of specific, concrete fear. On the other hand, one also hears God's inbreaking, transforming presence in these words. They announce that God's unfailing promises defeat the people's fears.

Second Isaiah provides homiletical support for the words "fear not" by looking backward and forward at Israel's life with God. After the first announcement of "fear not," Second Isaiah reminds Israel of what their God has already done for them:

> . . . for I am with you,
>   do not be afraid, for I am your God;
> I will strengthen you, I will help you,
>   I will uphold you with my victorious right hand. (v. 10)

God is with Israel and has undertaken powerful actions in their behalf: strengthened, helped, and upheld them. These actions are the story in which Israel moves. Second Isaiah then turns his eyes toward the future and announces what will happen as a result of the banishment of fear. Verses 11-12 promise that Israel's enemies will be rendered powerless. Second Isaiah invites his community to set aside its despairing, fear-filled vision of the future and to imagine instead what the future looks like when they trust God's promises. He invites them to replace their distorted story with God's faithful story.

The salvation oracle of Isaiah 41:8-13 ends in verse 13 with a repetition of the words of salvation, "Fear not, I have helped you." This repetition of the words *fear not* shows that the word of salvation is indeed the core of the promise of salvation. The repetition also shows that the community needs to hear these words again and again. We are timid, embedded creatures, and our fears reach deep into our being.

The words *fear not* of the salvation oracle resound as a persistent refrain in the preaching of Second Isaiah. The language of the liturgy provides a generative paradigm for all of Second Isaiah's preaching. The three elements noted earlier—the dynamic of speaking and being answered, speech that transforms, and a refusal to take the world in fear—are at the heart of Second Isaiah's preaching. Second Isaiah knows that the cries of Israel in exile have been heard by God and that the words *fear not* are God's transformative answer. This assurance is the ground of Second Isaiah's refusal to accept the seeming hopelessness of exile. He is therefore able to begin his preaching with the words:

> Comfort, O comfort my people,
>   says your God.
> Speak tenderly to Jerusalem,
>   and cry to her
> that she has served her term,
>   that her penalty is paid,
> that she has received from the LORD's hand
>   double for all her sins.
>
> (Isa. 40:1-2)

Second Isaiah addresses his people with a bold and sure word of comfort grounded in what God has already done. The term is *served,* the penalty *is paid,* Jerusalem *has received*—all past tense verbs reflecting the decisive change God has already wrought. Second Isaiah preached over and over again the decisive new reality already inaugurated by God. The cadences of Israel's liturgy redescribed the world for Second Isaiah, so that he was able to tell his people a story of courageous homecoming and a bold, new future. All of Isaiah 40–55 is an invitation into a world shaped by this transformative language.

Second Isaiah's preaching could not of itself make the Babylonian threat go away. His preaching could, however, invalidate the Babylonians' power by placing it in the context of God's promises. His preaching could remind his listeners how to speak the language that defines the world in terms of freedom and fullness of life and authorizes them to speak that language anew. Through his preaching he offered his community the sights and sounds of their authentic world, a world determined by God's "fear not" instead of by their fears. He knew that the only way to move his people out of despair and into the hope-filled future already initiated by God was to reassert God's promises over and over again, so that finally the language that shaped the life of the community would no longer be "I am afraid" but "do not fear."

THE "FEAR NOT" NEWS OF THE CHURCH

The fluidity of the language of Israel's liturgy did not end with Second Isaiah's use of that language in the exile. The early church adapted the language of Israel's core liturgy for its proclamation of the good news of Jesus Christ. The announcement of God's "fear not" and the announcement of the gospel of Jesus Christ are of a piece with each other.[17] Both speak a word that decisively changes the shape of the present and opens the way to a new future. The early church used the cadences of Israel's liturgy of *decisive speech, transformation,* and *refusal* in order to have its say about the new world inaugurated by the life, death, and resurrection of Jesus. It is therefore more than coincidental that within the Gospel accounts of Jesus' life, the announcements of the birth and resurrection of Jesus are cast in the language of the salvation oracle. The words *do not fear* (do not be afraid) provide the paradigm for the early church's proclamation of radical newness.

To a group of poor, struggling shepherds, working late into the night to keep their flocks in tow and thus somehow make ends meet, the Gospel of Luke records that this word came: "*Do not be afraid;* for see—I am bringing you good news of great joy for all the people: to you is born this day in the city of David a Savior, who is the Messiah, the Lord" (Luke 2:10-11; italics added).

Jesus' birth is made known to the shepherds through the angel's word of proclamation *(euangelidzomai).* Do not be afraid, the shepherds are told, for today your world has been changed by a decisive new beginning. The significance of Jesus' birth is not limited to the family group gathered around a manger in Bethlehem. The angel's proclaimed word makes clear that this event now opens the present and future of the shepherds to "great joy." The fears of the world have been transformed, and

27

the "old" language of faith provides the words to announce the new age.

Likewise, the Gospel of Matthew records that when the women come to Jesus' tomb "as the first day of the week was dawning" (28:1), they are greeted by an angel who announces: *"Do not be afraid;* I know that you are looking for Jesus who was crucified. He is not here; for he has been raised as he said" (Matt. 28:5-6; italics added). The words *He has been raised,* which constitute the core Easter proclamation of the church, are cast in the language of a salvation oracle. In the moment of the angel's speaking, fear is banished and the shape of the world is changed. The present and future are now to be governed by the hope-filled reality of the resurrection. The fearful power of death has been vanquished.

From manger to empty tomb, the word of assurance with which the followers of Jesus are greeted, is "do not be afraid." The language of Israel's core liturgy finds a new home in the proclamation of the Christmas and Easter promises of the church: Christ is born, Christ is risen; do not be afraid. The words *do not be afraid* provide language through which one can envision God's fresh future inaugurated by the coming of Christ.

The fullest example of the movement of the salvation oracle of Israel's liturgy into the preaching of the New Testament is found in the farewell discourse of the Gospel of John (chapters 14–17). Like Second Isaiah, the Fourth Evangelist transforms the cultic moment of decisive speaking into the preaching moment of decisive speaking.

The farewell discourse contains Jesus' words to his disciples prior to his crucifixion. They are words of assurance and comfort, spoken to meet the disciples' very real fears as they face the prospect of Jesus' death and departure. What is most remarkable about the farewell discourse is that even though it comes before the Passion in the flow of the Fourth Gospel narrative, it speaks from a clear post-resurrection perspective. That is, the words of hope, comfort, and assurance that Jesus offers his disciples are spoken from the certitude of the resurrection and the gift of the Spirit.[18] As in Second Isaiah, the disciples are encouraged to hand their fears over to the unfailing promises of God. Their present lives are thus transformed by the assurance of God's grace and support that will carry them into the future.

The preaching of the Johannine Jesus in the farewell discourse, like the preaching of Second Isaiah, simultaneously recognizes the reality of the community's fears and denies that situation ultimate power. The primary fear of Jesus' disciples was what their lives would be like in Jesus' absence. They had come to believe in Jesus as the source of their salvation (John 3:17), the agent of their redemption (1:29), the initiator of God's new creation (1:12-13), and the embodiment of God's love (3:16). Yet now Jesus told them it was time for him to leave them (13:31-35), and the disciples had to face the reality of life without him. Had all their hopes been misplaced? Were they to be abandoned by Jesus? Was God's love for them fickle? To these and other fears, the words of the farewell discourse provide a reply:

> "I will not leave you orphaned; I am coming to you.
> In a little while the world will no longer see me,
> but you will see me; because I live, you also will live."
> (John 14:18-19)
> "But because I have said these things to you, sorrow has filled your hearts. Nevertheless I tell you the truth: it is to your advantage that I go away, for if I do not go away, the Advocate will not come to you; but if I go, I will send him to you." (John 16:6-7)
> "So you have pain now, but I will see you again, and your hearts will rejoice, and no one will take your joy from you." (John 16:22)

These words of the Johannine Jesus meet the fears and despair of his disciples with comfort and assurance. The spoken word of the sure promise transforms the disciples' fear-filled present. Just as the preaching of Second Isaiah offered his listeners the assurance of homecoming from exile, the preaching of the

Johannine Jesus offers the assurance of his abiding presence even in times of seeming absence.

The three elements from Israel's liturgy that were carried forward into Second Isaiah's preaching are again present in the preaching of the farewell discourse: fears spoken and answered, speech that transforms the present reality, and a refusal to take the world in fear. The words of the farewell discourse attest to the power of the spoken word to dispel fear and open the way to a new world shaped by promise and fullness of life.

The connection between the preaching of Second Isaiah and the farewell discourse are most explicit in John 14:27: "Do not let your hearts be troubled, and do not let them be afraid." "Do not fear," the Johannine Jesus proclaims, and the possibility of a new world is created.

PREACHING AS SALVATION ORACLE

Like Second Isaiah and the preachers of the early church, those who are part of the contemporary church are children of Israel's liturgy. We are formed by a language that affirms the importance of speaking and being answered, of decisive speech that transforms, and of an unshakable refusal to allow fear to have dominance in the world. The words *fear not* are not simply vocabulary words but reflect a way of seeing the world in which God's hopes and promises, not our fears and weak resignation, are given prominence and credibility. Second Isaiah and the preachers of the early church viewed the world through Israel's transformative liturgy of hope and their proclamation was shaped, indeed engendered, by the language that bespoke that vision.

My urging, then, is that the salvation oracle provides a model for contemporary preaching just as it did for the preaching of Second Isaiah and the preachers of the early church. Joseph Sittler, in his final collection of essays, *Gravity and Grace*, makes an important distinction between an answer and a reply to fear.[19] He works at that distinction by imagining a nighttime scene between a mother and a child. The child awakes with a cry in the middle of the night, frightened by whatever shapes and sounds inhabit the nighttime space of children. The mother comes into the room to see what is wrong, and the child says, "I am afraid." The mother then goes through all the customary acts of looking under the bed and into the closet and tells the child that there is nothing there. But it is fear itself of which the child is really afraid, not simply the imagined goblin under the bed, and so the child's fear continues unabated until the mother says, "Do not be afraid; I am with you." With those words, the world is no longer a fearful place that the child must face alone, but the fearfulness of the night is transformed because the night is now inhabited by the mother's assurance and presence.[20]

The mother's words function for her child in the same way that the "fear not" oracle functioned in Second Isaiah's preaching and can function in ours. Sittler wisely points out that the mother's words are not a definitive *answer* to the child's fear, but they are a powerful and decisive *reply*. They cannot finally answer and solve the source of the child's fearfulness, but they can offer a reply to the child's fears that makes it possible for the child to move on.

My guess is that we often spend so much time despairing about our inability to offer a definitive answer to the fears of the world that we overlook the very real opportunity we have of offering a reply. As Sittler writes, "To the problem of evil there is, I think, no answer. But there are replies."[21] There are replies that enable us "to take, to contain, and to sustain faith in the midst of the valley of the shadow."[22]

The salvation oracle holds one key to those replies for the proclamation of the church. Preachers, therefore, need to become skilled in the liberating cadences of this language that offers the assurances of "fear not." There is no denying that the language of "I am/we are afraid" threatens to swallow up the language of "fear not" among contemporary Christians. Our fears may be more diffuse than those that immobilized Second Isaiah's community and our captors may be more well integrated into our own systems and conventions than the Babylonians that held Israel in exile, but the church still needs to hear and to speak a healing word against the tyranny of fear.

In our preaching, we are called to be like that mother sitting at the bedside of her child. We are called to announce God's "fear not" as a reply to the world's fears, even if we cannot answer for all that contributes to those fears. The words *fear not, do not be afraid* (in whatever particular form that core proclamation takes from week to week) provide fresh replies to situations of fear and give the church strength to believe again in God's promises and possibilities for the future. With that faith we can face our fears with new eyes. With the salvation oracle as a model, through our sermons we can create a world where it is possible to believe that "fear not" language has real power. The language of our faith tells a story of a world in which new life is possible. The language of the salvation oracle is one way to redescribe our lives in accordance with those possibilities.

CHAPTER TWO

READING AND PREACHING THE OLD TESTAMENT
Gene M. Tucker

I n his excellent introduction to method in biblical study, John Barton argues that the proper function of all methods of biblical criticism is to develop the literary competence of the reader and interpreter. Barton's particular notion of literary competence derives from modern structuralist linguistics: "Instead of saying simply that methods of biblical study aim to assist understanding of the text, we may say that they aim to make the student *competent in reading* biblical material."[1] Just as one must know the conventions of a language to comprehend it, so one must be aware of the conventions of literature to read it with competence. Examples from daily life abound. One who reads a spy novel as if it were an account of political events has only limited literary competence. Most readers of daily newspapers—hardly the best example of literature, to be sure—know the difference between news stories and editorials, and their sense of literary propriety is rightly offended when elements of the latter are introduced into the former. Moreover, reading competence entails awareness of the literary context of what one is reading. An anecdote or a scene in a novel is read quite differently from an otherwise similar narrative of events read in a textbook for a course on twentieth-century history.

READING THE OLD TESTAMENT

For more than a century, biblical scholarship has defined competent reading of the Old Testament mainly in terms of the

33

historical-critical method. A competent historical-critical reading involves awareness of the date, authorship, and historical circumstances of the text's origin and of its literary transmission. The contributions of such approaches have been and continue to be indispensable. Because the Old Testament is an ancient, oriental book, it encounters us as strange and alien, thus confronting us as a voice not our own and evoking critical reflection. Through the historical-critical method, readers, preachers, and congregations have made the acquaintance of ancient characters and have visualized themselves in ancient worlds. Moreover, the continuing investigation of the ancient manuscripts and languages enriches and improves translations of the Bible into modern tongues, an indispensable enterprise if the Bible is to be read at all.

But in recent years the problems and limitations of an exclusive reliance on historical-critical exegesis, particularly exegesis for preaching, have become increasingly apparent. Beyond the fact that the concerns of historical criticism and of communities of faith often have become estranged from each other—commonly expressed as the difference between what the text *meant* and what it *means*—the major problems are the following: (1) Historical-critical inquiry draws attention away from the text and to its context. Such inquiry is legitimate and important, to be sure, but more for the historian than the preacher. As a result, interpretation too often has become information *about* the text, its background and development. The more immediate interest of the preacher is the world created by the reading of the text rather than the world created by the historian, even by the preacher as historian. (2) Historical approaches have been driven by the assumption, often expressed but always implied, that there is a single "correct" meaning that can be abstracted from any given text. When different meanings are recognized, they are explained historically—for example, as the result of the development of the texts over time. (3) Closely related to this is the myth of historical objectivity, that the text will yield its univocal meaning to informed but disinterested inquiry.

It is obvious to all who have studied the Bible with

34

congregations—and that includes all preachers—that multiple and even contradictory readings of biblical texts are not only possible but actual. Every text of any significance is open to diverse readings. That is, read in diverse times and places—in distinct interpretive communities, to use Stanley Fish's term[2]—different meanings are evoked. In fact, those meanings are produced in the process of reading. That is why, in speaking of the theological authority of the Bible, it is more accurate to say that the word of God may come to expression in the reading and hearing of the text than to assert that the Bible *is* the word of God.

Thus one cannot, even by brute force, reduce a text to a single meaning. That does not mean, however, that the text is open to every possible meaning or that every reading is equally competent. If it is open to all possibilities, then one does not need a text. But what distinguishes a competent from an incompetent reading? There can be only one "rule": The competent reader struggles to pay close attention to the text itself in all its literary and linguistic details, and is aware of its full literary context. The text functions as a conversation partner in the search for and even the creation of meaning.

The best image I can think of for biblical interpretation is that of a conversation or a dialogue between two parties, in this case the text and the reader. Any good, serious conversation (by which I mean interesting, enlightening, or even disturbing) entails two factors: distance and intimacy. Distance refers to the recognition of the otherness of the partner in the dialogue. If two parties are to converse, each must know that the other's thoughts are not necessarily his or her thoughts, and each must respect the other's integrity. Otherwise each could only hear what was already in his or her mind. Part of the object of a good conversation is to bridge that distance, but it is never erased or ignored. There is little point in reading the Bible unless it is acknowledged as the other.

Likewise, any conversation presumes a measure of intimacy, at least that the partners have something in common. That common ground includes a language, and the conversation partners will need to identify with each other's language sufficiently to understand not only the surface expressions but the deeper meanings as well. We would not read the Bible if we did not presume a measure of identification with it, that it is our book.

Biblical interpretation is no more and no less than a disciplined and informed reading of the text, in its details and in its context. Moreover, the process does not—and need not—proceed without presuppositions. To be sure, one element of that disciplined reading is the struggle to hear the text on its own terms. Still, the process and the results of reading inevitably are guided by the interpreter's own experience, history, and social context, as well as the goal of the reading. Oppressed minorities, for example, have always gained understanding and strength through the interpretation of apocalyptic texts such as Daniel and Revelation. They know intuitively what historical scholars had to struggle to recognize: Such documents arose among oppressed minorities and expressed their hopes and dreams.

Individuality and experience therefore are by no means to be set aside in the process of interpretation. The reverse is true. What one is capable of understanding will be limited but also deepened by personal and social experience. It is difficult even to comprehend many of the individual complaint psalms which cry against impending death, or Ecclesiastes 12:1-8 which describes it, unless one has viewed death at close quarters. Those are not texts for children. Individuals who have experienced "the absence of God" will comprehend the book of Job in ways not available to those who have not.

When the importance of the reader and the reader's background is accepted, then the search for the "enduring significance," or the "eternal verities" of the text—the search for its single meaning—may be put aside. There are riches untold and almost infinite in individual texts. If one looks for the particularities, both preacher and congregation are continually enriched and renewed. New dimensions of the life of faith—its problems and potential—are opened up. One test for the competence of one's reading is to ask: "Have I seen something I did not see before, have I been confronted by the text as something different, perhaps even strange? Did I learn anything *from* the reading of text that I had not known before?" The "rules" of reading are transcended by the creative insight and interpretation of the reader. One of the factors that distinguishes a good painter is, of course, mastery of technique, including eye-hand coordination. But even more fundamental is quite simply the capacity to see—to recognize all kinds of details missed by ordinary folk, such as colors, shades of dark and light, and perspective. The competent reader is the one who has learned to see the details of the text, including the awareness of its literary context and the recognition of its genre.

There are some particular ways in which one's reading—like the artist's capacity to see—can be informed and disciplined. To return to the point with which we began: A particularly important dimension of reading competence is genre competence, something we take for granted in reading contemporary literature but requires thoughtful work when we read ancient and alien literature such as the Old Testament. Texts of different types invite different readings, and our presumptions about genre shape our reading. The reader is attentive not just to content but to the form and shape, the texture and mood, of the text.

An especially important point concerning the genre competence of the reader of the Old Testament concerns the long tradition that it is to be read as law. If one thinks of the Old Testament as a whole fundamentally as law, then one has made a theological judgment that is linked to and implies a literary judgment, a decision concerning genre of the whole will affect one's reading of its individual parts. The Hebrew word from which "law" derives, *torah*, is used in a variety of ways in the Old Testament, but its fundamental reference is to "instruction," or "teaching." To be sure, in many instances the Hebrew term applies to a formal body of authoritative instruction, as in "the book of the law," or to collections of individual laws, such as in Deuteronomy or Exodus. In Jewish tradition the term refers to the first part of the canon, the Pentateuch. But "law" is hardly the most accurate category for the Old Testament as a whole, and the interpretation of the Old Testament as such a genre has all too often led to distorted if not incompetent readings. If "law" is thought to be the overarching genre, then the reader tends to look for the "moral" of each text, to ask how it guides the reader's behavior.

The literature of the Old Testament consists of a great many different genres, including laws, collections of laws and instructions of various kinds. But law, however defined, is by no means the dominant or the most common genre, nor is it an appropriate overarching category for the whole. Mostly the Old Testament is narrative, stories of various kinds. Virtually everything from Genesis through II Kings, Chronicles and Ezra-Nehemiah—to name only the most extensive blocks of biblical literature—is narrative, the reporting and interpretation of events in more or less chronological order. "Narrative" is a broad generic category that includes a great many different specific genres. Some, such as the stories of Elisha, are legends; others, such as much of the material in the books of Kings and the account of the later life of David in II Samuel 9–20, are more like what we would call history. Still others, such as most of the accounts in Genesis 1–11, are stories of the primeval time that—from the perspective of the narrators and the readers—account for and interpret the present state of existence. To be sure, some Old Testament stories are didactic—that is, designed specifically to teach a point, to guide behavior, or to instruct. But that is the exception rather than the rule. If Old Testament narratives are designed to shape lives, it is at a level more fundamental than specific directions. The competent reader will therefore see the narrative shape of the whole and will work to understand the specific narrative genres of individual units.

READING COMPETENCE AND PREACHING

Preaching in particular is enriched by an awareness of the genre of the text—its type of literature, its mood, tone, and perspective. It has been taken more or less for granted that the *content* of the sermon should conform in some way to that of the text. Equally important is the relationship between the *form* of the text and that of the sermon. What mood, shape, genre, style, and tone is consistent with the text? Can the sermon, by being shaped by the literary features of the text, evoke the same response the text does? It is poor exegesis and bad theology, for example, to use the Beatitudes for moralistic talks. They are blessings, pronouncements of good news, and not laws or instructions for behavior.

One who preaches on Old Testament texts needs to know how to read narratives, and that requires a reading competence in which the preacher recognizes the genre of the story, its shape and function. Such a reading will begin with acknowledging that a narrative text is neither law nor theological propositions and will move on to understand its particular genre. Preaching narrative texts—stories of various kinds—is interesting and risky but consistent with good theology and good communication. It is consistent with good theology and communication because of the importance of indirection, openness, and the narrative form both of the Old Testament stories and of the Christian sermon. One of Fred Craddock's first books was *As One Without Authority*. In it he argued that preaching should not be a series of propositions, arrived at by deductive reasoning from generalities to application. Instead it should be inductive, the process of discovering meaning. The danger, of course, is that the answers are not so clear, and that the preacher as reader gives up some control over the message to the hearers. Biblical narrative is like that. It does not work with propositions but tells a story in which the hearer or reader can identify with more than one character in the story. Some biblical narratives, to be sure, contain explicit lessons, but in a great many cases the storytellers exercise remarkable restraint. They do not pass judgment on the characters or events, and thereby leave the reader to struggle with their meaning.

One can hardly do better with narrative texts than to tell the story. The retelling, the critical paraphrase, of biblical narratives requires attention to the literary genre, including the kind of plot, the characterization, the mood and tone, and the function of particular stories. The critical paraphrase is also enriched by an awareness of the contents and the genre of each story's context. Virtually all narratives in the Old Testament are parts of larger contexts. That may include the whole story that runs from Genesis through II Kings, from creation to the Babylonian exile. Certainly one does not need to summarize all of that story for a congregation each time one of its units is preached. How much one does depends upon the situation, the particular kind of story, and the aim of the sermon.

The preacher's sensitive attention to the genre of a narrative deepens the possibilities for the sermon. In presenting a reading of a narrative, one can recreate the perspective of the story itself; that is, bring the hearers into the world that the story creates, whether that world is "historical" or not. What are the characters faced with, their thoughts and motives, their wisdom and their folly? With whom are the readers invited to identify? How does the narrative set the boundaries between its world and the "real" world of the reader? That is fundamentally a literary perspective. Or one can present the perspective of the narrator. That approach could stress the historical dimensions and the history of the literature. When and where and why was the story written, and what issues did the writer and the audience face? At best one will be conversant with both those perspectives.

In any case, it is difficult to grasp the import of a narrative without knowing what kind it is. Some are historical, others didactic, others are legendary. Knowing the technical vocabulary is not as necessary as having a sense about the shape and purpose of different genres.

TWO OLD TESTAMENT NARRATIVES

The importance and value of reading and genre competence may be demonstrated through our reading of two texts from the book of Genesis. Attention to the internal details and the external relationships of Genesis 12:1-3 shows the value of considering the genre of a text in itself and in its broader literary context. With the analysis of Genesis 22:1-14 we will present a reading of a complex story whose genre is difficult to determine. The complexity of form as well as the depth of content in that story of the near sacrifice of Isaac evoke an equally troublesome range of meanings.

Genesis 12:1-3

The first verses of Genesis 12 contain a narrative of the simplest kind. Genesis 12:1-3 is a report of events from a theological perspective—the Lord is one of the characters. It also reports speech, fundamentally the speech of the Lord to Abram. The main genre of the divine speech is the pronouncement blessings, but there are instructions as well. This brief account of the call of Abram and the Lord's promise to him plays a decisive role not only in the book of Genesis but also in the entire story of ancient Israel. To examine these verses is to call attention to the importance of both genre and context, to show how a careful reading of these verses leads the reader to view the whole.

These verses that introduce the story of Abram/Abraham also introduce the patriarchal narrative as a whole. Moreover, the events recounted here are, in the framework of Genesis through II Kings, the pivot upon which history turns. That history concerns not just Israel but, ultimately, all of humankind, and it is a history of salvation.

Chapter 12 marks a change in both the subject matter of the book of Genesis and in literary genre. Genesis 1–11 is the primeval history, the account of beginnings, long ago and far away. Genesis 12–50 presents the stories of the ancestors of Israel through successive but linked narratives that focus upon family life. Genesis 12:1-3 in particular are the turning point in history, because up to this point the story had been a history of sin.[3] After the creation of the first pair (Gen. 2), there was the initial disobedience in the garden followed by its dire effects. Then follows a case of fratricide (Gen. 4:1-16), the disruption of the order of creation by the intermarriage of divine and human beings (Gen. 6:1-3), and eventually the corruption of the entire race leading to the flood (Gen. 6–9). Even after that new beginning, the story of the Tower of Babel reports how human hubris leads to the dispersion and division of people into different races and tongues (Gen. 11:1-11).

41

But a new history begins with the call of Abraham, identified as salvific by the promises of blessing that accompany the call. We can recognize at the outset what becomes more and more clear as the story unfolds—namely, that God sets history on a course that leads to blessing. The promise, reiterated to each succeeding patriarch, unfolds in three movements. The first is directed to Abram: "I will make of you a great nation, and I will bless you, and make your name great, so that you will be a blessing" (12:2). Although addressed to the patriarch himself, the blessing is a promise for the future, that one day his descendants would be a mighty and renowned nation. Implicit here and explicit elsewhere in the patriarchal traditions is the promise of progeny and land (12:7), both prerequisites for nationhood. The reader familiar with the preceding report will find the promise of a future for Abraham's progeny all the more remarkable, for Sarah was barren (Gen. 11:30). The second movement concerns God's solidarity with Abraham in his relations with others: "I will bless those who bless you and those who curse you I will curse" (12:3a). The final movement goes even further to include all peoples in the divine blessing expressed to this individual: "And in you all the families of the earth shall be blessed" (12:3b). There are no clear grammatical grounds for deciding whether the final verb in Genesis 12:3b should be read as reflexive ("shall bless themselves") or passive ("shall be blessed"). In either case, however, the universal goal of the divine blessing through the descendants of Abraham is clear.

Since the blessings reported here encompass the remainder of Genesis through Joshua, when the promise of land had been fulfilled, the implied addressees of this report are those who have experienced the fulfillment of the promises. The text possibly even implies the account of the rise of the monarchy reported in I and II Samuel in its mention of the "great nation." Built into this promise are two factors to temper any nationalistic pride that might arise. On the one hand, according to the genealogical scheme Abraham had other descendants besides Israel. On the other hand, the purpose of the blessing that eventfully comes to Israel is the blessing of all human families.

What follows this call? Abraham, like his parents (Gen. 11:31-32), was a migrant. Along with the narrator we know more than Abraham and Sarah knew, that they would never find a place they could call home, but would travel all their lives as resident aliens in a foreign land (Heb. 11:13-16). In the end, when Sarah dies, Abraham has to buy a burial place from one of the present legal owners of the land promised to his heirs (Gen. 23).

Abraham's obedient and courageous response to set out on such an adventure, especially in view of his advanced age (12:4), is an important dimension of the passage. However, the storyteller does not allow us to dwell too much on Abraham as an example of obedience. The divine promise of blessing is decisive. We are given here a picture of God's salvific purpose, and it finally is global in its direction and scope. In that context, Abraham's response in faith is a gift to the generations that follow.

Attention to the genre and literary details of Genesis 12:1-3 has revealed that it is, to be sure, a report of the vocation of Abraham and his faithful response, but more fundamentally it is an account of divine blessing. Moreover, the analysis has drawn the reader's attention to this report's key function in defining the longer narrative of which it is a part. All that follows in Genesis through Joshua may be read as the intricate account of how those blessings have their effects.

Genesis 22:1-14

The story of the binding or the near-sacrifice of Isaac is one of the most powerful, profound, and troubling of biblical stories. Although it is a carefully crafted story that follows a plot that moves through a climax to a clear resolution, it shows how biblical narratives can evoke more questions than answers. Moreover, with the characterization of a God who would threaten the life of an innocent child, the text is potentially subversive.

This story of Abraham and Isaac, momentous in and of itself, takes on particular theological meaning when read in its context as a whole. Abraham and Sarah had set out to a strange land with the promise that their descendants would become a great and powerful nation, possessing the land in which they and their immediate descendants would only be resident aliens. The report of the fulfillment of the promise begins in the book of Exodus and is not concluded until the books of Joshua and Judges. This pithy narrative is a chapter in the history of salvation—including Exodus, covenant on Sinai, wilderness wandering and settlement of Canaan. Awareness of this larger story heightens the drama—as if there were not drama enough already—for it is not only the life of a single child that is in jeopardy. The promised future is held captive to the outcome of the tale.

More directly, the immediate prelude to this chapter is the story of the birth of Isaac (Gen. 21:1-7). Long after the aged pair had given up hope for a son, and therefore for the fulfillment of the promise of descendants, Isaac was born to Sarah. His birth was a blessing in itself, but also the necessary first step in the fulfillment of the promise in Genesis 12:1-3.

The story begins with an explanation of what it is about: "God tested Abraham" (22:1). And as so often is the case in biblical narrative, the readers and hearers know more than the characters do. Abraham, not having been told that he is being tested, hears only the horrifying command to take Isaac to the land of Moriah and offer him as a burnt sacrifice. The narrator, who knows everything, gives the reader virtually no description but only action and dialogue, and that with great restraint.[4] There is no speculation on the emotions or feelings of the characters, but the language and pace lead the reader on. The repetition in the command, "Take your son, your only son Isaac, whom you love . . ." (22:2), stresses the deep affection and strong ties between father and son, as does the image of the father and son headed off on foot to the mountain with the instruments of death and the tools of sacrifice in their hands (22:6).

Although one may have heard or read the story many times, and knows how it turns out, to hear it again is to become engaged in its poignancy and power. Will the angel of the Lord arrive in time? The reader knows that it is a "test," but soon realizes also

44

that it is a matter of life and death. The question, "will Abraham pass the test?" (what the narrator had told us was the point) becomes less significant than the other one, "will Isaac live?" At the climax of the story both questions are answered at the same time. Abraham, who had never hesitated, is willing to obey, but God will not require the life of Isaac (22:10-12).

The story has evoked extensive reflection in the history of church and synagogue both because of the seriousness of the issues it considers and because of all that is left unsaid. When the boy asked the obvious question, "Where is the lamb for the burnt offering?" (22:7), Abraham's answer (22:8) was a foreshadowing of what would happen. But did he know, did he hope, or was the response a ruse to keep Isaac quiet, to end the conversation with a religious platitude? Why, we may ask but find no satisfying answer, did God need to test Abraham in the first place? At least in the story of God's testing Job the reader of the book is given the explanation of a contest between God and the satan.

It would be a serious mistake to reduce this rich narrative to a single point or meaning, for they are many. In one sense the genre of the story is etiology—an explanation of the origin—of a place and its name (22:14); that is its conclusion. But given the crisis that has just been resolved, that seems almost trivial. Like most of the narratives in Genesis 12–50, it is a family narrative, concerned with household events. More seriously, the story concerns the possibility of child sacrifice; that is the possibility that drives the plot. Since such practices were not unheard of in the surrounding cultures, it is tempting to consider that theme in the historical context, possibly at the level of the oral tradition behind the literature. The tale at least implies the question, Does our God require that we sacrifice our children? If that is the question (and it certainly is in the world created by the narrative), then the story's response is that failure to do so does not mean lack of faith, for our ancestor Abraham was willing but God did not—and will not—require it. The sacrifice of a ram will be sufficient.

Central to the story is the issue of faith, treated through the structure of this narrative genre. It is Abraham's faith that is tested, and in the process the biblical tradition leaves the reader

45

with a profound understanding of what faith is. It is not defined by means of a theological treatise or a set of propositions and readers are not left with admonitions to be faithful. Rather, the question is answered by means of example, with a story. But it is not a didactic tale that applies the lessons to the circumstances of the reader. It is the story of Abraham who trusted in God even when God appeared to be acting against his promise. Faith is like that. Faith is commitment, the directing of one's trust toward God. It entails the courage and risk of action. Whether Abraham knew that the God he worshiped would not require the life of his son we cannot know, for the narrator does not tell us. In this reading the story makes a powerful statement about human identity in relationship to God. But even that urgent and inspiring affirmation concerning faith is not the last word, the "meaning" of the story.

This is, of course, a ridiculous and utterly implausible story that makes no sense whatsoever in the modern world. No father in this enlightened age would think of sacrificing a child for his beliefs. Only primitive peoples would consider such a horrible idea. Is that true? Has there ever been a time when children did not die because of the faith of their parents? Every time people go to war it happens, and especially when it is a holy war. Thus the story of Abraham and Isaac, just as it presents the most powerful biblical statement about faith, also confronts the reader with the issue of the line between faith and fanaticism. Genesis 22 gives no explicit answer to the question. The story ends with the affirmation that the biblical God does not require such sacrifices, but it began and also concluded with the implication that the truly faithful are willing to lay the lives of their children before the object of their faith. Thus the story leaves the reader to struggle with that profound question.

Attention to the question of the story's genre, as well as other literary characteristics, has by no means resolved the issue of the "meaning" of this narrative. Rather, recognition of the elusiveness and the complexity of the genre has helped to inform a complex reading. Read at one level, Genesis 22:1-14 is an etiological tale explaining the name of a place ("So Abraham called that place 'The Lord will provide . . .' " vs. 14). In another sense it is an etiology concerning the possibility of child sacrifice. In yet another sense, and according to its own introductory framework, it is a story of a test (vs. 1), focusing on the faith of Abraham. But its narrative development draws attention to the threat to the life of the child Isaac, evoking the recognition that the question of faith has no simple answer. Like most of the other narratives in Genesis 12–50, it is a family story, here concerning father and son. But there is also that other character with whom the reader is left to struggle, the God who could initiate the horrible test.

READING AND INTERPRETING THE BOOK OF THE LAW: NEHEMIAH 8:1-12

Having argued at the outset that the Old Testament is more narrative than law, we conclude with a text about the law, Nehemiah 8:1-12. This text is particularly relevant to our topic because it deals directly with the question of reading and interpreting the Scriptures. It is not only the text's contents— what is said—that are instructive, but also its form and literary features—its genre. This is a particular kind of story concerning the law, set in something of a liturgical context, so recognition of genre and context inform and deepen our reading of a text concerning reading and interpretation.

Sermons based on texts from the Book of Nehemiah are rare in Christian worship. The book generally is regarded as a pedestrian account of events in the post-exilic period, perceived by most Protestants as a dull and legalistic age. An excellent recent study of the books of Ezra and Nehemiah was entitled *In an Age of Prose*.[5] These verses from Nehemiah 8 appear as the lectionary text for the Third Sunday After Epiphany in year C, undoubtedly because of its parallels with the Gospel lesson about Jesus interpreting the Scriptures in the synagogue in Nazareth.

Despite the virtual neglect of texts from Nehemiah in the life of the church, Nehemiah 8:1-12 is highly appropriate to a consideration of the process of reading, interpreting and preaching biblical texts. Our reading of this story in terms of its

47

literary features of genre, form, and content serves to provide a summary statement of our conclusions concerning reading and interpreting the Scriptures.

The meaning and even the implications of this account of the reading of the law seem rather simple and straightforward. Upon first reading, the story does not appear to be subtle or complicated—it is just what one might expect from a mundane book such as Nehemiah. The scene is easy to reconstruct, and it is not difficult for readers and hearers—especially if they are preachers or teachers—to identify with the characters in it. On the assigned day the people assembled in the Water Gate in Jerusalem to hear the reading of the law of Moses. Ezra is up front. All his assistants are arranged beside him while the people stand facing the leader. Differences of status and authority seem clear. Once everyone is assembled the reading can begin. Ezra will read, the assistants will interpret, and the people will listen and learn. Ezra—the leader, scribe, and priest—is standing on a podium. He needed a little box to stand on, made especially for the occasion. The people are standing there, looking up, patiently listening. Ezra read and the interpreters taught from early morning until noon, when they had to break for lunch.

Nehemiah 8:1-12 seems to be the perfect text to endorse the authority of texts, readers, and interpreters such as preachers. Those who want to stand where Ezra stood, or even with his assistants the interpreters, should read and study the Scriptures, and their congregations will listen with bated breath to their words from on high. The text appears to endorse a hierarchical if not an authoritarian and legalistic understanding of the community of faith in relationship to the Scriptures and interpreters of the Scriptures.

A closer reading reveals something else. To be sure, the account calls attention to the importance and power of readers and interpreters. But more than that, it helps to put those roles into context. And not so incidentally, the more closely we look at this story about the law, the more we hear about the importance of the story itself as well as the process of interpretation.

First of all, it is not Ezra and his assistants who take charge and stand in the center, but the people—the men, women, and children. Ezra did not call them; they called him. They gathered as one, and they *told Ezra* to go and get the book of the law and read it to them. Attention to the literary details reveals the importance of this point. One recent interpreter of this text counted thirteen references to the people in this story.[6] "The people" and "all the people" ring like a litany through the account.

The implication of this point is unmistakable. No one can stand to preach or to teach unless someone has asked them—called them—to do so, either explicitly or implicitly. The lesson of the text, remarkably, is not one of heroism, or of center stage, but of humility. Of interdependence, of the reader and interpreter of the law as part of and responsive to the community of faith. If that is a word of judgment on a hierarchical self-understanding, it is good news as well. The good news for interpreters in particular is that they are not and could not be alone, that they need not be heroes, that what they do is in and with a community of faith.

Reading and interpretation and understanding are profoundly corporate enterprises. They always take place within some interpretive community. What one says as a preacher or teacher is what one is in the process of learning with a congregation or community, in this case the broad community of those who want to understand and be faithful to the law, to the will of God. Recent anthropological studies of prophetic figures have demonstrated that their messages are shaped over time by their audiences, that communication is not a simple one-way street from speaker to hearer, but that there is a "feedback loop" in which the audience affects what a speaker says.[7] This is no less true for preachers than for prophets.

Second, the location of the ceremony in Nehemiah 8 is striking. As consideration of this text in its literary context reveals, a major concern of the books of Ezra and Nehemiah had been with the rebuilding of the Temple and the revival of the sacred rituals after the return of the exiles from Babylon. Now that the work is done, where do the people hold their service and carry out their interpretation of the will of God? Out in the city, in the public square before the Water Gate. Not in the new

Temple, or even its outer courts, but on a street corner, in the middle of the everyday political, legal, and economic life of the ordinary people. This has been a subtle theme of Ezra and Nehemiah all along, represented by the rebuilding of the walls of Jerusalem. Theirs is not a secular city. To the contrary, all of the city has been made sacred.

Third, the central object in this story is the book of the law of Moses, and the central activity is its interpretation. That little podium is not mainly to elevate Ezra, but to lift up the book that he holds in his hands. This emphasis on the written law means that divine revelation is available to all who can read or who can understand the reading. But without continual interpretation, translation, application, and even extension to new circumstances, the book becomes merely an icon, an object to venerate.

The story does concern the law, the Torah. Laws—at least in the broadest sense of the term—surround us from the day we are born to the day we die. Most of them have such power over us that we are unaware of them. They are customs, practices, prejudices, and patterns of thought that our cultures teach us. Law and community go hand in hand. We are shaped and influenced by the communities of which we become a part. The advantage of a written law—and tradition more broadly—is that it becomes available for analysis and interpretation, and even criticism. A book is an external basis by which to evaluate all the laws we take for granted.

Where is the good news in the reading of the law in the Water Gate? When the people first heard Ezra read the law they wept. Their reaction was sadness, fear, and implicitly, confession of sin and repentance. But the story does not end there. When the law was explained to them, it became a cause for rejoicing. What were they expecting? Condemnation of their behavior, judgment? What they finally experienced was forgiveness.

There is an important gap in the story. What did the interpreters say that turned the people's weeping into celebration? Except for one line, we are not told how the law became good news through its interpretation. I suspect it was because in the biblical tradition the law is *always* set in the framework of divine grace. The Decalogue begins: "I am the Lord your God who brought you out of the land of Egypt. [The summary of the story of salvation from slavery.] You shall have no other gods besides me." Moreover, the law is incomprehensible apart from a covenant in which God says, "I will be your God and you will be my people." In its context in the book of Nehemiah, this reading of the law is a prelude to the reestablishment of the covenant between God and people. Thus Ezra could send the people on their way with the words, "Do not be grieved, for the joy of the LORD is your strength" (Neh. 8:10). So the role of the scribal interpreter and the role of the priest are inseparable, at least according to this story. It is good to know that a scribal interpreter of the Scriptures can also be a priest, one who pronounces the divine blessing.

A close reading that is attentive to the story of the reading of the Scriptures takes the reader to the substance of the text: God has sanctified the city, and all the places where people live and work. The judging and redeeming word of God has been and continues to be revealed to those who read, interpret, and hear the text. That word comes to life in the reading and hearing of the text. There in the Water Gate, the people responded to the interpretation of the Scriptures by repenting and by rejoicing in the grace of God. Then they ate and drank together. That "book of the law" was not the word of God until it was brought out into the middle of the city, read, interpreted, and evoked a response by the people. That is the Old Testament's model for reading and preaching the Old Testament.

CHAPTER THREE

RHETORIC, RIGHTEOUSNESS, AND THE SERMON ON THE MOUNT

M. Eugene Boring

Compare these two lines:

"If it weren't for the fact that God is better to me than I deserve, I could be in a really bad situation like that person over there."

"There, but for the grace of God, go I."

Or these:

"I think I know whose woods these are."

"Whose woods these are, I think I know."

One might say that the pairs of sentences above have the same "what"; the only difference is their "how." And yet even this statement, though in the right direction, would not be entirely correct. In each instance, the second form is not merely a repackaging of the content of the first. "Meaning" is not confined to the content of a communication, with form as an optional means of delivering the content. Meaning is itself a product of form and content, a "how" as well as a "what." The parable of the sower not only means a different *thing* from the Twenty-third Psalm or the Lord's Prayer, but means in a different *way*. A Gospel, as narrative, means in a different way than an Epistle—or a sermon, including the Sermon on the Mount if it is considered apart from its narrative setting. How a text means as well as what it means is always the concern of the preacher who desires to release the meaning of a text for the congregation, which means—fearful thought—it is the concern of the preacher who dares to listen for the meaning of a text himself or herself.

None of this is news to those who preach. Every person whose

53

responsibility, dread, and delight it is to stand before the congregation and attempt to communicate the Christian message knows that "outline" (structure) is an important dimension of the meaning of the sermon. One can look over a sermon that has "worked" and discover that it was not only a matter of solid content, but that the elements were arranged so that they flowed toward the desired result, bearing the hearers along with its movement. Whether or not the movement of the sermon followed the listing of "points" one had constructed as the "outline," such an analysis will disclose that an effective sermon has a flow of its own, a movement leading the hearers through the process of coming to a conclusion, replacing a defective image, or entering into a new commitment. The "outline" that emerges from looking back over the sermon may bear little resemblance to the surface outline imposed on the material in advance, but will be a discovery of the sermon's actual rhetorical structure.

I use the word *rhetorical* advisedly. The Greek word for "flow" is ῥέω, *rheo;* the art of constructing and analyzing the "flow" of persuasive speech was called rhetoric. It is unfortunate that, in contrast to the noble and robust reputation of the ancient term—Augustine, for example, was a professional teacher of rhetoric—*rhetoric* in our time and place often connotes speech that is superficial, manipulative, or deceptive. Rhetoric is a matter of how what is said *works* on and in the hearer/reader. Preachers are interested in rhetoric because they are interested in what they say having an effect. Rhetoric is a matter of result, not of decoration. A rhetorical analysis of one's own sermons will look for the subsurface signals of order, arrangement, pattern, structure, and calculated repetitions that help the sermon to flow, and make the experience of hearing the sermon into a trip that moves the congregation toward its own encounter with the message of the biblical text.

Rhetorical structure is a fundamental factor in the effectiveness of our own speaking and writing—a matter of homiletics. But rhetorical structure is also a fundamental factor for the normative text on which our preaching is based, the Bible—a matter of exegesis. Thus "rhetorical criticism" is an (perhaps new) item to add to our kit of exegetical tools.[1]

In this article, I am interested in exploring the ways in which the structure of Matthew's Gospel facilitates the communication of what he has to say about righteousness. Matthew uses the vocabulary of *righteousness/justice* (both are translations of the same Greek word δικαιοσύνη) as much as all the other Gospels together.[2] Most of this vocabulary is peculiar to Matthew rather than derived from his sources. All the occurrences of *righteousness* in Matthew are redactional. In Jesus' first and greatest speech in Matthew, the Sermon on the Mount (Matt. 5:1–7:27), the Messiah explicates the meaning of the righteousness he has come to fulfill and demand. Five of Matthew's seven references to righteousness occur in this sermon. In the following, we will thus attend to discovering insights into Matthew's compositional techniques and the structure of his Gospel as a whole, with a view to applying them to an analysis of the setting of the Sermon on the Mount in the narrative and its internal structure.

Instead of imposing an outline on the Matthean text, I would like to discover the structure lying beneath the surface of the text itself, placed there by Matthew himself as his strategy of communication.[3] This is not done in the first place as an aid to *preaching* the text—though that may be useful later on—but as a way of *hearing* the text in its own terms. One of the ways of getting within hearing distance of the text is to inquire after its structure, to ask if there is a "strategy of communication built into the form of the text."[4]

Whoever believes that authentic preaching requires coming within understanding distance of the text at hand needs to investigate the macrostructure of the biblical book from which the text is taken. Spending some time at this task is not a matter of preparation for only one sermon, but the foundational spadework that supports the long-term project of authentic preaching. It is an expression of the first rule of responsible interpretation: context. Thus consideration of the rhetorical structure of the Sermon on the Mount must begin with an examination of the structure of the Gospel as a whole, in order to determine the meaning Matthew gives to the Sermon in the structure of his Gospel. Also, by examining the Gospel of

Matthew as a whole, we will gain a sense of Matthew as a composer, obtain a solid impression of the extent to which he imposes his own structure on traditional materials in order to reinterpret them, and gain some insight and confidence in looking at the Matthean structure of the Sermon on the Mount or any pericope within it.

I. THE STRUCTURE OF THE GOSPEL

A. External Factors

Matthew did not compose freely from his own imagination alone, but was influenced by factors in his tradition and situation. When one reads carefully through the Gospel as a whole in search of Matthew's "outline," one readily discovers he does have a number of structural points of contact with material external to his own text, as well as patterns and techniques he devised himself. We will deal with the external factors first. There are four possible external influences that could have been significant for the structure adopted or created by Matthew: (1) the actual history of the life of Jesus, (2) a pattern derived from the Hebrew Bible, (3) the lectionary and liturgical year, and (4) the Christian documents and traditions sacred to his community, usually called his "sources."

1. The Life of Jesus

Since the Gospel of Matthew, whatever else it is, is a story in which Jesus is the central character, one might readily suppose that the structure of the Gospel is determined by the chronological order of Jesus' life. A first glance at the order of the major elements of both Matthew and what must have been the actual order in the life of Jesus seems to confirm this: The order of birth, baptism, ministry, crucifixion, resurrection is the order of both the Gospel and of Jesus' actual life. While Jesus' life necessarily had to unfold in this particular chronological order, this is not the case with Matthew's narrative. Matthew could have *told* even these events in a different order, for example by the use of flashbacks, or by beginning at the end or the middle and having a character narrate to the reader what had happened before.[5] Nothing *must* come in the narrative at any particular place. The author, even if interested in recording only purely historical facts and placing them in the presumed historical order, need not structure his text to narrate them in that particular sequence. In fact, when we look more closely at Matthew, we see that Matthew's order is not oriented to the "real" order in the life of Jesus. We have all long ago learned that neither Matthew nor any other Gospel is historical or biographical in that sense.[6]

2. The Hebrew Bible

Until recently, the most widespread view among Bible scholars, still held by some first-rank exegetes, was that Matthew structured his Gospel into five "Books" analogous to the Jewish Pentateuch.[7]

Prologue	The Birth Narrative	1:1–2:23
Book I	Narrative	3:1–4:25
	Sermon on the Mount	5:1–7:27
	Concluding Formula	7:28-29
Book II	Narrative and Debates	8:1–9:35
	The Mission Discourse	9:36–10:42
	Concluding Formula	11:1
Book III	Narrative and Debates	11:2–12:50
	The Parable Discourse	13:1-52
	Concluding Formula	13:53
Book IV	Narrative and Debates	13:54–17:21
	Discourse on Church Discipline	17:22–18:35
	Concluding Formula	19:1
Book V	Narrative and Debates	19:2–22:46
	Eschatological Discourse	23:1–25:4
	Concluding Formula	26:1
Epilogue	The Passion and Resurrection	26:2–28:20

This is an attractive proposal, and its wide influence is understandable. Like the Pentateuch, Matthew is indeed an alternation of narrative and discourse. Strikingly, Matthew has gathered the teaching of Jesus into extended speeches, exactly five of which conclude with almost the same formula unique to Matthew, "Now when Jesus had finished saying these things . . ." (7:28; compare 11:1; 13:53; 19:1; 26:1).[8] And it seems clear that Matthew's story of Jesus is told with the Pentateuch's story of Moses as a model: the birth and early life of Jesus is reminiscent of the birth and early life of Moses (birth narrated, preservation from attempted murder by the wicked ruler, journey to Egypt, appointed by God to be the savior of his people, forty years/days testing in the wilderness, then ascending a mountain to teach the people of God). That Jesus' teaching the meaning of true righteousness in the Sermon on the Mount has some structural correspondence to Moses' revelation of the Law on Sinai is too neat a fit to be a coincidence on Matthew's part or creative imagination on the part of the modern interpreter. The issue of the Law and how to interpret it was clearly and understandably a central issue in Matthew's church; that the Christian message from/about Jesus should be communicated in a structure that portrayed Jesus as a Moses-like authoritative teacher of the Torah for the eschatological people of God would seem to be a brilliant move on Matthew's part. Yet the problems with seeing the above arrangement as *the* outline of Matthew have been increasingly noticed in recent years, such as the secondary status to which the birth story and the story of Jesus' crucifixion and resurrection must be relegated ("Prologue" and "Epilogue"), and the way the text must sometimes be forced to get exactly five great speeches.[9] The "Five Books" view of Matthew's structure is illuminating and has support from data both internal and external to the text, but we must look further before adopting it as *the* key to Matthew's structure.

3. The Lectionary and Liturgical Year

A different external factor, a "given" in Matthew's situation, figures in the proposal of Michael Goulder that Matthew's shape is determined by the Jewish lectionary.[10] Goulder's proposal—argued with a fascinating combination of erudition, charm, and no small amount of rhetorical skill—is that Matthew takes over the Gospel of Mark, the authoritative tradition in his community, and writes a creative midrash on it analogous to the way the author of Chronicles interpreted the books of Samuel and Kings. Matthew's outline for his midrashic composition was provided by the synagogue lectionary. Goulder's interpretation has not been widely accepted, being neglected especially in North America,[11] since it dispenses with Q as a source for Matthew and regards everything not found in Mark as product of Matthew's midrashic creativity. The lectionary pattern requires some forcing of the material, and in addition the Jewish lectionary is generally regarded as having been developed too late for Matthew to have made use of it. Nonetheless, that Goulder's study is full of relevatory insights makes clear that Matthew should be interpreted in relation to the context of the lectionary—which included traditional modes of Jewish thought—and brings home to the contemporary interpreter the importance of one's view of structure in interpreting the Gospel of Matthew—or any Gospel text.

4. Sacred Christian Documents and Traditions

An additional value of Goulder's work is that he focuses the attention of the contemporary interpreter on Matthew as an interpreter of his sources—although Goulder believes Matthew was working with only one source, the Gospel of Mark. Of the four possible external factors that might have influenced Matthew's structure, this last one is the most important. Matthew is not preeminently the interpreter of the life of Jesus, the Old Testament, or the lectionary (though the first two were certainly very important to him). As is the case with us latter-day interpreters, the impact of the original revelatory events is mediated to Matthew by the community and its sacred tradition and documents, especially Mark and Q. Matthew is therefore primarily the reinterpreter of the Christian texts and traditions that had become of central importance to his community. In this, the contemporary preacher may come to regard Matthew as a partner in the task of interpretation. The Gospel of Matthew is not an inert object to be subjected to our hermeneutical skill or lack of it, but represents the work of a fellow interpreter. Instead of regarding the Gospel of Matthew as a passive object to be interpreted, we might better think of his text as representing an active process of interpretation in which we are still involved, extending his hermeneutical work into our own present.

Matthew interprets the written texts Mark and Q, and the M traditions peculiar to his Gospel, some of which may have been written.[12] Matthew was not a solo writer working in splendid isolation, but was an interpreter of documents and traditions that had become important for his church and that he wished to reinterpret for a new situation.[13] Matthew's readers, too, were familiar with Mark and Q, and respected them as authoritative Christian tradition that had been read and heard for years in the Matthean church.

Thorough and illuminating studies exist elsewhere of how Matthew has used Mark and Q, but the contemporary interpreter can do no better than to work carefully through a synopsis twice, once following Mark as the lead text and noting every change of order and wording that Matthew makes, and once following the order of the pericopes common only to Luke and Matthew (roughly equal to Q), noting the differences in the Matthean and Lucan versions.[14] Of the numerous insights that dawn as a result of this kind of comparative study, two are important for the interpretation of the Sermon on the Mount. The first observation resulting from the process of observing how Matthew has handled his major source is that the Sermon on the Mount is the only one of Matthew's five major discourses that does not have a basis in Mark. In each of the other speeches, Matthew begins with the brief speech of Jesus already present in the Markan narrative and expands it with material from Q, M, and his own editorial creativity. But the Sermon on the Mount is entirely Matthew's own composition.[15] The very idea of including such a sermon in the story, corresponding in some way to Moses' delivery of the Law from the mountain, is Matthew's own rhetorical strategy. It is all the more important, then, to notice that it is the *first* speech of Jesus in Matthew,[16] and that it is perhaps the *longest* one.[17]

The second observation is that the Sermon comes at a key point in the structure created by Matthew in 1:1–12:21. Beginning at Matthew 12:22 (equal to Mark 3:22), Matthew adopts the Markan order of pericopes and never departs from it. Although Matthew often alters the Markan vocabulary, adds new material within and between Markan pericopes, and occasionally rearranges the material within pericopes, including unpacking some of Mark's intercalations, from Mark 3:22 on he never changes Mark's order. The first-century hearer/reader of Matthew's community would, from Matthew 12:22 on, feel that they were in familiar territory—but strangely familiar territory, for the familiar Markan story has now been placed in a new *structure,* and thereby given a new *meaning.* The importance of this for interpreting the Sermon on the Mount is that the Sermon comes in the early part of Matthew, the extensive section where Matthew is not following Mark's structure but is creating his own. By the time the hearer/reader gets to the once-familiar stories in the Markan order, he or she has been given a new structure within which to understand the old stories afresh.[18]

Matthew chose the conflict scene in Mark 3:22-30 as the point in the Markan story line toward which his own composition 1:1–12:21 builds. This scene (Matt. 12:22-32) portrays the explosive conflict ignited by the charge that Jesus has Beelzebul—namely, that he is in league with Satan and works by Satan's power (12:24, 26). This accusation, attributed by Matthew specifically to the Pharisees (Mark 4:22 "scribes"; Luke 11:15 "some") was very important to Matthew. Had members of his own community faced this charge from the emergent Pharisaic leadership? (Compare 10:25!) In any case, Matthew had obviously reflected deeply on this theological indictment, found in both his major sources, and has made it central to his own structure. Beginning with this scene in the Markan narrative, and using materials from Q, Mark, and the traditions of his own community, Matthew has composed an extensive "introduction," the entire first part of his narrative, that builds toward this key scene of conflict in Mark. Already this is a hint that conflict is the clue to the plot of Matthew's story. The story begins with the announcement of the advent of a new "King of the Jews" (1:1-25). But there is already a king representing the power of this age. In the conflict that necessarily results, the Jewish leaders side with the earthly ruler, while the king sent from God is worshiped by Gentiles (2:1-23). John the Baptist appears with the message of the near advent of God's kingdom, and Jesus begins his ministry only after being baptized by John, who is then arrested and imprisoned by the kingdom of this age (3:1–4:17). Jesus then calls his own disciples (4:18-22), who are witnesses to the word and works of the messianic king (4:23–9:35). The disciples are called to follow Jesus, who empowers and equips them for their mission representing him, but they still live in this age and are tempted to waver (9:36–11:1), as is John the Baptist himself (11:2-19). Thus the conflict continues (11:20–12:14), even though the new king is a servant figure who, when the Jews reject him, does not retaliate, but withdraws in order to bring salvation to the Gentiles (12:15-21). Using a chiastic pattern, Matthew has carefully arranged, rewritten, and expanded his traditional materials into a narrative with the following structure:

A. Jesus as Messianic King,
   Son of David and Son of God — 1:2-25
   B. Conflict with the Kingdom of This Age — 2:1-23
      C. John the Baptist — 3:1–4:17
         D. The Disciples Called — 4:18-22
            E. The Authority of the Messiah in
               Word and Deed — 4:23–9:35
         D1. The Disciples Authorized and Sent — 9:36–11:1
      C1. John the Baptist — 11:2-19
   B1. Conflict — 11:20–12:14
A1. The Servant King — 12:15-21

This narrative then attaches to the Markan story at 12:22 (equals Mark 3:22), and the conflict continues. Matthew's church, previous hearers/readers of Mark's Gospel and Q, have now been given a new framework for interpreting their sacred tradition. In this framework, Jesus himself as messianic king is central, filling not only the pivotal central section 4:23–9:35 (E), but the beginning and ending units that frame the entire section as well (A, A1). The Sermon on the Mount (chapters 5–7), along with Jesus' messianic deeds of power (chapters 8–9), forms the centerpiece of this structure, framed by the practically identical summary statements in 4:23 and 9:35.

B. Internal Factors

Just as the structure of an effective sermon may be best perceived after the fact, by analyzing the actual flow of a sermon we have already delivered, so also the best approach to Matthew's structure is to observe carefully the finished product with the question of structure in mind. What are the structural clues embedded in the story itself? Study of Matthew has so far yielded a long list.

1. Topical Collections

Matthew is "easy to outline." We all recognize that Matthew has an easily-remembered structure when we try to locate something in the Gospels, for it is often its Matthean location that comes first to mind. Matthew has organized much of his material topically. Parables are in chapter 13, miracles are in chapters 8–9, eschatology is in chapters 24–25, Beatitudes are in chapter 5, and the Lord's Prayer is in chapter 6 along with other teachings on prayer. It is clear that topical organization is a factor in Matthew's structure, but it cannot be *the* structural key, for it misses the flow of the narrative. Matthew is a story with movement, not a list of sayings and events arranged under topical heads.

2. Geographical Notices

Unlike John, which has Jesus commute regularly from Judea to Galilee, in Matthew Jesus makes only one trip to Jerusalem. In this regard Matthew is following the structure of his major source, Mark. Like Mark, Matthew can be divided into a two part outline, "Galilee" (chapters 1–18) and "Jerusalem" (chapters 20–28), with a brief transitional section occupied by the journey (chapters 19–20). Matthew has tightened the narrative connections in Mark and given notice each time the story changes location. Thus some scholars take geography to be the sole clue to Matthew's structure, arranging the outline into "First Galilean Ministry, Sermon on the Mount, Second Galilean Ministry," and so on.[19]

3. Summaries and Transitional Statements

Summaries and transitional statements are important structural considerations since they are mostly editorial. In addition to transitional statements made after major speeches (7:28; 11:1; 13:53; 19:1; 26:1), Matthew includes summaries of Jesus' preaching, teaching, and healing activity (4:13-17; 4:23-25, 9:35; 12:15-21). That some of these have structural significance is clear—for example, in the way 4:23 is repeated almost verbatim in 9:35, framing the Sermon on the Mount in chapters 5–7 ("the authority of the Messiah in word") and the collection of miracle and discipleship stories in chapters 8–9 ("the authority of the Messiah in deed").

4. Recurrent Phrases or Sentences

a. "From then Jesus began . . ."

It has long been noticed that the phrase "from that time Jesus began . . ." plus an infinitive expressing Jesus' communication of his message occurs at both 4:17 and 16:21, that the phrases are introduced by Matthew himself, and that each introduces a turning point in Jesus' ministry. This older view has recently been revived and amplified with supporting literary evidence, so that the book is divided into three major parts:[20]

I. The Presentation of Jesus (1:1–4:16)
II. The Ministry of Jesus to Israel and Israel's Repudiation of Jesus (4:17–16:20)
III. The Journey of Jesus to Jerusalem and His Suffering, Death, and Resurrection (16:21–28:20)

Not only are the phrases in 4:17 and 16:21 strikingly identical, the periods they introduce are characterized by a particular audience and message. Matthew 4:17–16:20 is a public message of announcement of the kingdom of God and call to repentance, while 16:21 is the private announcement to Jesus' disciples of the suffering, death, and vindication of the Son of Man. There is thus some agreement among Matthean scholars that 4:17 and 16:21 are important turning points in the structure of Matthew's story, but there is no consensus that this three-part division represents *the* outline of Matthew.[21]

b. Old Testament formula quotations

Matthew includes a number of "formula quotations," references to the Bible that are introduced by something like "All this took place to fulfill what had been spoken by the Lord through the prophet. . . ." One may count from ten to fourteen in all, depending on how rigidly one looks for the exact formula: 1:23; (2:6), 2:15, 2:18, 2:23; (3:3); 4:15-16; 8:17; 12:18-21; (13:14-15), 13:35; 21:5; (26:56); 27:9-10.[22] They are all from Matthew's hand, not from his sources, and are unevenly distributed throughout the Gospel. They seem sometimes to be placed at strategic locations in the narrative, such as 12:18-21, which comes at the precise point where Matthew concludes his own creative structuring of the narrative and begins unwaveringly to follow the Markan order. The formula quotations are very important for understanding Matthew's theology;[23] our interest here is their potential structural role in Matthew's composition.

c. Passion predictions

In a carefully structured segment of Mark, Jesus three times predicted his suffering, death, and resurrection (8:31; 9:31; 10:32-33). Matthew includes these same three Passion predictions in the corresponding locations (since this is the section in which he is following the Markan order exactly), and adds a fourth (26:2), but it is not clear that they serve the same structuring function as in Mark.

d. "When Jesus had finished these words . . ."

With reference to Matthew's structure as purportedly based on a typological adaptation of the pentateuchal pattern, we have already noticed the influence this repeated formula at the end of major speeches has played in the efforts to determine Matthew's outline. But apart from the validity of this typological approach, the five concluding or transitional statements do serve as internal structural clues to Matthew's structure.

5. Framing Devices, Ring Composition, Inclusions

Sometimes the repetition of phrases serves as a frame around a group of items to bind them into a unit. A good preacher may "set up" the hearer by intentionally using a particular phrase early in the sermon, so that when it occurs later, the hearer relates it to the first occurrence, binding the intervening material into a unit. We know that Matthew uses this kind of "ring composition," for example in 4:23 and 9:35. That this is not the literary critic's imagination is made clear by 11:4. "Tell John what you hear and see" looks back to chapters 5–7 ("hear") and chapters 8–9 ("see") and binds them into a unit, "the words and deeds of the Messiah." Matthew has changed Q here to get this pair. This is a clear example of framing, and demonstrates that Matthew intentionally used this rhetorical device.

Like an elegant "periodic" sentence in the old style of composition, Matthew sometimes arranges his material to return to an introductory theme or phrase, "rounding off" the thought or section by coming back around to the beginning. The theme of "God-with-us" brackets the entire Gospel, occurring in key beginning and ending statements (1:23 and 28:20). "Law and the prophets" is an inclusio-formula that binds together a major section of the Sermon on the Mount (5:17 and 7:12).

6. Chiastic Structure

Some scholars have seen in Matthew an elaboration of this framing technique in which the entire section, and not just beginning and ending, form a series of corresponding frames in the pattern ABCDEFE¹D¹C¹B¹A¹. Both Peter F. Ellis and C. H. Lohr see the entire Gospel arranged according to this chiastic structure, an arrangement correlated to the "Five Books" scheme discussed above:[24]

A	1-4	Birth and beginnings	Narrative
B	5-7	Blessings, entering the kingdom	Discourse
C	8-9	Authority and invitation	Narrative
D	10	Mission discourse	Discourse
E	11-12	Rejection by this generation	Narrative
F	13	Parables of the kingdom	Discourse
E1	14-17	Acknowledgment by disciples	Narrative
D1	18	Community discourse	Discourse
C1	19-22	Authority and invitation	Narrative
B1	23-25	Woes, coming of the kingdom	Discourse
A1	26-28	Death and rebirth	Narrative

The neatness of such charts is beguiling, and although they do not fit the text exactly, the general pattern does not seem to be accidental, even if it is not *the* key to Matthean structure. The five discourses do seem to be arranged in a roughly chiastic pattern.[25] The Sermon on the Mount (5:1–7:21) and the last discourse (23:1–25:4) correspond: blessings and woes, entering the kingdom and the coming of the kingdom. Chapters 10 and 18 are a pair: sending out the missionaries and receiving the little ones, and both deal with apostolic authority. In this arrangement, chapter 13 becomes the central core: the centrality of the kingdom of God and its relation to the church as a *corpus mixtum,* a mixed bag in the present to be sorted out only by God at the eschaton. This corresponds to a central tenet of Matthean theology.

7. Triadic Patterns

The recent work of W. D. Davies and Dale C. Allison, Jr. has brought to light another striking aspect of the structuring hand of Matthew, namely his propensity to compose in triads. The narrative power of triadic structure in storytelling has long been noted—how many stories about "The Three . . ." do you know?

Matthew, too, has structured much of his own composition in a triadic pattern. The opening line, which functions as a title, contains three names (Jesus, David, Abraham). This is followed by a genealogy explicitly and somewhat artificially structured in three sections. In Davies and Allison's analysis, each of the remaining stories prior to the Sermon on the Mount falls naturally into three sections:[26]

I. The Conception and Infancy of Jesus
   A. The virginal conception (1:18-25)
   B. The visit of the magi (2:1-12)
   C. The infants and Herod (2:13-23)[27]
II. John the Baptist and Jesus
   A. John introduced and described (3:1-6)
   B. John's words (3:7-12)
   C. John baptizes Jesus (3:13-17)
III. The Beginning of Jesus' Ministry
   A. The (three-fold!) temptation (4:1-11)
   B. The return to Galilee (4:12-17)
   C. The calling of four disciples (4:18-22)

Then comes the Sermon on the Mount, in which triadic structure is fundamental (see below). Following the Sermon on the Mount is a collection of ten miracles, 8:1–9:38. But Allison and Davies point out that though there are ten miracles, there are nine miracle *stories,* arranged in groups of three.[28] That triadic structure is a part of Matthew's own compositional technique is apparent from two additional striking facts documented by Davies and Allison: (1) When Matthew takes over and expands a Markan speech, the section derived from the source is not triadic, but Matthew's additions are structured in tripartite units. This is clearly seen in both the Matthean additions to the Markan collection of parables (Mark 4 parallels Matthew 13) and to the Markan eschatological discourse (Mark 13 parallels Matthew 24–25). (2) The triadic structure is very carefully worked out in the early part of the Gospel where Matthew is creatively composing, but disappears as soon as Matthew begins to follow the Markan order at Matthew 12:22

(Mark 3:22), except, as noted, for the Matthean *additions* to the Markan speeches.

8. Narrative Rhetoric

The fundamental insight about Matthew's structure is that it is a narrative, a story. The Gospel is not a collection of texts arranged topically, structured by whatever obvious or subtle pattern, but a connected story that moves from Abraham in its first sentence to the end of the age in the last, with Jesus the Messiah as the primary character. This means that the Gospel (as narrative) was an *in*direct communication already to the ancient reader, and is doubly so to the modern reader.[29]

C. Matthew as Composer

We may now present a summary of the insights derived from a study of Matthew's structure as a whole relevant to interpreting the Sermon on the Mount:

1. Matthew is a composer who has structured his narrative for rhetorical effect, not merely a collector or editor. A major hermeneutical method of Matthew is that of arrangement.

2. Matthew's structure is not obvious. He has no "first," "second," and "third." While there are numerous rhetorical patterns and techniques, they do not all function at the same level. It is thus not possible to divide the Matthean narrative into one linear, flat-surface arrangement that represents *the* outline of the Gospel of Matthew. Theoretically, this lack of a conspicuously visible structure could mean that he has no unified outline at all, but is careless or simply rambles. Closer examination of how the rhetorical structures function, however, points to Matthew as a skilled communicator who does not make his outline obvious.

3. That Matthew's structure is not neatly meticulous, obvious, or architectonically consistent is also because he is not composing *ex nihilo,* but is interpreting a tradition and sources which he has treated with both respect and freedom. He made structural changes that seem drastic (not to speak of changes of content),

yet also retained elements that were not particularly meaningful to him, because they are part of his tradition which he does not abandon lightly.

4. Matthew has composed a narrative into which speeches are inserted at crucial points. The Gospel of Matthew is not a collection of speeches connected by narrative. The narrative is primary. The Sermon on the Mount cannot be interpreted apart from its setting in Matthew's narrative "sermon"-story about Jesus, which is his Gospel as a whole.[30] Jesus as proclaimed by Matthew in his Gospel as a whole precedes Jesus the proclaimer of ethics in the Sermon on the Mount. Here we gain a valuable insight into interpreting anything in the Sermon on the Mount. We cannot understand it as Matthew presents it to us if we take it as discursive statements, abstract principles, wise sayings, or commands of Jesus. It is not a self-contained entity, but is embedded in the story of God's act in Jesus.[31]

Jesus' story is a segment of an ongoing story. The story of Jesus represents *God's* saving act. Thus what Jesus says in Matthew 5–7 is embedded in the story of what God has already done in Jesus. This is analogous to the covenant Torah given on Sinai being embedded in the Pentateuchal narrative. Neither the imperatives of the Book of the Covenant nor even the Ten Commandments can be understood if they are abstracted from the story of the saving history.

II. THE RHETORICAL STRUCTURE OF
THE SERMON ON THE MOUNT

We may now see why it is hermeneutically important to recognize that the structure of the Sermon on the Mount is Matthew's structure, not Jesus'.[32] Every perceptive reader who has asked the historical question about this "sermon" has noticed how difficult it is to imagine the Sermon as a discourse the historical Jesus actually delivered in this form. The difficulty of trying to imagine it as a sermon actually preached by Jesus is evident from every Hollywood version which attempts to have Jesus effectively recite Matthew 5–7 and to have the listeners look suitably impressed. The variety of materials and abrupt transitions show that the Sermon on the Mount is not an actual sermon, but a collection of traditional materials rhetorically arranged into an effective literary pattern. Real people on a 30 C.E. Galilean hillside would hardly sit still for it, and they would not understand it, unless they already shared the Christology of the post–Easter Matthean community. On the other hand, the Matthean hearers/readers are attentive because they know who Jesus is from the narrative, and because they recognize that each of these sayings is part of the distilled essence of Jesus' teaching, many of which they have repeatedly heard in the liturgy of their church as Q and other traditions regularly read in the congregational worship. They will read/hear the Sermon as part of Matthew's restructuring and reinterpretation of their sacred tradition, the story of Jesus.

Matthew and his church had long been familiar with a sermonic structure in the opening section of Q, roughly identical with the "Sermon on the Plain" in Luke 6:20-49. Examination of the parallel material in a synopsis reveals that Matthew takes over all the material in the Q sermon, beginning with the Beatitudes (5:1-12) and ending with the House Built on the Rock (7:24-27), and keeps all the intervening materials in exactly the same order except for one small but significant exception.[33] Matthew slightly rearranges the sayings in the Q section "On the Love of One's Enemies" now preserved in Luke 6:27-36. He extracts verses 27-29 and constructs a separate unit from it, reformulating it into one of his "antitheses," Matthew 5:38-42. This makes six Antitheses, corresponding to Matthew's structuring in triads. That Matthew thinks of two pairs of three Antitheses is clear not only because he has reformulated his Q material in order to obtain six, but also by his beginning the second triad with the conjunction "again" in 5:33. The other significant result of Matthew's rearrangement of this one pericope is to relocate the Q text found in Luke 6:31 and make it the conclusion of the extensive didactic core of the Sermon at 7:12, at the same time adding his characteristic phrase "law and prophets" to make an inclusion with 5:17, the beginning of the didactic core of the Sermon. Matthew's original hearers/readers acquainted with Q would recognize the familiar sermonic summary of Jesus' teaching, but would hear it in a new way because of its new narrative setting and modified form.

If W. D. Davies' hypothesis is correct, Matthew's hearers would also recognize another pattern in Matthew's restructured Sermon.[34] A familiar rabbinic saying attributed to Simon the Just affirmed, "By three things the world is sustained: by the law, by the Temple service, and by deeds of loving kindness."[35] The Christian reformulation of these "Three Pillars of Judaism" would have been recognized in the Sermon by those familiar with the pattern, since 5:17-48 deals with the Law, 6:1-18 is concerned with worship and religious practice, and 6:19–7:12 deals with social relationships and action. Matthew has added all of the material in 6:1-34 to the Q sermon in order to get this pattern. Again, this is not to say that this three-part outline is *the* outline of the Sermon on the Mount, but that the structure created by Matthew would make contact with this pattern from the hearers' cultural context and evoke the kind of associations Matthew wants his hearers/readers to think about—the message of Jesus as the fulfillment of the Law and the revelation of the ultimate will of God. Thus the structure Matthew has devised by his reformulation of Q would call forth in the minds of his hearers contacts with both the traditional Christian sermon in Q and the traditional synagogue pattern, and fuse them into a new unity set forth by the Jesus in Matthew's story, the Jesus who came not to destroy the Law but to fulfill it.

Within this modified structure, Matthew makes additional rhetorical moves. First, he introduces the theme of righteousness/justice and weaves it into the structure of the Sermon. Even a casual reading of the Sermon reveals that the theme of righteousness/justice dominates the content, as signaled by the occurrence of the words "righteous" and "righteousness" (5:6, 10, 20, 45; 6:1, 33). None of these was in Matthew's source; all are introduced editorially, with striking results. The Q sermon had already made the indicatives of the Beatitudes the foundation for the imperatives in the rest of the Sermon.[36] But the Q sermon had not mentioned "righteousness." Matthew makes righteousness a constituent element of the foundational pronouncements of the Beatitudes (5:5, 10); declares programatically that the disciples' righteousness must exceed Pharisaic and scribal righteousness (5:20); subsumes all exercise of piety, service, and worship under the heading of "righteousness;" (6:1); and virtually identifies the traditional key themes of Jesus' preaching, the kingdom of God,[37] with "righteousness" (6:33).

Matthew's second key rhetorical move is to make the Sermon on the Mount the explication of the righteousness Jesus came to teach, and which the hearer/reader has come to anticipate, for the burning question alive in Matthew's Jewish-Christian setting, "what is right" and "what is the meaning of righteousness" has been subtly woven into the narrative from the beginning. Matthew's story opens with Joseph on the narrative stage. The first thing said about him is that he is a "righteous" or "just" (δίκαιός) man (1:19). In Matthew's context, this surely means that he lives in accord with the Law. Yet Joseph has an ethical problem. His fianceé is pregnant, and not by him. The Law considered such a situation adultery, and the punishment was severe (see, for example, Deut. 22:23-27; Lev. 18:20; 20:10). Joseph, the righteous man, had already decided to abide by what the Matthean reader already knows to be a higher law, the law of love.[38] When we first meet Joseph in the opening scene of the narrative, he has already resolved that, painful as it will be to both Mary and himself, he will divorce her quietly, robbing her of neither life, future, nor dignity. Here Joseph is presented as a δίκαιός person who affirms the Law, yet "fulfills" it not by literally adhering to it, but by acting according to the higher law of love. Sympathetic hearers/readers in Matthew's community may have recognized analogous situations in their own lives and affirmed Joseph's resolved course of action as "Christian," and yet wondered *how* could it be that one is "righteous" and yet does not abide by the letter of the Law? The tensive question is only subtly posed here; it is not resolved.

The second, and only, reference to "righteousness" in Matthew prior to the Sermon is in 3:15, again a Matthean addition to the Markan account. The result is that in the Gospel of Matthew the first words the readers hear Jesus say are "Let it be so now, for thus it is proper for us to fulfill all righteousness." This terse keynote address signals that Jesus' ministry which now begins is oriented to righteousness, that the path of justice has something to do with following Jesus. Yet there is no immediate response to the question at issue in Matthew's community in its struggles with Pharisaic Judaism: "*How* can followers of Jesus do what is right if they do not live in accord with the Law? Does not discipleship to Jesus come at the price of rejecting the Law?"

The contemporary preacher comes to the Sermon on the Mount via an analogous path. When we "turn to the text," it is with some of the same concerns as Matthew and his church: in a world of ethical relativity, we want to do what is just and right; we want to respect our own sacred tradition which now includes not only Matthew's Bible but Matthew *as* Bible; and in the cause of what we believe is right and just we sometimes find ourselves acting against the clear word of the Bible.[39] Matthew's picture of righteous-Joseph-who-does-not-keep-the-Law (1:19) has already set up the problem with which the modern reader resonates, and so it is good news when Jesus-who-comes-to-fulfill-all-righteousness appears (3:15) as somehow the resolution of this problem. When Jesus, who has been painted in Mosaic colors, ascends the mountain to give his disciples instruction in righteousness (5:1), readers who have come to this point by the rhetorical path created by Matthew will expect to hear something from Jesus that they will take with utmost seriousness. This Jesus will not dismiss either the Bible or the concern for righteousness, but will claim that his way fulfills both. But readers who have been led to this mountain by the Matthean narrative will have learned from Joseph, Jesus, and Matthew not to expect a simple law or principle that tells them what to do in their changed situation. The Jesus who speaks from the mount is both more demanding and more flexible, calling for radical obedience and yet providing situational applications (5:21-48), calling for perfection and yet assuming the hearers will continue to be sinners in need of forgiveness (6:12; 7:11). A sermon

74

that allows the word of Jesus to be heard will not reduce the Sermon on the Mount to some useful principles or raid it for useful imagery, but will be so structured as to help the congregation approach the mount by the rhetorical path prepared by Matthew, so that when Jesus speaks from the mount, the hearer/reader is ready to listen and to do.

CHAPTER FOUR

ROMANS IN THE PULPIT: FORM AND FORMATION IN ROMANS 5:1-11

Leander E. Keck

R omans is the Everest of the Pauline range. Scaling its heights proves to be a challenge few students of Paul can refuse—because, like Everest, it is there.

Exegetes respond to the challenge by writing ever larger commentaries, but for preachers the task is even more daunting because they have a limited time in which to interpret a slice of Paul's tightly constructed argument. The relentless theologizing that marks the first eleven chapters contains neither glimpses into the turbulent life of the congregation, as do the Corinthian letters, nor passages that reveal the humanity of the Apostle, as does Philippians—either of which would relieve the text's demands for concentrated thought. In dealing with Romans 1–11 one must come to grips with Paul's theological argument, and that requires close attention to the ways in which he gave it structure and persuasive force.

It has become evident that it is not enough to understand Paul's concepts (e.g., justification, faith, law), as essential as this is. One must also attend carefully to the freedom with which he reformulated them, sometimes with a different vocabulary. Above all, one must note carefully how he connects his concepts by prepositions (e.g., *in, with, through*), and especially by various connecting phrases, for it is these that give shape and texture to the argument. Fred Craddock has been alert not only to the significance of form for understanding the content of the biblical text, but also to the role of form in communicating the content of the sermon. He knows that attending to the form of Romans while in the study will determine what happens to Romans in the pulpit.

THE PUBLIC READING OF ROMANS

Romans is normally read to the congregation before it is interpreted—as was the case at first. Paul knew it would be read aloud, and in dictating it he relied on his rhetorical skill to create a text through which he would, in effect, "speak" to the congregation. Perhaps he counted on the reader to comment on it as he went along, pointing out what Paul had emphasized. Apart from such pauses, we must assume that it was read through, from beginning to end, so that Paul could have his say. "Church services" were not confined to sixty minutes before Sunday noon, and the Christians were not eager to get to the restaurants early. Instead, congregations met at night, probably assembling gradually since there was no five o'clock quitting time. If Acts 20:7-12 is a clue, the meetings might last until daybreak—plenty of time to hear Romans. (One wonders how many hearers fell asleep, like young Eutychus who, having dozed off "as Paul talked still longer," fell out the window!) Today, however, one cannot take for granted what Paul assumed—that the content of the letter would be communicated in the very act of reading it aloud.

For this situation, Romans alone cannot be held accountable for it is our attention spans that have contracted, especially when there are no moving images to keep us alert as we listen. Only the visually impaired continue the art of listening. How, then, will one read Romans aloud so that its message will be heard?

If we attend to the text, Paul himself can help us. And so can children. Whoever has read to children knows that one uses the voice to distinguish narrative, explanation, and dialogue. Paul knew this too, and so varied his style, thereby inviting the public reader to reflect this orally. Readers to children also know that pace is important. Romans is usually read too rapidly, and without due attention to phrasing. Even in a text without fluff, all the words and phrases do not count equally, as is true also of notes and phrases in music. Hearing Romans read rapidly, and without change of pace or inflection, is as satisfying as hearing Mozart on a player piano. Readers to children have also learned to pay attention to unusual words and phrases, as the late Dr. Seuss knew very well. Romans abounds in unexpected phrases deliberately created by Paul to convey certain dimensions of the gospel. For example, "under law"/"under grace" (6:14-15); "slaves of righteousness" (6:18); "put on the Lord Jesus Christ" (13:14). One's oral reading should invite the hearer to reflect for a moment, and perhaps to savor the language as well.

In Romans 1–11, more than in any other letter, Paul shows his capacity to weave diverse kinds of materials (forms, genres) into an argument that, as it moves along, alternates rhetorical styles. As a result, the alert reader is not wearied by a relentless sequence of declarative sentences. The most important rhetorical device in Romans is the *diatribē*.[1]

Whereas the Platonic dialogue was designed to allow the several participants to explore aspects of the theme, the *diatribē* propels the argument by questions and answers, both of which the speaker (author) controls. Sometimes the speaker puts a question to the imagined hearer, as in Romans 2:21 ("You, then, who teach others, will you not teach yourself?"). Sometimes an imagined interlocutor poses a question to the author, as in Romans 3:1 ("Then what advantage has the Jew?"). Such questions are not requests for information but objections, which the speaker proceeds to answer, in diverse ways, in order to move the argument forward. In the *diatribē*, the counter-questions never develop alternative views; they are devices by which the speaker sets up the next point.

One of Paul's favorite *diatribē* devices in Romans is to ask a double question, the first alerting the reader/hearer to the second, which formulates an inference to be rejected with the vigorous formula, "By no means!"[2] For example: "What then are we to say? Should we continue in sin in order that grace may abound? By no means!" (6:1-2; see also 6:15; 7:7, 13; 9:14; 11:1).

In responding to the wrong inference Paul sometimes poses a counter-question (as in Rom. 6:2, "How can we who have died to sin still live in it?"), which is put in such a way as to allow only one, self-evident answer (here: "Impossible!"). At other times he can launch an explanation, as in 7:7-12. Shifting to the *diatribē* gives a conversational quality to the argument comparable to actual dialogue in stories.

This should be reflected in the public reading of Romans. There is no need to be melodramatic. Sensitivity to the forms in the text, basic to comprehending its content, will do—especially if one's reading is disciplined by practice. There is no more reason to think that without practice one can read Romans communicatively than one can assume that a village choir can sing the "Hallelujah Chorus" without a rehearsal. These matters are so elemental that one is reluctant to put them into print. One thing overcomes this reluctance—memories of hearing Romans on a player piano in the pulpit.

Paul's skill with language is manifest also in the architecture of those paragraphs in which he relaxes the relentless exposition for a moment before pressing on. Romans 5:1-11 is such a passage. The discussion that follows will focus, therefore, not on Paul's ideas but on the ways in which he relied on structure and form to communicate them. To see this, one must overcome the format in which Bibles are printed, for they do not print the text for what it originally was—a script to be spoken. As a result, one cannot *see* what Paul intended the ear to *hear*—phrases as units of thought, the specified relation between them, and the careful structure of the sentences. To discern Paul's craftsmanship, one must observe precisely the details which are commonly overlooked.

STRUCTURE AND FORM OF ROMANS 5:1-11

The fact that some commentators regard Romans 5:1-11 as the conclusion of the first part of the argument begun at 1:18, and others as the introduction to the next part (chapters 5–8) probably confirms the conclusion that it is both—a transition passage, a hinge between the two major sections. Recognizing this is an important clue to understanding it, for as Craddock insisted, one must ask, What does the text *do*?[3] By definition, transitional paragraphs echo what has already been said and alert one to what will be said next.[4] They facilitate the flow of thought by reiterating and by anticipating. One looks for three things in a linking, transitional paragraph: repetitions and reformulations, new ideas or perspectives, and the rationale by which they are connected. All three are evident in Romans 5:1-11. To understand this paragraph, then, one must follow its clues closely.

Instead of beginning with an analysis of the structure of the passage as a whole, we will first examine its initial sentence, for this was the oral/aural event that alerted the original hearers to what was afoot—a transition.

> Therefore, having been justified on the basis of faith we have peace with God through our Lord Jesus Christ, through whom we have also come to have access to this grace in which we stand and we boast of hope of the glory of God. (author's translation)

The initial sentence (vv. 1-2) alerts the reader/hearer to expect a transitional paragraph because it first reformulates what Paul has been talking about since 3:21 ("having been justified by faith") and then introduces two new elements into the argument—present consequences ("we have peace with God" and "we boast," the main verbs) and the future, expressed as the content of the boasting (hope of the glory of God). What the syntax makes clear is that apart from the prior act of God[5] (the passive "having been justified" implies divine action), there would be neither peace with God now nor boasting in view of the future hope. Paul does not simply lay concepts end to end, as he does in I Corinthians 1:30—Christ "became for us wisdom from God, and righteousness and sanctification and redemption." Rather, he dictates a sentence that both indicates how these concepts are related and uses verbal forms that relate the readers' experience to what has been argued: *(we)* having been justified, *we* have peace, *we* boast. This also signals a turn in the argument toward the experiential (hinted at in the phrasing at the end of the previous sentence: *our* trespasses/*our* justification) as McDonald (see note 4) rightly sees. Whereas 1:18–4:25 explained Paul's theology of justification as such, chapters 6 and 8 will continue the exposition by interpreting the readers' experience of baptism and the Spirit.

The opening sentence has additional allusions to what Paul has already said. "We have peace with God"[6] expresses the resolution of the situation prior to justification—living under the wrath of God (1:18–3:20). That this situation changed "through our Lord Jesus Christ" also paraphrases what Paul had argued in 3:21-26.

The rationale of the clause, "and we boast because of hope of the glory of God" is more complex. First, it surprises the reader by introducing a positive meaning of *boast*. At 3:27 Paul had pointedly rejected "boasting" because there he had in view pride, either in one's achievement or in one's status as a Jew; at 2:27 he had indicted "the Jew" for "boasting in God"—a phrase repeated almost verbatim at 5:11. Here, however, because of justification on the basis of faith, "boasting" is affirmed, because it is grounded in what God will do in the future: "because of hope of the glory of God." Moreover, this "glory" also refers to what Paul had already said: all persons "fall short of the glory of God" (3:23). But now, having been justified on the basis of faith, what had been the condition of deprivation (sharing in Adam's loss of God's glory, as many Jewish traditions held[7]) has become the hoped-for condition to be regained. By introducing the theme of hope, Paul's opening sentence also points ahead to this "glory," of which he will speak in 8:17, 21, 30. The original hearers did not know this, of course, but Paul could expect them to listen for it as the reading continued—a rhetorical strategy of anticipation.

In terms of theological content, this initial sentence also signals a fundamental dimension of Paul's thought—the present life of the Christian is marked by the tension between the "already" (peace with God) and the "not yet" (glory of God). Indeed, that this is the theme of the whole passage is evident from its overall structure, to which we will turn presently. But first we must look at the central part of the initial sentence.

According to v. 1, "peace with God" is only one of the things the justified enjoy "through our Lord Jesus Christ"; the other is even more important if the length of the phrase is a clue: "[we also have] obtained access to this grace in which we stand." Here, too, "grace" reminds the reader that according to 3:24, justification occurs "freely by his grace through the redemption which is in Christ Jesus," and that Abraham's justification, too, was according to grace, a sheer gift and in no way a recompense for "work" (4:4). More important, here Paul signals another way of talking about grace—a status or realm within which one "stands" and which therefore is the determinative field of force for one's life. This view will be reasserted in 6:15, where "under grace" also suggests a controlling influence. Even silent readers of Paul's Greek text will note that he calls the Roman hearers' attention to this clause by relying on the rhetorical device of alliteration: *eschēkamen* ("we have obtained") . . . *hestēkamen* ("we stand"). Modern readers who study the text of Romans can recognize what the original hearers would have learned as they continued to listen to it—that by speaking of grace as "space" Paul is readying the reader to follow him as he expounds Christian existence in terms of participation, "being in," or being transferred to another sovereignty. It is this way of thinking that comes to the fore in chapters 6–8, for which the subsequent paragraph about Adam and Christ (5:12-21) sets the stage.

If these observations about the initial sentence have shown anything, it is that Paul was not dictating "off the top of his head" but carefully structuring the expression of his thought in order to facilitate communication.

Turning now to the composition and structure of the passage, we note that despite the remarkable number of concepts, Paul gives it a shape that is consonant with its theme by effective use of repetition. (a) By repeating in v. 9 the initial word *dikaiōthentes* ("having been justified"), he signals a transition to the second part of the passage. (b) Although *hope* had intimated that Paul's thought is now moving toward the future, in v. 9 he makes this move explicit by beginning the sentence with "How much more, having been justified now" and by shifting, for the first time, to the future tense of the main verb, "we shall be saved." (c) By having v. 11 repeat three phrases from the first sentence ("not only this, but we boast," "through our Lord Jesus Christ," and "through whom") he creates a "frame," an *inclusio*—a common device indicating that the thought unit has been completed.

Having been justified . . . through our Lord Jesus Christ
through whom. . . .
Not only this, but we boast. . . .
How much more, having been justified . . . shall we be saved.
Not only this, but we boast . . . through our Lord Jesus Christ
through whom. . . .

Moreover, he gives movement to the thought by repeating a key word from the previous sentence:

v. 2 we boast
v. 3 we also boast
   v. 4 the love of God
   v. 8 [God's] own love
     v. 9 we shall be saved
     v. 10 we shall be saved
       v. 10 reconciled (twice)
       v. 11 we received reconciliation

The structure of the long sentence in vv. 3-5 allows Paul to correlate a number of ideas without losing the hearer. (a) By beginning with "not only this but" he signals that what is to follow is even more important than what he had just said: "we also boast because of sufferings." (b) "Knowing that" states the warrant for such boasting. Cosby points out that here Paul uses three rhetorical devices "to formulate a string of statements that rhetorically builds to a climax":[8] *epezeugmenon* (one verb, *produces*, unites three clauses, obscured by NRSV which uses it three times for the sake of clarity), *polysyndeton* (a series of *and*s connects the phrases), and *gradatio* (a stair-step sequence that puts the most important item last for the sake of tension and climax).

> knowing that *(hoti)* suffering produces endurance
>   and endurance   character
>   and character   hope
>   and hope does not disappoint[9]
> because *(hoti)* God's love . . . into our hearts

The careful structure of the paragraph is marred, however, by vv. 6-7, which separate the two references to God's love in v. 5 and v. 8. Moreover, they interrupt the flow of thought. They could be omitted without loss. In fact, previous scrutiny of these verses showed that there are good reasons for regarding them as additions to the text.[10] The issue is important enough to summarize the main arguments here. First, omitting vv. 6-7 removes those lines that disturb the pattern that governs the whole passage—repetition of key words in adjacent sentences. Second, v. 6 is a virtual paraphrase of v. 8; none of the other repetitions involve entire sentences. Third, although v. 7b ("though perhaps for a good person [or "the good"] someone might actually dare to die") is formulated in light of 7a ("rarely will anyone die for a righteous person"), the difference between a righteous and a good person is not clear. Since Christ died for sinners, the distinction is irrelevant in any case. Verse 7 appears to be a maxim in which the second part reinforces the first by repetition.

Finally, v. 7 expresses a view of voluntary dying that verges on the heroic, as Käsemann saw. But nowhere else does Paul either view Christ's death in this way or compare it with such dying. Verse 7 is a moralizing analogy, foreign to Paul's thinking about Christ's death. It was probably a comment that an early copyist found in the margin of his manuscript. The copyist, assuming that a predecessor had accidentally omitted v. 7 but had noted it in the margin lest it be lost, sensed the need for a transition from v. 5 when he included it, and so formulated v. 6. In doing so, he anticipated the "while we were . . ." phrasing of v. 8 and v. 10, on the one hand, and echoed "ungodly" from 4:5 on the other. In creating this rhetorically effective sentence *(asthenōn,* "weak"; *asebōn,* "ungodly")* he construed Paul's "ungodly" as weakness, which is not Paul's view of the human condition for which Christ provides a solution. In short, instead of holding Paul himself responsible for this unPauline digression—as if his mind wandered as he dictated until he resumed his train of thought in v. 8—it is better to see here traces of early reflection on what Paul wrote.

Detecting post-Pauline additions to the paragraph reminds us that Romans, like most Pauline letters, was edited for church use, though hardly as extensively as has sometimes been claimed.[11] It is close attention to the literary and rhetorical structures in the text, as well as to subtle shifts in content, that alert one to such passages, as is the case also where it appears that Paul is quoting. In other words, this paragraph is particularly instructive because it reminds us, first, not to take anything in the text for granted and, second, that when trying to account for strange turns of thought one has a choice. One can either attribute the phenomenon to Paul's mind—a psychological explanation—or to the nature of the text—an historical explanation that reckons with the possibility that it embodies three phases: traditions older than the text itself, what Paul himself formulated, and what might have been added or changed (including variant readings) subsequently.

Before resuming the analysis of the composition of our paragraph, it is useful to reflect on another matter—the implication for preaching of the possibility that vv. 6-7 are post-Pauline. One can, of course, ignore the possibility by either treating these verses as Pauline or by developing the sermon from other parts of the passage. It is more productive in the long run, however, to take the possibility seriously, not by emphasizing it in the pulpit, but by reflecting on its import for the way Christ's death is treated. Concretely, in preparing to preach about this event, vv. 6-7 invite the preacher to ponder the danger of turning the event into an example, albeit one of surpassing magnitude, of what is generally true about self-sacrifice. Such a construal, no matter how true, runs directly counter to v. 8, with its stupendous assertion that what Christ's death demonstrates is not his love for God (or for sinners; Paul can say that, too, in Gal. 2:20) but God's love toward us. Christ's dying for us and God's love coincide. If that is missed, the point of the whole paragraph is missed because this is the ultimate warrant for everything said in both of its parts.

In vv. 9-11, everything said about the believer is the result of Christ's action:

justified now	by his blood[12]
we shall be saved	through him
reconciled	through the death of his Son
we shall be saved	by his life
we boast	through our Lord Jesus Christ
we received reconciliation now	through him

The composition of vv. 9-11 reflects Paul's agenda—an explicit emphasis on the future in light of the presently experienced change from the past. The opening phrase in v. 9 announces that everything said until now, astounding though it be, is destined to be surpassed: "How much more . . . shall we be saved."[13] By repeating the sentence structure, Paul reinforces the point:

how much more	justified	shall we be saved
how much more	reconciled	shall we be saved

The repetition shows that the change from justification to reconciliation is not a shift to a different theology of salvation but simple metonymy—the substitution of synonym.[14] This not only holds the hearers' attention but also accents the content.[15] The role of v. 11 in creating an *inclusio* with v. 1 has been observed; to be noted here is the function of the "now" in vv. 9 and 11. If one tries to read the sentences without this word, its contribution becomes evident. In v. 9 "now" promises that the "how much more" will be expressed in terms of time—a promise kept in "we *shall be* saved." In v. 11, on the other hand, it reinforces the present basis of the boasting in God through Christ.

That the future salvation will be "from the wrath" ("of God" being added by the translators) is a clear reminder of the theme in 1:18–3:20. This allusion is important for the interpretation of "the wrath," for 1:18–3:20 does not speak of God's wrath only as a coming event. Rather, just as 1:17 says God's righteousness "is being revealed" (present tense, *apokalyptetai*), so 1:18 says God's wrath "is being revealed" *(apokalyptetai);* the one is as much present as the other.[16] Consequently, the human condition portrayed in 1:18–3:20 is not simply what the wrath of God will come to punish but is itself the sign of God's impending wrath (2:5-11), God's over-againstness seen now as the obverse of God's rectitude. What 5:9 promises, therefore, is full salvation from this situation for those whose relation to God has already been rectified. If God's wrath were only God's imminent anger and recompense, those who now "have peace with God" (v. 1) would already have been "saved from the wrath."

The structure of the next sentence (v. 10) indicates that its function is to provide the warrant for what is said in v. 9: For, if X, then how much more than X is Y. That X is nothing other than a paraphrase of v. 9 is indicated not only by the metonymy of "reconciled to God"/"justified" but also by the fact that "through the death of his son" reformulates "in his blood"—in effect a double metonymy. That Y is "we shall be saved" is obvious. What is new is that this salvation will be "by his life," thereby balancing the negative aspect ("from the wrath") with the positive.

Perhaps *en tē zoē autou* should be translated literally: "in his life," since chapter 6 will point out that one has a new life now by being baptized into Christ's death (v. 4), and one will also share Christ's resurrection (v. 5). Participation in, or solidarity with, the resurrected Christ who will never again die is the solution to human mortality. Indeed, eternal life is *"in* Christ Jesus" (6:23). In other words, what 5:10 summarizes, chapter 6 spells out: Christ's death brings about a new relation to God (and a new relation to righteousness, 6:18), and participation in (or solidarity with) the resurrected Christ will bring ultimate salvation. The unity of the cross and resurrection is the unstated basis of the argument from present (having been justified/reconciled) to the future.

Finally, when Paul created an *inclusio* he deliberately repeated the phrasing about boasting (vv. 3, 11). This suggests that the two uses of "boast in" should be considered together. In v. 11 boasting "in God" means that God is the ground and content of the boast, just as "in the law" equals "about the law" (2:23) or "in persons" equals "about persons" in I Cor. 3:21. Since v. 3 uses the same formulation, it appears that "in sufferings" also states the ground and content of the boasting. Does Paul really mean that Christians boast *because* they suffer pain (like everyone else)? This does not comport well with 8:18-25 (where the word for sufferings is *pathēmata*). Or does "in sufferings" refer to the situation in which one boasts? Or does he have in mind a special suffering that Jewish apocalyptic often associated with the end of the age (the "messianic woes"), frequently paired with persecution.[17] The common word for this suffering is *thlipsis*— Paul's term in v. 3. Since plausible cases can be made for various understandings, the interpreter must make a judgment call. Attending closely to the form of the text is sometimes of more use in identifying an issue than in settling it. But better to be left with the question than with premature confidence that one knows what Paul surely must have been talking about.

Romans in the Pulpit

What has this examination of Romans 5:1-11, detailed though far from exhaustive,[18] shown about preparing to take Romans into the pulpit?[19] First, understanding this particular passage requires one to see it in its specific relations to what has been said already and to what is about to be said. It is not simply a matter of noting the literary context; it is a matter of discerning what is being alluded to and what is being anticipated in an argument. The more solid one's grasp of the flow of Paul's thought in chapters 1–8, the more firmly grounded will be one's exposition of what Paul says here, precisely because of the nature and function of this paragraph.

Second, the more one grasps the character and content of Paul's thought as a whole, the freer one is to allow Paul's formulations here to shape the sermon. The paragraph is *not* a summary of Paul's thought, though it taps his thought in order to express particular assertions and inferences.

Third, Paul's point is in the sentences that relate concepts in a particular way. What needs to be preached more often is what these sentences actually assert, rather than the themes they reflect. That is, preaching should reflect the syntactical and rhetorical details of Paul's letter and not content itself with theological generalities.

Fourth, the specific content of the sentences cannot be separated from their specific structure or from their relation to one another, which Paul builds into the text. The fact that rhetorical considerations have shaped both the parts and the whole does not detract from the content or from its import. To the contrary, they are vehicles for highlighting memorably what Paul deems necessary to say at this point. Rhetoric is a matter of neither sheer oratory nor mere ornament; it is a sophisticated science of making communication more effective. Paul knew that. Fred Craddock knows it. The rest of us can learn it.

PART II
TURNING TO THE SERMON

CHAPTER FIVE

THE REVOLUTION OF SERMONIC SHAPE

Eugene L. Lowry

When Fred Craddock's work *As One Without Authority* was published in 1971, a new era in North American homiletics was born. Certainly it was not that he dropped a brand new bombshell on the homiletical world; rather, it was that by means of a masterfully executed *gestalt,* he gave birth to a new mentality, beginning what Richard Eslinger has called "the Copernican Revolution in homiletics."[1]

Gathering up recent work in numerous related disciplines represented by such voices as Walter J. Ong, Carl Michaelson, Amos Wilder, Joseph Sittler, Gerhard Ebeling, Ernst Cassirer, and Eta Linneman, building on the homiletical work of H. Grady Davis and R. E. C. Browne, as well as naming the experiences of countless parish preachers, Fred Craddock reshaped the sermon. Certainly the time was ripe. The blossoming of post–World War II piety in the United States was pretty well spent. Flowering instead was a renewed interest in social action inside and outside the church along with a growing "minimalization of the power of words to effect anything,"[2] as Craddock put it.

The practical disciplines within the theological school curricula, which were drawing enthusiastic interest, were found principally in pastoral counseling and social action courses. An "actions speak louder than words" mentality was in vogue. At a deeper level, Craddock observed that the "loss of power and meaning in words may lie in the nature of traditional religious language."[3] He noted other developments that served to exacerbate the problem. For example, the power of the television medium was thought to have "changed [the] shape of the human sensorium"[4] from oral to visual. Moreover, there was a questioning of authority, which resulted in a "new relationship between speaker and hearer."[5] In short, Craddock granted that "we are all aware that in countless courts of opinion the verdict on preaching has been rendered and the sentence passed."[6]

OPENING A NEW DOOR

It was with this just cited statement that Fred Craddock began his first writing on the subject of homiletics. And it caught the homiletical world's attention. Modestly, he continued: "All this slim volume asks is a stay of execution until one other witness be heard."[7] And listen the homiletical world did. *As One Without Authority* was published only three years after I had accepted a position to teach preaching in a theological seminary. When I read his first sentence I remembered immediately the welcome I had received by one of my new colleagues, who in partial jest (I think) said: "Welcome. I understand you are going to be teaching blacksmithing."

What Craddock did was to open fully a new door. He called it "inductive preaching," but many of the people who have walked through that door have worn name tags saying "narrative preaching." Admittedly, the term *narrative preaching* is vague—a banner of many colors and stripes. Interestingly, Craddock does not often use the term *narrative preaching*, except in *Overhearing the Gospel,* in which he notes that "the shape of the communication is paramount in the business of effecting listener experience, and if the experience being sought is overhearing, the structure most congenial and with greatest potential for effectiveness is narrative."[8]

I have no doubt that Craddock wishes that some of us who have walked through that door would have turned another direction instead. Indeed, we need to become clear as to what the elusive term *narrative preaching* really means. Does one mean story preaching, à la Jensen, or narratively shaped sermons (as I would hold)? What might be the connection between inductive and episodal preaching? Do first person sermons count? What do you do with Buttrick's methodology?

What apparently happened is that by prompting a fresh reappraisal of sermon shape, Craddock gave the homiletical world permission to entertain radically new ideas about preaching. Coming together on this scene were diverse people with excitement about such areas of interest as biblical narrative criticism, linguistic studies, literary criticism, story theology, media analysis, and much more. The ensuing confusion is a tribute to the creativity of the times—and to be expected when something really new happens.

Meanwhile at the local church level, pastors were growing weary not only of their own preaching, but of the all-too-familiar table of contents of available books on preaching: "the preacher's study life, the preacher's prayer life, the preacher's preparation time, the shape of the parish," and so forth. Of course there were precursors who had set the stage. In a recent essay, Professor Lucy Rose has demonstrated how certain sections in the classic works of John Broadus and H. Grady Davis pushed the door ajar.[9]

Yet such powerful evocation of a new epoch in preaching theory could not be lured into being by just anybody. It would need someone firmly placed within a well-established, "foundational" discipline, such as New Testament studies. It required an analytical and analogical mind that could sense and then name connections among quite diverse fields of study. It would necessitate wit and wisdom. It would require someone of pastoral sensitivity with an uncanny sense of others' frustrations. And it needed to be a linguistic artist whose language could capture experiences in such a way that the reader might have a "shock of recognition." Fred Craddock was the one.

The result, as we peer back over twenty years, *appears* as a paradigmatic shift involving moves from deductive to inductive, from rhetoric to poetic, from space to time, from literality to orality, from prose to poetry, from hot to cool, from creed to hymn, from science to art, from left brain to right brain, from proposition to parable, from direct to indirect, from construction to development, from discursive to aesthetic, from theme to

95

event, from description to image, from point to evocation, from authoritarian to democratic, from truth to meaning, from account to experience. But note that I said *appears* "from . . . to . . . ." The matter is not quite as simple as that. Before we explore carefully the nature of this fundamental paradigm shift, we need to gain some clarity about our subject and its diverse yet intertwined categories of concern. What precisely are we talking about when we use the term *narrative preaching*?

DEFINING THE TERMS

In a recent article, John S. McClure has attempted to define some terms and issues. In "Narrative and Preaching: Sorting It All Out," he identifies "four ways that the word *narrative* is used in relation to preaching."[10] First, when the term focuses on biblical material, the subject of inquiry is "narrative hermeneutics."[11] Second, when the focus relates to sermonic shape, McClure speaks of "narrative semantics."[12] He identifies the third focus as "narrative enculturation,"[13] suggesting exploration of "the use of culture and human experience,"[14] linking narrative elements such as metaphor and image with current interest in imagination—in short the connection between "sermonic meaning and culture."[15] Finally, McClure identifies "narrative world view"[16] by which he intends the role of preaching in the cultivation of a "theological world view or 'faith story.' "[17]

His first category, "narrative hermeneutics," is clear. The focus on biblical literary forms and their impact on the sermon is quickly identifiable, building on the important work of biblical narrative criticism in our time. His explanation of the category "narrative semantics" is clear, identifying those of us working primarily on the question of narrative sermonic shape. The title, however, may throw people off. The term *semantics,* denoting the study of meaning, diverts the focus somewhat. This second category might be more aptly designated "narrative homiletical

96

form." Then everybody will understand precisely the focus. Understandably, McClure's third and fourth categories are a bit more confusing inasmuch as such various concerns as metaphor, imagination, and world view (I would name Crite's "Narrative Quality of Experience," and Fackre's "Narrative Theology") are difficult to corral. Yet some categorical definition is crucial. McClure has provided an important service to the field in naming these categories. Even if others of us will quibble or cut the pie another way, still it now will be difficult to speak responsibly about narrative preaching without naming one's central focus or point of entry. His work is timely, particularly as some of us want to claim a paradigm shift in the homiletical discipline.

Likewise, Lucy Rose has attempted to provide the same crucial service. Rose also divides the concerns into four areas of focus: the purpose of preaching (sensing a move from persuasion to transforming event), biblical hermeneutics (moving from central idea to saying and doing), the language of preaching (moving from clarity to engagement), and the arrangement of sermonic material (moving from logical reasoning to plot).[18] My preferences of categories are narrative homiletics, narrative hermeneutics, and narrative theology.

Two matters are crucial at this step of identifying our concerns. First, one needs to recognize the interconnectedness of the various foci. Often distinctions have to do with point of entry. For example, with Craddock it probably was his keen observation about the process of biblical exegetical work that prompted his concern for sermonic form. Charles Rice's entry point seems to be the affinity of storytelling to "the content and form of Christian revelation."[19] I moved from preliminary focus on sermonic shape toward exploration of biblical parable work being done by such people as Via, Crossan, and Perrin, and consideration of the issue of narrativity, reflected in such thinkers as Scholes and Kellogg, Stephen Crites, and Gabriel Fackre.

The second crucial matter is to recognize the great diversity of current voices and emphases. Not everyone who is writing on the subject of narrative preaching has the same point of view as any other writer, let alone the same entry point of concern. Neither those who hope to be critical of this shift in North American homiletics nor those of us who are advocates can simply presume that the terms *story, inductive,* and *narrative* are synonymous.

For example, story preaching (at least in Jensen's view) is concerned with the content of the entire sermon consisting in one story told. Narrative preaching more typically focuses on the plot shape a sermon may take—moving from opening disequilibrium to final resolution—whether or not a story is involved. Craddock explains:

> Finally, by narrative structure I am not proposing . . . a long story or a series of stories or illustrations. While such may actually be the form used for a given message, it is not necessary in order to be narrative. Communication may be narrativelike and yet contain a rich variety of materials: poetry, polemic, anecdote, humor, exegetical analysis, commentary.[20]

Rose notes that when the identifying focus is upon *story,* we have a less radical shift in homiletical mood, namely that story preaching is viewed as one of many options of preaching still governed by conventional rhetorical principles. On the other hand, narrative preaching (at least as just now defined!) involves a departure toward a newer set of principles.

Again, are *inductive* and *narrative* (as I define it) synonymous? The answer is not easy. I hazard a yes and a no. In one sense, both terms are describing the same kind of process from different vantage points, or through the lens of identifiably different issues. Craddock's reference point concerns the movement of ideas, contrasting deductive (general to particular) and inductive (particular to general). He makes his claim succinctly: "The plain fact of the matter is that we are seeking to communicate with people whose experiences are concrete. Everyone lives inductively, not deductively."[21] My point of entry is the shape of plot, which works its way from opening conflict into increased complication through a decisive turn toward resolution.

One might ask, How do you go about complicating a plot? The answer: probably through inductive reasoning, but not always.

Sometimes simple juxtaposition of conflicting conceptual ingredients will do it. Another might ask, What is the ongoing consequence of the inductive reasoning process? The answer: probably increased tension or complication, but not always. Sometimes one piece of inductive reasoning will resolve itself nicely into a subsequent arena of inductive reasoning with a sense of an actual lessening of complication. Hence, whereas inductive process may result in increasing clarity (and thus less conflict), plot is working toward increasing conflict (and thus less clarity), but only sometimes. Other times the two processes are virtually identical.

Indeed, note particularly what they always have in common. With either inductive or narrative models one never begins with the conclusion. As McClure says it, they both "promote sermonic forms built around the delay of the arrival of the preacher's meaning."[22] Craddock hopes the congregation will experience the shock of recognition. I hope the meaning of the sermon is encountered, not just reported. Technically, one might point out that a plotted sermon moves with inductive process throughout approximately three-fourths of the sermon until the decisive turn or reversal, at which point it flips over to deductive reasoning the rest of the way. Yet in both cases the goal of any sermon is *event*, "a sharing in the Word," says Craddock, "a trip not just a destination."[23]

Again, one might name another sermon form as *episodal* preaching, which appears to incorporate elements of both inductive and narrative preaching by the utilization of apparently unrelated vignettes successively accumulating until a final ideational *gestalt* unites the whole. In terms of movement of ideas, it is inductive, and in effect implicitly narrative.

Then we have Buttrick's *moves*. Although he is more likely to reserve the term *narrative sermon* to preaching in the mode of immediacy,[24] nonetheless his nomenclature of "moves" suggests his concern for process. Says Buttrick: "The word *plot* may be applied to all kinds of hermeneutical acts; it is not restricted to stories."[25] Nonetheless, in comparing methods I have often said that if you imagine a sermon as a string of pearls, Buttrick would

99

be interested primarily in the pearls; I am interested primarily in the string.

African American preaching in the United States often appears to follow traditional rules of preaching, except that underneath the formal organization of ideas is a narrative expectation. Says Henry Mitchell, "The final role of celebration is that fitting climax to a balanced proclamation which has already included exegesis, exposition, explanation, application, and deeply meaningful illustration. . . . All else leads up to this climactic moment."[26] Because the congregation knows the sermon will not be completed until the final climax, the people can afford to tell the preacher to "take your time."

EXPLORING THE VARIABLES

All of which is to say that numerous kinds of preaching today are marked by commonalities that simply will not fit the older paradigm of preaching, which grew out of rhetorical principles and structures. Clearly it is a new day. Yet we will bear false witness if we move forward with a simplistic either-or mentality of opposites. Earlier I alleged a paradigm shift that *appears* to move from deductive to inductive, from rhetoric to poetic, from space to time, from literality to orality, from prose to poetry, from hot to cool, from creed to hymn, from science to art, from left brain to right brain, from proposition to parable, from direct to indirect, from construction to development, from discursive to aesthetic, from theme to event, from point to evocation, from authoritarian to democratic, from truth to meaning, from account to experience. But why the term *appears*? Because otherwise such an exclusionary mode of work will create great mischief of confusion (and arrogance on several sides as well).

Although there are some ingredients so sharply delineated as to justify either-or categorization, more often than not the paradigm shift is more an alteration of emphasis, with one aspect becoming dominant in concern while another aspect becomes subordinate.

In many instances the change can be described accurately as a *figure-ground shift*. All of these kinds of differences will become evident now as we begin to explore the specifics of several variables of the sermon. Any one of them may be less than decisive, perhaps even appearing to be of minor import. Taken together, they represent a major shift in the way preaching is thought and practiced. These variables can be classified under such categories as *shape, content,* and *goal*—although they are significantly intertwined.

(1) Shape

Because the central focus of my work has concerned sermonic shape, we will begin here, remembering that lying beneath this focus are concerns related to both the content and the goals of preaching.

(a) Deduction/Induction

After noting that people think inductively, that biblical exegesis is engaged inductively, and that even "the Incarnation itself is the inductive method,"[27] Craddock observes how "the route from exegesis to preaching is made unnecessarily difficult in traditional practice by the radical reversal of the mental processes in the transition from the study of the text to the structure of the sermon itself."[28] In short, the inductive process of sermon preparation is turned on its head in the delivery itself. That is, the traditional sermon announces its conclusions first, and then divides into particulars by means of amplification, application, and illustration or other means of proof. So Craddock asks: "Why not re-create with the congregation . . . [one's] inductive experience of coming to an understanding of the message of the text?"[29] Inductive process in moving from particular to general attempts to build anticipation rather than unpacking a thesis, just as a joke does not begin with the punch line.[30]

So here we have an instance of a radical "either-or" situation—well, almost. Actually, in an overall inductive process, there may be deductive moments. For example, in pursuing some central sermonic issue and hoping for final resolution of it, the preacher might make reference to the work of some social scientist or biblical scholar. That moment might accurately be called deductive, inasmuch as it announces a conclusion. Yet that conclusion is in the service of a larger inductive process. My point is that inductive movement does not consist wholly of climbing unknown mountains in the fog without the clarity of some known reference points. It is likewise true that when the deductive preacher pauses for illustrative purposes, the story told is inductive in shape: "The other day I was driving toward. . . ."

(b) Authoritarian/Democratic

Because narrative preaching focuses first upon an issue, textual or pastoral, and moves toward the gospel's intersective power for resolution, the new homiletic reflects a quite different relationship of preacher and congregation. In reflecting upon traditionally shaped sermons Craddock observes: "There is no democracy here, no contributing by the hearer. If the congregation is on the team, it is as javelin catcher."[31]

The question here is, With whom does the preacher stand—with the people as the first listener to the text or with God as the most recent teller? Narrative preaching by its shape maximizes the sense of shared exploration rather than detailed explanation. I have observed how often the classically trained preacher utilizes a particular illustration perhaps as much to reveal identification with the congregation ("I am like you, you know") as for the conceptual point in question.

Indeed, one may notice how illustrative materials are utilized differently in the contrasting models of preaching. In the traditional homiletic, many illustrations concretize the point just made; whereas in the narrative model, illustrations more likely further the exploration of an issue. Illustrations in narrative preaching are more likely to precede a point rather than follow it.

(c) Creed/Hymn

This set of polarities might well be engaged later when we are considering the *goal* of preaching. Yet it will serve our present concern to note the differences relative to sermonic shape. Although creeds often reflect narrative shape in the sense of moving from creation to eschatology (the Korean Creed) or processing through the Trinity (the Nicene Creed) nonetheless such movement is not absolutely necessary. That is, there is a sense of completion or discrete integrity to each particular affirmation. Certainly a Barthian could design a creed beginning with the incarnation rather than creation. The primary question for a creed is comprehensiveness.

In a hymn, on the other hand, every note requires the immediately preceding one for anything to make sense. The complete melody line of a favorite Protestant hymn contains the following notes: CCCCCCDDDDFFFFFFFFFFFFGGGGAAAA-AAAAAC1C1C1. The hymn is "Amazing Grace," but of course one would have to be told this, because the notes, as listed, are out of sequence; and sequence is central to its meaning. When a traditional sermon is divided into three points—parallel to one another and equally subservient to the main thesis—often it is possible to shift point "I" to "III" with old point "III" becoming "II" ("The Three Qualities of Love" or "Three Marks of Discipleship").

When in fact one discovers that it is impossible to play musical chairs with the three points and maintain the meaning, then it is time to observe that some narrative principle is at work, at least implicitly. In narrative preaching, succession of ideas is crucial for the meaning to be grasped (as indeed it is with Hegel's thesis, antithesis, and synthesis).

(d) Literality/Orality

Not unrelated to the question of authority, the matter of language reveals an important distinction between traditional and narrative preaching. Again, in part this distinction may be due to educational processes, the journey through formal education. Yet I observe that syntax and word choice are typically more formal in the traditionally shaped sermon. Explanation and elaboration seem to lean toward declaratory compositional style, whereas narrative exploration will often prompt greater syntactic variety.

Craddock once noted how it is that the preacher, perhaps sensing things are not going well in the sermon, may set the manuscript aside and just begin to talk with the folks.[32] My hunch is that at least two things are likely to happen here: The preacher moves to induction *and* the grammar gravitates from connection with the eye to connection with the ear. Obviously this is not always so. I have known of traditional preachers whose speech is clearly within the orality genre (I think of David H. C. Read) and I have known preachers utilizing narrative procedures with language gravitating toward literality (Harry Emerson Fosdick, for example). Yet I perceive a clear leaning overall. While Craddock notes how we think inductively, perhaps it is also true that speech more resembling conversational oral style is more likely to happen.

(e) Construction/Development

The term *construction* has long been a favorite in describing the preparation process for the traditional sermon. Indeed, it is apt. *The Craft of Sermon Construction* by W. E. Sangster is a classic. When the focus of preparatory work is upon a thesis divided into separable parts (and put in proper place), the image of assemblage is noteworthy. Ideational division is key for organization. Ilion T. Jones asks, "Does each point constitute a distinct phase of the thesis?"[33] Preachers will sometimes speak of having *put the sermon together*. The images are clearly spatial and suggest the sermon as some*thing* a contractor erects. (Note J. Randall Nichols' title: *Building the Word.*) The proper rhetorical question is, Will the argument *stand*?

Then, along came H. Grady Davis with another classic work, *Design for Preaching*—and one senses a greater imagistic dynamic—particularly when later he explains that a sermon is "like a tree" which is a "living organism."[34] Craddock reminds the preacher that to be effective one will have as "primary methodological concern the matter of movement."[35] "Traditional preaching . . . is as old as Aristotle," Craddock reminds us, and involves a deductive movement downward, "a most unnatural mode of communication."[36] He later observes, "Looked at geographically, a three-point sermon on this pattern would take the congregation on three trips down hill, but who gets them to the top each time?"[37]

Narrative preachers, believing that form and content are not divisible, focus not merely on the content of ideas but their possible movement in homiletical time. One likely will never hear a composer speak of organizing or constructing an overture, because music as performed also is a narrative art form. Shape and sequence are compositional realities having to do with a temporal event, not simply ideational building blocks. As Buttrick explains, "Sermons are a sequence of plotted moves"[38] that are "decided by what we intend to bring out, by the world we intend toward."[39]

It bears repeating that the contrast is *not* an either-or dichotomy, reducible to saying traditional preaching is all ideas and no movement and narrative preaching is all movement and no ideas! Nor is the issue one of simple priority. It may have more to do with *primary point of contact.* In the sermon itself, does the preacher engage the ideas with the people on hand or engage the people with the ideas in hand?

(2) Content

(a) Discursive/Aesthetic

Nowhere in our discussion is it more important to avoid mutually exclusive categories than here. Especially when story preaching is viewed as belonging under the larger umbrella of narrative preaching, we need to be as inclusive as possible within the framework of particularity. There is already enough stereotyping going on about how the genre of narrative preaching really suggests anecdotal preaching with story after story barely connected with any ideational glue. One can become really alarmed when as late as 1985 Killinger suggested that one of the purposes of illustrative material is to " 'rest' the congregation" from thought. "It requires great concentration," he says, "especially if the material being listened to is very tightly argued. The use of an illustration in the midst of a sermon permits people to relax for a few moments."[40] Again: "Illustrations . . . let the congregation breathe more easily before plunging back into the thought line of the sermon."[41]

Presumably we have here a sharp dichotomy between "thought" and "feeling" being applied to illustration. With such a notion, no wonder there are those who muse about the different purposes of "story" and "argument." But such a dichotomy simply will not survive close scrutiny. To the contrary, sometimes a story is the more economical, precise, and powerful means *of* argument—witness the parables of Jesus. R. E. C. Browne cites Austin Farrer: "There is a current and exceedingly stupid doctrine that symbol evokes emotion, and exact prose states reality. Nothing could be further from the truth: exact prose abstracts from reality, symbol presents it."[42] Browne concludes, "In religion the manifoldness of truth is declared through the use of imagery that stirs the whole mind into action."[43] The point here is not to establish some kind of "this is always better than that" argument. It is to say that if one grants *story* the capacity to carry the freight of thought, then it is possible to move on toward some kind of both/and consideration.

Again, R. E. C. Browne observes that the doctrine of revelation is at stake in how we preach. "Those who hold that divine revelation is given in propositional form will regard preaching as the statement of doctrine in a series of propositions expressed in definable terms." Yet, he notes that "many who deny the literal inspiration of the Scriptures govern their work as preachers by doctrinal principles which assume that divine revelation is given in propositions. The form of their sermons denies implicitly what they state explicitly about the mode of revelation."[44]

Gabriele Lusser Rico, in building on left brain/right brain discussions, notes the power of metaphor to bridge the two spheres—or types—of thought. She cites Denise McCluggage in the *Centered Skier* who claims metaphor is a bilinguist, functioning as a bridge between discursive and aesthetic thought, "drawing on the power of both hemispheres: verbal for the left and image for the right."[45] Indeed, is it not the case that when one is encountered by a powerful metaphor, first the "right brain" *gets it* with a shock (or doesn't) and then the "left brain" begins *scrambling* to make "left brain" sense of it?

What is important to affirm here is that both discursive and aesthetic modes are modes of thought—both are epistemological categories. Moreover, the field called narrative preaching does not operate in only one mode. In a typical narrative sermon—moving, for example, from opening conflict into complication—it is often the case that rational discourse is the means being employed in order to "thicken the plot."

What is noteworthy in contrasting traditional and narrative forms of preaching is the high value placed on rational argument within the rhetorical tradition. Perhaps that is why the deductive outline has been so commonly used. Don W. Wardlaw notes that as "the church moved solidly into the Hellenistic world . . . preaching adopted a discursive style. . . . Church fathers from Origen to Chrysostom, while imbued with the mind of Christ, exegeted and preached with the mind of Plato and Aristotle."[46] Hence, "when preachers feel they have not preached a passage of Scripture unless they have dissected and rearranged that Word into a lawyer's brief, they in reality make the Word of God subservient to one particular, technical kind of reason."[47]

One function of narrative forms of preaching is opening up greater options of content and shape in the proclamation of the gospel. Utilization of aesthetic knowing in preaching is not ornamental; neither does it constitute a denial of discursive knowing. It may reopen the door toward an enriched discursive understanding of what H. Richard Niebuhr had in mind when, in defining revelation, he chose for the chapter heading "The Story of Our Life."[48]

(b) Propositional/Parable

At stake here is the question of how we go about communicating the gospel, which has difficulty fitting into the tight packaging of propositional thought. In *The Prophetic Imagination,* Walter Brueggemann names the cultivation of prophetic consciousness as the primary task of our work. If we grant his assessment, and I do, the question is, How best to shape that vision? Recent work in biblical literary criticism, and parable study in particular, is offering important resources. As William Beardslee notes, "*Poetics*-inspired style of literary study, though it has been far more fruitful than that derived from the *Rhetoric* in the interpretation of general literature, has until recently been of relatively limited use in the study of the New Testament."[49] He notes how the critical approach to biblical study "looks for the intellectual meaning of a work, for its ideational content."[50] When allied with traditional homiletical style, this approach tends to subordinate the form of the text to propositional truth. Cut off from its literary moorings, this truth may float toward universal principles.

Narrative criticism seeks to keep form and content intact. "This type of criticism," states Beardslee, "regards literary form as an essential part of the function of the work, and not as a separable, instrumental addition to the intellectual content."[51] Likewise, narrative preaching not only attempts to maintain the integrity of the text, but also by analogy it seeks the same kind of integrity of form and content in sermonic shape itself. We will deal further with this issue in a later discussion on sermonic goal. Suffice it to say here that, just as a parable seeks not to make a point but to be one, so narrative preaching seeks not simply to report some extrinsic gospel truth, but to be the truth. At the back of this concern is an understanding of revelation as event.

(c) Hot/Cool

It was Marshall McLuhan who made common parlance of the phrase *hot and cool media.*[52] A radio newscast is a hot medium, he said, meaning it was of high definition (dense with data) so that the listener had little to do but take the data in. Television, on the other hand, is of low definition, leaving great room for participation by the viewer. Some of us are old enough to remember that many "hot" radio personalities did not fare well in the new medium of television. On the other hand, some aspects of radio are cool—highly participatory—particularly in radio theatre. I remember in particular the radio version of the Lone Ranger program. I had the perfect image of the Lone Ranger's horse in my mind—big, beautiful, and fast. Then I watched the new television version of the program. What a disappointment. Where did they get that puny pony for my hero?

So it is with storytelling as contrasted with rhetorical reasoning. The latter tends to be dense with data. One goes along with the argument—or drops out. The storyteller's parabolic way is cool, leaving the listener to complete the sketched picture, and the tale. The print media is perfect for the hot medium and Greek rhetoric. Not only is the picture of high definition, but one can step back a sentence or two to review the line of thought. Oral speech is much cooler, allowing the listeners to participate more fully. So with the recent work with the parables we are beginning to recognize afresh the power of metaphor with its tensive symbol system evoking the imagination. Given its plotted motion, narrative preaching is ideal for the powerful evocation of metaphor and image. Some would say the entire sermon ought to be experienced as parabolic in form. Yet it is also true that the coolness of metaphoric symbol provides a remarkable juxtaposition inside traditional homiletical form.

Typically, the most powerful deductive preachers are those who, for example, understand how images can work to evoke participation of listeners inside the rational movement of the sermon. Clearly, it would be inaccurate to describe one style of sermon as always "hot" and the other as always "cool." It would be better to ask how any model works to incorporate both ends of the spectrum in its proclamation.

(3) Goal

(a) Theme/Event

Perhaps the issue finding the central place in all the various models or understandings of narrative preaching is the goal of sermonic event. One can feel this thread moving through every volume of Fred Craddock's writing on preaching. In *As One Without Authority,* he argued that "fundamental to induction is movement of material that respects the hearer as . . . deserving the right to participate" in the anticipation that "moves from expectation to fulfillment."[53] In *Overhearing the Gospel,* he asserts that the listeners' experience "is the alpha and omega of the whole effort,"[54] that the purpose of narrative structure is to "reproduce and recreate events."[55] "The *nod* of recognition precedes the *shock* of recognition,"[56] he observes in *Preaching.* Linking recognition to anticipation, Craddock continues, "the goal is not to get something said but to get something heard."[57] Indeed, my discussion regarding form and content is really subservient to the basic issue of sermon as event. The goal of any sermon ought to be evocation of the experience of the Word.

While philosophers may be centering on the question of truth, the preacher's goals focus on *experienced truth.* Buttrick hopes to shape consciousness, Mitchell plans for the sermonic celebration. I try to move toward an event-in-time. Craddock summarizes his hope for preaching in our time by observing that when the preacher begins to ask,

> why the Gospel should always be impaled upon the frame of Aristotelian logic, when . . . muscles twitch and . . . nerves tingle to mount the pulpit not with three points but with the Gospel as narrative or parable or poem or myth, . . . then perhaps the preacher stands at the threshold of new pulpit power.[58]

Deductive preaching by its structure tends toward rational conviction. Inductive preaching attempts evocation. The danger of deductive preaching lies at that end of the continuum where a sermon becomes mere report. The danger of inductive preaching is at the other end of the continuum where matters are so open ended that people do not know what to do with the message.

I recall hearing a student sermon, after which another student responded by saying, "I am not sure what you want us to do, or really what your point was." The preacher responded, "Oh, good"—but that was not my response. It is one thing for a sermon to end in such a fashion that the ball is left finally in the listeners' court, and quite another for the ball to evaporate in the drift toward concluding indefiniteness. I know no one so creative at precisely this point as Fred Craddock, who invariably turns away from the pulpit just when the listeners think there must be at least one more sentence. After the momentary shock, the listeners provide the closure, precisely because the preacher had cued its inevitability.

(b) Rhetoric/Poetics

Finally, the transformation of homiletical theory and practice in our time can best be understood as a form of figure/ground shift. What is going on simply cannot be labeled with pejorative either/or designations. The shift is indeed a radical one, but not involving mutually exclusive entities or goals. For a long time we have been following instructions drawn from rhetoric as we ask the central question about sermonic form. Inside the rhetorical envelope, we have learned to insert *poetics*-inspired narrative components. The effective traditional sermon, for example, has always included illustrative material. Indeed, my experience of listening to sermons suggests that the traditionally-shaped sermon is likely to have more illustrations than narrative sermons because, of course, the shape requires it.

Suppose we imagine that *instead of the sermonic envelope being governed by rhetorical principles with poetics inside, that the reverse be true—a narratively shaped envelope with rhetorical ingredients inside.* I believe that is exactly the transformation that is happening in preaching today. Inside the narrative flow one may find reason at work, discursive rationality in all its strength, with the process

111

including the use of metaphoric image, story, and so on. One should no more label a narrative sermon as *mere story* than one would name a traditional sermon *mere logic*. Both story and logic are proper. The question is: *What specifics are to be included inside which overall shape?* Which are the eggs; which is the basket? The changing answer to that question is the revolution of preaching in our time.

CHAPTER SIX

PREACHING AS THE CHURCH'S LANGUAGE

Richard Lischer

The pastor of our congregation stands on the pavement in the center of the chancel when he preaches. He stands there rather solidly like a tree planted by the rivers of water and speaks directly to us from a pastoral heart. His sermons always explore the meaning of a biblical passage for our life together and our callings in the world. With the altar behind him and the baptismal font just to the side, he finds it natural to reflect on our baptismal identity or the blessings that we share at the Lord's table. Standing in such proximity to the pews, our minister's words seem to arise from the congregation. When he says "we," he really seems to mean "we," that is, *us*, the people of God.

CORPORATE CHRISTIANITY

Such preaching is a reflection of the corporate character of the Christian faith. Early in the *Church Dogmatics* Karl Barth says that the task of theology is to assess the relationship of the church's "distinctive talk about God with the being of the church."[1] The church's preaching, along with its liturgy and ministry, constitutes its "distinctive talk." According to Barth, that talk must reflect and promote the church's common life as the people of God. It must do so not because the consensus among social scientists now favors "community" above individualism, but because the nature of Christianity itself demands it.

Critical theology has long debated whether the historical Jesus ever intended to found a church. New Testament scholar Gerhard Lohfink has shown that the question is misplaced in that Jesus could not have founded a church since one already existed when he began his ministry—God's people of Israel. Lohfink argues that Jesus came to "gather Israel," an intention symbolized in his calling of the Twelve, in his healing the sick (as a sign of the eschatological fulfillment), in the communal life of his "family," and in his followers' witness to the nations.[2] "What we now call church is nothing other than the community of those ready to live in the people of God, gathered by Jesus and sanctified by his death."[3]

What Jesus introduced by his ministry and death was given substance and organization by the early Christian communities. Believers in Christ understood themselves to be the *ekklesia*, not only a public assembly in the political sense of the word, but the *qahal Yahweh*, God's covenant people who have been separated from the nations. Later, the disciples in Jerusalem referred to themselves as "saints," a word that denotes holiness and separation but, significantly, does not occur in the singular in the New Testament. The book of Acts and the epistles of Paul document the richness of the community's life. Its members broke bread together daily and had all things in common. The Holy Spirit worked wonders among them. The social barriers of race, position, and sex were broken down in their midst. They ordered their life in such a way as to promote the "building up" of the group, which Paul metaphorically identified as the body of Jesus Christ. The gifts of individuals were coordinated for good within the needs of the whole organism. New Testament Christians lived according to "the praxis of 'togetherness' " a clue to which Lohfink finds in the ubiquity of the pronoun "one another" *(allelon)*:

—"outdo one another in showing honor" (Rom. 12:10)
—"live in harmony with one another" (Rom. 12:16)
—"welcome one another" (Rom. 15:7)
—"wait for one another" (I Cor. 11:33)
—"have the same care for one another" (I Cor. 12:25)
—"be servants of one another" (Gal. 5:13)
—"bear one another's burdens" (Gal. 6:2)

—"comfort one another" (I Thess. 5:11)
—"build one another up" (I Thess. 5:11)
—"bear with one another lovingly" (Eph. 4:2)
—"be subject to one another" (Eph. 5:21)
—"forgive one another" (Col. 3:13)
—"confess your sins to one another" (James 5:16)
—"pray for one another" (James 5:16)
—"be hospitable to one another" (I Peter 4:9)
—"have fellowship with one another" (I John 1:7)[4]

The church's witness to the nations was not distinct from or added on to its essential "togetherness." The radical unity of the body of Christ constituted its witness to the world as well as its uniqueness within it. Although the New Testament does not explicitly call the church what Lohfink terms a "contrast-society," everything about its biblical portrayal supports that designation. Precisely because the church does not exist for itself as a separatist society but completely and exclusively *for* the world, "it is necessary that the church not *become* world, that it retain its own countenance."[5] This position was vehemently defended by Justin Martyr, Tertullian, Origen, and many other apologists and fathers until the official Christianity of the Constantinian era all but destroyed it. Summarizing Origen's position, Lohfink concludes, "The most important and most irreplaceable service Christians can render society is quite simply that they truly be the church."[6]

This church exists for the world, but it renews its identity when it gathers for worship. It speaks in the world, but it learns its "distinctive talk" when its members come together around word and sacrament. Worship is often misconceived as a series of special ceremonies intended for the edification of the individual believer. Yet baptism is not an episode of private initiation but an action involving the entire church. Confession is not a formula for personal remorse but a moment in the ongoing mutual admonition and absolution of the brothers and sisters. Eucharist is not a ritual following the sermon from which one may or may not excuse oneself, but the community's meal with the risen Lord. Doxology is not a hymn to be sung but a life to be lived. Preaching is not a virtuoso performance but the language of the church that accompanies the laborious formation of a new people.

No speaker preaches a sermon, then, and no hearer receives it apart from a *medium* of encounter, and that medium is the church. Although the Word of God created both the cosmos and the church, it does not follow that the preacher's job is to distance the Word from the church or to prove its superiority to the church. Because of God's act in Christ, the church embodies the Word and makes it flesh in the world. Preachers, therefore, do not need to re-invent the priority of the Word. When they do so, they tend to abstract their individual hearers from the church and create the false impression that it is possible for individuals, as individuals, to participate in the Word apart from the community that embodies it. Protestantism has a long history of flaunting the Word above the sacraments and liturgy, as if, in Barth's words, preaching were not an interpretation of the sacrament, having the same meaning, "but in words."[7]

It must be remembered that no interpreter enjoys historical access to unprocessed information about Jesus. From the beginning, the story of Jesus was encoded by the church. The Apostle Paul and the Evangelists were stimulated by the church to write their stories, which were read in the midst of the assembly. No biblical writer envisioned a reader curled up alone reading the Bible. The form critic Martin Dibelius said, "In the beginning was the sermon," by which he meant that when we open the New Testament we encounter a rendering of Jesus whose many features have already been shaped to the needs of a community of believers. The New Testament preaches from church to church. Preaching is the church giving voice to its experience of God's salvation.

THE SCENE CONTAINS THE ACT

The view of preaching that locates the Word within a community of faith corresponds to a theory of rhetoric that encloses language within the situation that evokes it. Classical rhetorical theory engaged little in audience analysis or psychology. It assumed that the occasion—whether the courtroom, senate, or civil celebration—determined the quality and purpose of the speech.[8]

The modern theory of rhetoric that most clearly reflects this view is Kenneth Burke's dramatistic pentad. According to Burke, every rhetorical action is a drama made up of five components: act, scene, agent, agency, and purpose. In terms of preaching, the act is the physical action of speaking, the scene is the environment and tradition of worship, the agent is the preacher, the agency is a crafted piece of work called a sermon, and the purpose is, broadly speaking, formative.

Burke's first law is "the scene contains the act," which he follows with "the scene contains the agents." By this he means that under normal circumstances language does not possess communicative properties outside the community that authorizes and understands it.[9] The words *communicate* and *community* come from the same root. The speech's environment supplies its meaning and purpose. Language is not neutral with regard to place. It is not transferable to other environments. Drop into a seminar on torts when you expected a lecture on liberation theology (or vice versa), and you find yourself in an alien world. English is spoken in both, but in one nothing makes sense. Or, to give another example, the "sweet nothings" that lovers speak to each other are not really "nothing" at all. They are the mutually agreed-upon acts and agencies that have meaning within the narrow confines of the lovers' "scene," which is the history of their relationship.

So far, we have asserted two principles, one theological, the other rhetorical. The first is that the preaching of the gospel refers to *the church's* experience of Jesus Christ and the church's unique purposes in using language about him. The specific context of sermons is the worship-scene in which the congregation gathers to remember, renew, and reportray its identity and mission. The way the church "talks to itself" at worship ultimately constitutes its witness to the world. The second principle states that the occasion of the speech, including the community for which it is given and the many circumstances

117

surrounding it, will shape its language and define its meaning and purpose.

THE "TURN TO THE SUBJECT"

Modern Protestants are the inheritors of a theological culture that undercuts both of the above principles. We live in a theological ecosystem in which one of the elements necessary to health, the communal experience and practice of faith, has been sorely depleted. How this occurred is a familiar story that hardly needs retelling. It is *our* story.

Under relentless pressure from Enlightenment philosophers, the unquestioned solidity of Christian truth broke into perspectives, principles, theories, and fragments of meaning. After Kant's epistemology, which relocated truth from the external cosmos to the subjective faculty of mind, the traditional proofs of God's existence would never again unite the church against an unbelieving world. Textual critics separated the Bible's history from the history of the world. Biblical history was exchanged for "stories" that illustrated some divine truth to be sure, but were not true in themselves. The Protestant Reformation had already divided the church into churches, thereby weakening the authority of tradition in theology and biblical interpretation. The voice of the people drowned out the proclamations of emperors and monarchs. Individual rights supplanted the divine right in every realm. The only "turn" available to modern Christians was the turn away from the massive authority of an objectively true reality to the convictions and experience of the individual. George Lindbeck has detailed the "turn to the subject" in terms of the church's rejection of a cognitive model of doctrine in favor of the "experiential-expressive" in which doctrine (and, eventually, preaching) becomes an expression of individual piety.[10] The guarantor and judge of its truth is the degree to which the doctrine (or sermon) correlates to human experience. The key is experience. *There,* amidst the shifting currents of political and ecclesiastical authority, lay the island of true certainty. By the end of the

118

nineteenth century the influential historian Adolf von Harnack was able to describe the essence of Christianity as "religious individualism and subjectivism" without a trace of critique. Indeed, he read the story of Jesus in precisely those terms: "The kingdom of God comes by coming to *individuals,* making entrance into their *souls,* and being grasped by them. The kingdom of God is indeed God's *rule*—but it is the rule of a holy God in individual hearts."[11]

The homiletical corollary to the individualist hermeneutic can be seen in Phillips Brooks's *Lectures on Preaching:*

> It is the disposition of the preacher to forget that the gospel of Christ is primarily addressed to individuals, and that its ultimate purpose is the salvation of multitudes of men. . . . All successful preaching, I more and more believe, talks to individuals. The church is for the soul.

In a later lecture Brooks insists that the congregation is greater than the sum of the individuals in it, but he does so in order to show its "general humanity."[12] The congregation is a cross-section of humankind, not an instance of the body of Christ. The universal qualities in which it participates have less to do with the Lordship of Christ than with the ecumenicity of human nature.

A more conservative inheritor of the modern "turn to the subject," Charles Grandison Finney, followed a similar line of practice if not reasoning. He unleashed the torrent of his rhetoric on the individual affections. Preaching relies on experience (the more riveting the better), and its purpose even in an established congregation is persuasion, or conversion. Although the Holy Spirit oversees the project, both the preaching and the repenting are carried out by individuals. Conversion is not the work of the Spirit but the result of the skilled application of religious techniques.[13] The preacher must know which buttons to push, which angles to work, and when to go soft-focus. If the New Testament's preaching is from *church* to *church,* Finney's—and all that he continues to represent—is from *person* to *person.* The *formation* of a people has been replaced by the *persuasion* of individuals.

119

If one asks Protestant preachers what they are doing on Sunday morning, many, depending on accidents of birth and tradition, will sound a bit like Brooks or Finney or some combination of the two. They will assume that in their best moments they are "touching the lives" of individuals with the Word. They will frequently allude to their quest for effective "human" illustrations with which to do this touching. Because they do not recognize the churchly matrix of the New Testament or have been trained to reject it, they inadvertently claim the privilege of unmediated access to sacred information, which is the true source of Protestant arrogance with regard to the Word. With the Word poised over against the larger life of the church, many preach as if to convert their hearers who, for the most part, already hold membership in the body of Christ.

Our theological culture has produced churches that do not comprehend their own nature. Although they promote orthodox Christology, they represent biblically heterodox ecclesiology. They project a worldview at radical odds with the New Testament's teaching on community. Too often our members stand or kneel close to one another but do not love one another because they have not been formed to love one another. The pronoun *allelon* is missing from their vocabulary. A liturgically and sacramentally-enriched *koinonia* has not been developed within many of our congregations. Those who attend worship may be more definitively shaped by common Western values than by the Christian story. To use Robert Bellah's terms, the "community of memory" in which members are nurtured by tradition has given way to the "life-style enclave" in which convenience and a common mode of consumption are the most important factors.[14] The churches in which we preach too often are not contrast-societies but mirrors of the individualistic culture that surrounds and infects them.

HOMILETICS AT THE CROSSROADS

All over the world, in cathedrals and storefronts, clapboard meeting houses and base communities, there are preachers and congregations who are determined not to bow the knee to their own cultural and political environment. As a part of their mission to be the church, they are attempting to allow the church to shape the character and purpose of their "distinctive talk" about God and the world. It is time for homiletics to acknowledge their mission and to assist them in the recovery of the communal nature of preaching. It is time for homiletics to make its "turn to the church."

(1) *Preaching as event.* Protestants must rethink the metaphor of *event* with which they have long described the nature of preaching. The event may come from "above" as in most Lutheran and neoorthodox thinking, or it may arise from "below" as in liberalism's greater appreciation of the human sources of revelation. In both approaches, though the former would not acknowledge it, preaching mediates an *experience.* Moreover, it is an experience that has the potential, at least, of isolating the hearer in a private encounter with the Word and abstracting the worshiper from the church.

Preaching-as-event cannot be traced to any one theologian or theological school. For theologies that operate with revelation from above, the Word of God symbolizes a judgment, a *krisis,* knifing through history and meeting humankind in the religious consciousness, the conscience, the soul, or at what Luther called "the mathematical point" of encounter.[15] Any attempt to prepare for such an encounter leads to works righteousness. The Word of God happens, said Barth, wherever and whenever God makes it so.[16] The "experience" of this Word—and Barth was willing to retain the word *experience* to describe the encounter—has solely to do with God's breaking into human reality.[17] This theological truth, however, can lead to a false picture of the Christian life. For event-theology, the Word is not a story or an explanation by which a community forms its identity over time, but a call to repentance, an announcement of justification, or, as in Bultmann, a summons to authentic existence. It leaves the hearer not with a new way of life or a new "world" to inhabit, but a new status before God.

The mode of this event-from-above is always proclamatory, and its medium is pure sound. Faith is an acoustical affair. No rhetorical theory can explain it, and no form can do it justice. The truth of the Word cannot be affected in any way by the formal characteristics of its language-conveyance. Indeed, Barth argued that the form of the sermon served only to obscure the Word of God.[18] Rhetorical form exists only for the sake of persuasion, which is but another attempt to supplement the intrinsic eventfulness of the divine Word with a human technique.

And what of preaching-from-below? The event it describes also mediates an experience of revelation. Where preaching-from-above flows from Christology, preaching-from-below operates with a more general view of revelation. Scratch deeply enough into ordinary experience and you will discover intimations of or analogies to the divine life. The Bible's primary purpose is to provide the clues as to where to scratch. Preaching-from-above stresses hearing; preaching-from-below facilitates recognition. Thus it is the preacher's task to help the hearer *see*. Preaching-from-above prefers Romans and the feast of the Resurrection. Preaching-from-below enjoys the Synoptics and revels in Christmas and Epiphany. Word theology stresses content, with the sermon's form serving as so much conduit for the message. Analogical theology, on the other hand, knows that every content necessitates a form and that form is never accidental to content. Rather, the gospel must be attentively shaped to the capacity for its reception. Truth is nothing without its experience. In one, preaching is an event which mediates an experience of God on *God's* terms. In the other, preaching does the same but on *human* terms.

What finally makes both versions of the *event* untenable is their inattention to the church. The community is not trusted to interpret or embody the Word. The Word falls on the conscience of the individual but does not *render* or inform the life of the community. Neither Bultmann's call to authentic existence nor liberalism's reliance on experience creates an imaginative world of the church in which Christian hearers can find a home.

A word-event, someone has said, is hard to trap. It is as fleeting as a momentary encounter with grace or an inspirational feeling of acceptance, but it says little about the kind of people we shall be. Because of the abstract theological properties that Protestants often attribute to the word-event, the preacher is obliged to create an equally abstract "world" in which this Word will appear to be effective. Ignoring the real life of the church, the preacher tries to conjure the real world with observations from life. Once this "world" is established in the sermon, hitting it with the Word is as easy as shooting ducks in a gallery.

(2) *Preaching as translation.* Stymied by the two abstractions of Word and world and failing to consider the richness of the ecclesial medium that connects them, the preacher is left to construe the sermon as a work of *translation.* How to get from Word to world? The hymnist's haunting lament becomes the preacher's broken record: "What language shall I borrow / To thank thee, dearest friend?" Save for the massive exception of Karl Barth, twentieth-century theology (and preaching with it) has dedicated itself to finding the philosophical, therapeutic, or political equivalents to the gospel of Jesus Christ.

Translation is a form of apologetics. Its tendency is to promote not the particularity of the Christian faith but its universality. Revealed particulars may subtly become examples of a larger, more universal truth, as when the preacher speaks broadly of the human thirst for eternity and then adds, "Jesus called it the Kingdom of heaven." Preaching-as-translation often bypasses the most distinctive elements of Christianity, thereby producing religion without "myth," ethics without eschatology, worship without ritual, and death without resurrection (or, more frequently, resurrection without death). *Traduttore traditore,* goes the Italian proverb—a translator, a traitor. Translation discards words and concepts that are specific to the Body of Christ in favor of their interpersonal analogues. In the late 1960s William Malcomson reported one group's attempt to render the Christian vocabulary into a universal language:

> Instead of using the word *salvation,* we spoke of getting to know people more deeply and getting to understand ourselves more fully. Instead of *redemption,* we spoke of caring about other

123

people, being really concerned. . . . Instead of *divine,* we spoke of not knowing how to express what we feel, of trying to reach out toward another person.[19]

The point here is not to criticize a sincere attempt to communicate the gospel, but to remind us what that gospel looks like when it has been uprooted from its environment in the church's liturgy and ministry.

(3) *Preaching as illustrations.* The mania for translation produces a familiar result: the sermon illustration. The very notion of translation implies that a gulf is fixed between the Bible and the contemporary world. The preacher is thus obliged to seek to join the two. In liberal preaching, particularly, the bridge is usually built from the secular side of the gulf. Not only in liberal preaching, however, but in *most* preaching, the middle term between the biblical world and our own is often assumed to be the enduring and universal stuff of human experience. The more relevant the portrayal of that experience, the more satisfying the sermon. Thus the prodigal son was as callow as your typical seventeen-year-old, spoiled brat. The disciples in the boat with Jesus were as anxious as any person thrown into the "storm" of a personal crisis. The early workers in the vineyard were angry, just as I am when a lazy student receives a better grade than mine. The cleansing of the Temple reminds me that it's all right to vent my anger at unjust institutions, and so on.

Books of homiletical helps present pages of sample "joins" between religion and the contemporary world. Preachers have traditionally called this join an *illustration.* So important are these tidbits of experience that illustrations often assume a life of their own, and neither the preacher nor the congregation can remember what they were illustrations *of.* In the hands of experiential-expressivist preachers, illustrations are not sanctioned by their reflection of the text or appropriateness to the gospel, but the accuracy with which they reproduce our favorite or most fearful experiences. Rhetorician Richard M. Weaver reminds us that an illustration "implies that *something* is being illustrated, so that in the true illustration we will have a conjunction of mind and pictorial manifestation. But now

. . . the tendency is for manifestation to outrun the idea, so that illustrations are vivid rather than meaningful or communicative."[20] The sermon becomes little more than a vehicle for free-floating inspirational experiences, which are at best tangentially related to a religious truth or a vivid detail in a Bible passage.

When the communal context of preaching is forgotten, the preacher blithely "borrows" language from every conceivable "scene" except the one that is given—namely, the church. For some perverse reason, the preacher often seeks illustrative material from the most exotic realms possible, as if he or she were intentionally trying to detach the gospel from its moorings in the local community's life in Christ. Instead of picturing what it means to be the people of God, the preacher validates the gospel by ransacking literature, history, the movies, and his or her diary in order to show a correspondence between Christianity and the modern world. The measure in which these correspondences create an experience that is emotionally gratifying will often determine the degree of the preacher's "effectiveness."

It is time to make the turn to the church. Not human nature or experience but the *church* is the middle term that connects the text and the present community. The church is not a piece in the hermeneutical puzzle but the means by which it is solved. The church is the interpretive community that encloses the most primitive New Testament groups as well as today's Old First Church.[21] The church is the *scene* that historically and liturgically contains the acts and agencies of our individual sermons. Today, as twenty centuries ago, a fellowship that names itself after Jesus gathers around the sacraments and the proclaimed Word in order to be equipped for mission. Today, as then, the community envelopes the communicator and gives meaning and purpose to the message. What might our sermons be if preachers seriously acknowledged the church?

NEW CHOICES FOR PREACHING

(1) From event to formation. As attractive as the *event* is as a metaphor for God's action in the sermon, it does not deliver the

125

moral and theological formation necessary for God's people in the world. The alternative image of the journey or pilgrimage suggests that the sermon does not merely strike the conscience or create an existential experience, but that preaching, as opposed to individual sermons, forms a community of faith over time.

Preaching does this by consciously aligning itself with its primary scene, which is the worship service. The basic unit of meaning on Sunday morning is not the sermon but the service. What the service is trying to express in its lessons, prayers, order of worship, and sacramental actions, the sermon also articulates. Most worship services contain a gathering of the congregation, songs of praise and doxology, recitations of God's mighty acts, reminiscences of Jesus, the celebration of the sacraments, and a blessing and sending of the people into the world. These elements occur by means of responsive speech, song, repetition, and ritualized behavior. Should not preaching partake of this, its liturgical scene, by incorporating into its own language the spirit of gathering, the telling of the story, the attitude of doxology, and all the other dimensions of worship? Isn't it incongruous that the president of this assembly, the minister, should insert into this corporate observance a speech that focuses either on individual needs or universal truths but does nothing to reinforce the identity of this community, to train it in mutual love, or to equip it for ministry? No one will deny that individuals are convicted and justified by the Word and otherwise experience the blessings of God in church. But just as the New Testament was written to guide and sustain communities of Christians, so our preaching is meant to form a people of faith.

Preaching-as-formation is not content with its own eventfulness. It does more than announce a new standing before God or hold up fuzzy correspondences between religion and meaningful experiences. It directs the faithful into the implications of their redemption in Jesus Christ. Instead of demonstrating the likeness of Christian teaching to conventional values, which is the usual method of sermon illustrations, preaching-as-formation explores the differences. In so doing, it becomes the voice of the church as a contrast-society.

(2) From Illustration to Narrative. Aside from their skeletal structure, our sermons create a "world" composed of the characters, stories, anecdotes, allusions, and proofs with which we enflesh our basic arguments. Each of us has a limited field from which we fashion this world, and that field corresponds to our own understanding of God's relationship to the universe. If we imagine that God acts primarily in the lives of individuals or upon humankind in general, we will tend to package our illustrations as discrete units of experience. They will function analogously to the "topics" or commonplaces of classical rhetoric. The topics were all-purpose arguments that could be inserted into in a variety of situations. They were the orator's sure things. Similarly, the accomplished preacher may call up sure-thing illustrations, match them to various texts or truths as the situation requires, and punch them into the sermon like numbers on a jukebox.

But illustrations do not form a people for discipleship in the world. Illustrations that are solely premised upon the likeness of revelation to human experience cannot embolden a contrast-society. What is needed is the recovery of the narrative that has given identity to God's people. Homiletics' discovery of story over the past two decades does not indicate a full recovery of narrative. Story-preaching has actually done more to confuse the issue, for it has reinforced the use of illustrations and blurred the true purpose of narrative in preaching. Many homileticians and most preachers still think of stories as a way of making contact with the hearer by displaying familiar experiences in narrative form. An apt comparison in and of itself gives pleasure. The identification-stage of storytelling is followed by the lesson-stage in which the story then confirms some moral or religious truth which is implicit in the sermon.

But the church is not saved by stories but by the God who is rendered by them and emerges by their means. Our God has but a single story. Its most important purpose is neither identification nor illustration (of some other truth?), but *incorporation*. Preachers tell the story of God's faithfulness to Israel and to the church in the ministry, death, and resurrection of Jesus in order to incorporate their hearers into the very communities that have served as vessels of the story. The point is not to tell bunches of substitute-stories or to recount meaningful experiences that are vaguely analogous to God's story but to tell that one story as creatively and powerfully as possible, so that present-day communities will live it. Its message is not the entelechy of personal fulfillment—"You can be all that you were meant to be!"—but the narrated promise of God's ongoing rule in the world: "The Lord invites you to participate in the coming Kingdom—now!" The story we tell does not nail down important truths, but it enables a people to go on. Storyteller Isak Dinesen claims "Any sorrow can be borne if a story can be told about it." If such retelling appears repetitious, it is repetitious like the liturgy is repetitious—like the eucharist, like the church year, like the mercies of God are repetitious. Thus the apostle John reminds his congregation, "I write to you, not because you do not know the truth, but because you know it . . ." (I John 2:21).[22]

(3) From Translation to Performance. Neither our worship nor our preaching has as its ultimate purpose the examination of a religious text for the sake of the lessons that can be derived from it. Just as the liturgy is not a text but an action, so preaching is not a translation of an ancient text but a "performance" of it.

And the ultimate "performer," after the preacher has led a run-through of the story, is the Christian community. This is nowhere truer than in the book of Acts. Although Acts dramatizes "sermons" in which an individual speaker and his audience have a role, its more comprehensive theology of the Word associates preaching with a Spirit-charged complex of words, communities, and actions. The Word of God is portrayed as a movement that "grew and multiplied" (12:24) and "prevailed mightily" (19:20). The book of Acts does not reflect upon the hermeneutical gap between then and now or Jesus and the believer because that distance was daily being overcome in the life of Christian communities. Preaching is not represented as one person's persuasive address. It is the ceaseless activity of the church (see Acts 5:42).

The Christian church read, preached, sang, enacted, and otherwise "performed" the biblical words, and it continues to do so, thereby re-creating for itself a living figure from ancient materials. As it is used here, the word *performance,* like the word *act,* does not indicate falsification or charade, but enactment.[23] The performance of the Word of God is characteristic of traditions as varied as Orthodox mysticism, Roman Catholic sacramentalism, Puritan typological exegesis, and Pentecostal and African-American ecstasy. Without the community's performance of and participation in the Word, the chasm between the Book and the contemporary community is unbridgeable. The Bible remains a dead letter. There is no "meaning" that lies dormant in the text. Meaning is disclosed in the community's performance of the text in worship and in its witness in the world.

The African-American congregation is one of the best examples of a people that involves itself in the performance of the gospel. The Enlightenment taught biblical scholars (and preachers) to step *back* from the text in order to extract lessons from it. The black church did not pass through the Enlightenment and therefore is not as susceptible to modern alienation from the biblical story. Rather, it found salvation by stepping *into* the text and identifying the suffering and hope of its community with the stories of the Bible. In many African-American congregations, therefore, the preaching of the gospel is not a story of past events or a series of illustrations. The gospel coincides with the experience of the people. Even the preacher who dramatizes "How *I* got over" is voicing the community's joy in deliverance. When the Bible is preached according to the history and imagery of the community, its stories do not entertain but enable a people to go on. The community interprets the Word, and the Word interprets the community. That precarious balance gives to preaching an emergent character. Instead of descending from above, the Word emerges, or sometimes erupts, like a spring from the depths of a people's history and experience of the Word of God.

The community's experience of the Word transcends the perennial questions of translation and illustration. Shall I begin with the text or experience? Use the language of Zion or Cana? Bible in one hand, newspaper in the other? When the sermon's

129

language and imagery reflect the world of the living church and when its purpose is formative rather than persuasive, such questions lose their relevance. As recognition of the church's existence as a contrast-society continues to grow, contemporary preaching will move from *event to formation, illustration to narrative,* and *translation to performance.* These moves do not represent new rhetorical skills that must be mastered by the preacher, but new perspectives from which to view the entire enterprise of the church's ceaseless witness to Jesus Christ.

CHAPTER SEVEN

BEYOND NARRATIVE: IMAGINATION IN THE SERMON
Paul Scott Wilson

Without writing much that specifically focuses on the subject of imagination, Fred B. Craddock has perhaps done more than anyone else in recent memory to promote it in the pulpits of the United States and Canada. His sermons, lectures, commentaries, and homiletical books—initially about what he called "inductive" preaching—in various ways have each contributed to this. It is appropriate, in this volume celebrating his contribution to homiletics, first to clarify what we mean when we speak of imagination by way of a brief historical review, then to identify some specific functions of imagination in the sermon, and in the process to outline some homiletical strategies for enhancing it in our preaching.

THE FALLACY OF IDENTIFYING IMAGINATION WITH NARRATIVE PREACHING

To encourage *imagination* in preaching is not to encourage a particular *form of preaching,* although many people commonly identify homiletical creativity with story or narrative. Imagination is more than a mere synonym for creativity. It is helpful for preachers to understand the term within the history of Western thought as part of larger discussions about metaphor, rhetoric, and contemporary philosophy and language theory, for then the uniqueness of imagination can begin to emerge. The history is rich and diverse, but even a tour that is brief can enable the preacher to begin to grasp what is at stake.

131

Many people may still tend to think of imagination in the manner that Aristotle understood metaphor. Metaphor for him was a mere figure of speech, an ornament in language, an image—beautiful, highly valued, emotionally and aesthetically effective, but ultimately dispensable. A quality of one thing is attributed to another for effect, as in the metaphor, "She gave him *an icy glance.*" Aristotle and his followers argued that other words could easily be substituted in place of a metaphor without radically affecting the meaning, in order to communicate more precisely (simply saying, in this case, perhaps, "She hated him."). This understanding of metaphor, known as the substitution theory,[1] has been dominant throughout history. It seemed to be given tacit theological support and homiletical emphasis by Calvin and the Puritans who sought, where possible, to banish art from worship as a distraction from the Word of God. Their plain-style preaching minimized metaphor, imagery, and rhetorical divisions in favor of an unembellished presentation of the truth. Aristotle's understanding of metaphor would eventually be challenged by an appreciation that metaphor was more than just a figure of speech.

A second area of changing historical understandings concerns rhetoric or the art of persuasion. It, too, has affected our understanding of imagination. The result here was to make imagination and reason into adversaries. Classical rhetoric had five "canons" or sets of rules for creating speeches: *invention* (the discovery of potential arguments to use); *arrangement* (the order in which an argument is to be developed); *style; delivery;* and *memory.* In these canons, rhetoric and logic were intertwined. Logic was one of three kinds of appeal a speaker might use to persuade an audience: the other two were ethos and emotion.

By medieval times, rhetoric had largely lost its fundamental "oral" roots; it became linked with rules for written composition. The canon of invention tended to receive less emphasis, and as a result the attention given to logical argument diminished. The canon of style received increased importance, particularly in the Augustinian-Ciceronian schools.

Peter Ramus (1515–1572) recast rhetoric in a significant way. By his time, logic and rhetoric were no longer easy partners, and the ancient connection between them was largely lost. Ramus sought to restore logic and to clarify its difference from rhetoric. He introduced a dichotomy that formerly had not existed.[2] He assigned to rhetoric all matters of "style," "dress," and "delivery." He assigned to logic all matters of "invention" and "arrangement" of argument. Rhetoric became the property of imagination; logic became the property of reason and intellect.

A dichotomy between imagination and intellect was one of the results of the new rhetoric. The split was greatly reinforced by Francis Bacon (1561–1626)[3] and by other philosophers of the Enlightenment. They conceived of the human soul as possessing a number of attributes that could be ordered in a hierarchy of "faculties." In this "faculty" understanding of human psychology, imagination and reason are distinct and separate, and imagination is inferior to reason. These philosophers called a necessary halt to the popular preoccupation with individual words and ornate style, and called for primary attention to be given to "weight of the matter, worth of the subject, soundness of argument, life of invention, or depth of judgment."[4]

There were a number of other results: rhetoric, as ornament, was made subservient to logic (hence our use of the pejorative phrase, "It is just rhetoric."). Mental images were understood as products of the senses, and imagination was therefore seen as reproductive rather than as productive. While these images were necessary for thought, they were separate from ideas which were the product of reason. Thus form and content, image and idea tended to be conceived as separable.

John Locke (1632–1704) helped to frame the predominant eighteenth-century view of imagination. He identified wit with *imagination* and saw it as the power to see *similarities;* he identified judgment with *reason,* the power to see *differences.* Because imagination was as likely to produce fictions, dreams, visions, and emotions as it was likely to assist reason, and because it was akin to an instinctive or sensory power, it tended also to be suspect as a wild, unpredictable faculty that threatens natural order, needs tight control, and that should, if necessary, be minimized. This conviction that imagination was dangerously opposed to the status quo was not new. Aquinas's famous phrase that imagination made "everything other than it is" simply echoed classical mistrust. These ideas formed the seeds from which sprang popular eighteenth-century assumptions that imagination is opposed to both reason and science, instead of being integral to each.

It was left to the Romantic movement of the late eighteenth to mid-nineteenth centuries to begin overcoming the separation of imagination and reason. Two English-speaking theologians in particular (the first more known for his poetry), in different ways linked imagination with God's self-revelation. Samuel Taylor Coleridge, inspired largely by German idealism, defined imagination as the "reconciliation" or juxtaposition of "opposites," an act of self-conciousness in the individual mind that was identical in manner with the primary imagination of God.[5] He identified primary imagination with reason and absolute knowledge. (Kant had similarly spoken of a hidden art in nature, "a blind but indispensable faculty of the human soul without which we would have no knowledge whatsoever.") Coleridge identified secondary imagination with individual acts of poetic creativity, individual acts of reconciliation of opposites. I have argued elsewhere that his "opposites" were not simply logical opposites; they were any identities that were separate, distinct, and independent. His idea of "reconciliation" did not imply neutralizing "opposites," but rather meant the formation of new or third identities that "interpenetrated" opposites by the act of juxtaposition.

Profoundly influenced by Coleridge, Horace Bushnell in New England thought of all language as symbolic and metaphoric, and anticipated Paul Tillich in denying the possibility of a strictly literal (non-metaphoric) reading of the Bible: "Human language is a gift to the imagination so essentially metaphoric, warp and woof, that it has no exact blocks of meaning to build a science of." Bushnell used the word *imagination* in a positive way to mean the penetration through language to discover Christ, "the metaphor of God; God's last metaphor."[6] He thought that truth could be offered most fully within paradox or contradiction.[7]

It was thinking such as this that began the monumental modern shift of metaphor theory away from Aristotle's

134

restricted notions of "figure of speech" or "ornament of thought." William F. Lynch, Paul Ricoeur, Sallie McFague, and others in our own century have told us that *the way we think* is fundamentally metaphoric. Metaphor is not simply a figure of speech rooted in language. Rather, language and consciousness are rooted in metaphor.

Imagination is now sometimes used as a synonym for metaphor conceived as this larger creative linguistic *process*. Thus Urban T. Holmes III discusses imagination as a form of deeper perception beneath the surface of language;[8] and Eduard Riegert speaks of it as the power to "un-arrange" the mind: "An arranged mind, of course, is resistant to seeing."[9] (Ricoeur called this imaginative capacity to see old things in new ways a "second naïveté.")

Imagination is used in philosophy as a synonym for a related process, the process of ethical and social transformation. Richard Kearney's recent study of imagination in modern philosophy, *Poetics of Imagining: From Husserl to Lyotard*, summarizes imagination as, "the human power to convert absence into presence, actuality into possibility, what-is into something-other-than-it-is. In short . . . our ability to transform the time and space of our environment into a specifically human mode of existence *(Dasein)*."[10] Imagination is for Kearney the ethical human dimension. It has three ethical functions:

> *Utopian, testimonial* and *empathic*—[all] intimately linked to the poetic activity of imagining otherwise. How could we commit ourselves to utopian possibilities of existence, recount the stories of past heroes and victims, or respond to the ethical call of fellow humans, without the imaginative ability to *listen* to other voices from other times and places? And is it not this aesthetic acoustic which enables us to record a new voice for those others here and now?[11]

These and similar understandings of imagination as either a quality or process of thought have wide-reaching implications for homiletics. At minimum, they imply the reintegration of form and content, medium and message, image and idea, art and subject, and, as Coleridge encouraged, heart and head.

Beyond this, they encourage further identification of the affinities between imagination and Christian faith, from both linguistic (the characteristic language used for each) and ethical perspectives.

Unfortunately, the subject of imagination still represents a dividing line in contemporary homiletics. In our discipline, informed understanding of imagination seems lacking. Some continue to treat it as a synonym for unfocused, nonconceptual thought,[12] while others may be read to imply that doctrinal reflection precludes imagination.[13] This is simply the Ramus dichotomy in new clothing. In such thinking, imaginative preaching becomes identified with narrative form and inductive learning, and propositional preaching becomes identified with abstract thought, deductive learning, and detachment from experience.

I have found it most helpful homiletically to think of imagination not as a particular figure of speech (e.g., simile, metaphor) nor as a form of speech (e.g., poetry or story) nor as one kind of logical thought as opposed to another (i.e., induction verses deduction). Rather, it is a mode of thought that contrasts logic and, yet, is its necessary complement.

Imagination and *logic* may be understood as *two ways of thinking,* or as *two qualities of thought* that are, to some extent, mutually dependent. Logic is primarily unidirectional or linear, moving step-by-step to a specific purpose or intent. It finds meaningful connections between ideas primarily on a temporal axis of cause and effect.

By contrast, imagination finds a meaningful connection between two apparently dissimilar ideas that have no causal relationship. Advertisers imaginatively connected the idea of a city with fruit to get "The Big Apple." It has been common to think of logic as the only means of human knowledge. That understanding is inadequate. Imagination not only brings two ideas together, it also perceives a unity between them, or, to use Coleridge's words, it "reconciles" them as a new identity. Imagination produces something like a spark or a flash of new insight between them.[14] This perception of unity is not random; it is an act of discernment, a means of knowledge.

136

If we consider the metaphor, "love is a red rose," the two ideas (poles, opposites) that are brought together are "love" and "a red rose." At a literal level, it represents a falsehood or contradiction (love is not in fact a rose). Paul Ricoeur called this the "no" of metaphor. However, at a deeper level there is a "yes" as well: the "yes" in this case has something to do with the beauty or fragility of love and perhaps also with the color of the heart. This "reconciliation of opposites" to produce new meaning is the signature of imagination.

There are a variety of specific *forms* imagination may take. Metaphor is one. Paradox or contradiction is another. Parable is another (the poles being a mundane everyday story, on the one hand, and a religious idea such as "the Realm of God," on the other). Simile is another. Symbol is another. In fact there are many possible forms of imagination (even as in logic there are many different forms).

Part of the problem in identifying imagination with the particular homiletical form known as story or narrative is that there is no reconciliation of opposites intrinsic to narrative form *per se,* any more than there is to propositional form *per se.* Story operates primarily by inductive logic. Poor narrative technique, for instance the mere recital of events in a chronological order, results in simple linear thought. Moreover, imagination can as easily use propositional form as it can narrative, to incorporate polar sparking at a variety of levels, as we will explore. Both forms are potential fields for imaginative expression.

Imagination and logic, as two qualities of thought, should be used to complement each other. They exist not as enemies, apart from each other, but as aids to each other in a relationship of mutual support and dependency. When preachers emphasize imagination to the exclusion of propositional thought, the result can be a random collection of images or ideas that suggest possible sparks of meaning that ultimately fail to coalesce in a unified or purposeful whole. Similarly, when preachers become entirely propositional to the exclusion of imagination, their sermons become intensely linear, abstract, preoccupied with categories and removed from experience.

137

When we think of the movement of imagination in the sermon, we may start, then, by erasing what may be some of our presuppositions about imagination. Form (or medium or image) is not the issue on its own, nor is content (or message or argument) on its own. Some "interpenetration" is necessary. Imagination may be discerned operating in the sermon in various ways, at various levels, in various forms, in conjunction with logical thought. We want to be thinking of a variety of possible linguistic or conceptual poles that are in meaningful relationship with one another, such that new ideas, emotions, and perceptions are generated. It is within this bipolar context that imagination offers some genuine creative linguistic and ethical possibilities for preaching.

SOME SPECIFIC FUNCTIONS OF IMAGINATION

In addition to similes, metaphors, symbols, parables, paradox, and other formal expressions of imagination, we may identify some specific functions of imagination in preaching. Here I will examine imagination's role in three areas that are vital for excellent preaching: interpretation of the Bible (the revelation of God in the past); discernment of God's action in the world (knowledge of God in the past and present); and presentation of the mystery of God (past, present, and future). We may speak of these areas using Kearney's three ethical functions of imagination: testimonial, empathic, and utopian. Within each area it is possible to identify some strategies for enhancement of imagination in the sermon.

(1) Testimonial Imagination and Biblical Interpretation

Testimonial imagination, as defined by Kearney, looks to " 'exemplary' narratives legacied by our cultural memories and traditions for ethical guidance."[15] Of course for Christians our primary narrative is found in the Bible, and it is not always or ever simply exemplary; it is revelatory. It is nonetheless the standard by which we measure our doctrines and actions. We

138

search the Scriptures for understanding of who we are in relationship to God.

When we read the Bible, we want to read with imagination to determine what the testimony was and is. This does not mean reading into the Bible something that is not there. Rather, it is reading with greater precision and more accuracy, such that we begin to experience the richness of meanings that are in fact present. Imagination here implies perceiving metaphorical and symbolic possibility where it in fact exists, not just in the text but in our lives as well. The interpretive task is never one-way. Even as we engage a text, we find it affecting us, altering the way we think, or if you like, reinterpreting our lives. We read best when we read critically, and critical reading requires the creativity and discernment that are present in different ways in both imagination and logic.

There are a number of reasons for our failure as preachers to acknowledge the cornucopia of meanings present in a biblical text. First, we may have been taught that the details of a text do not matter, just as some people have been taught to skip descriptive passages in novels. "Get to the point," we may say to ourselves. Many of the details of a biblical text can in fact open valid new horizons in the text. The details are not separate from whatever legitimate understanding of the text may unfold; they are part of it because they are in relationship to every other aspect of the text. They remain unseen and their significance overlooked simply because we are over-familiar with the text and can no longer experience it afresh, with the "second naïveté" of Ricoeur.

Second, we may have been mistakenly taught that a text has only one meaning, one point. Some commentaries reinforce this impression as do some preachers when they preach and shut down all other possible interpretations for their listeners by insistence that their meaning is the only one. It is best to understand that there are many correct and many incorrect interpretations of every text. Our task is not to present the full range of possibilities, but to present one responsible interpretation that can be an effective bearer of the truth to us today.

Third, familiarity with our own church traditions may prevent us from seeing other possibilities. We assume that a text means what we remember it to mean or have been told that it means. For instance, if we had been taught from early days in Sunday school that Lot's wife was wrong to look back, we might be blind to exploring what was right about her action. Was she not right to have second thoughts about all those who were left behind?

Here are some homiletical strategies using testimonial imagination:

(a) Think of the text as being like a diamond with many facets; through any one of them you can see the center. There are many ways of looking at a text. Choose one way that interests, excites, or even bothers you and let that be your starting place. If we are bored by the text, we may bore with our sermon.

(b) Any idea with which a text is concerned may be called a concern of the text. These concerns of the text may be stated in very short sentences (e.g., Jesus healed the blind man; the man thought the people were trees). Try taking a biblical text and seeing how many of these concerns of the text you can identify. You will start to notice things you did not see before.

(c) Whenever we come upon a fresh idea about a text, we have come upon a concern of the text we had not noticed before. They may come from three sources: the details of the text itself, the commentaries with which we test and expand our interpretations, and our background knowledge of the time (e.g., the nativity commentaries may not mention the concern of the text, *Shepherds were outcasts,* but by Jesus' time this was a fact).

(d) Concerns of the text deal with the past: They are located in the text's ancient time (e.g., Jesus used the absence of wine as an occasion to manifest God's glory). If we now put this same idea in the present tense, we have an idea that may have truth for our time (e.g., Jesus comes to us in our need to manifest God's glory). This present-tense idea can be called a concern of the sermon. Already there is a spark between the two concerns. You can find similar sparks with each of your concerns of the text.

(e) This is an unconscious process that we do each time we prepare to preach. By making it conscious, we identify theme statements for individual paragraphs (or groups of paragraphs)

140

in a sermon that moves, possibly several times, into the text and then back to our situation. We only need a few of these paired concerns to plot what David Buttrick calls the "moves" of the sermon.

(f) When we present the textual material in the completed sermon, it is best to remember its testimonial nature. Testimony implies giving witness under oath. Often we are tempted to report about the testimony, rather than allow the congregation to hear the testimony as an action or event. The difference is one of style between preaching as though we are writing an essay, and preaching as though we are talking about real life events (albeit events 2000 or more years ago).

(2) Empathic Imagination and God's Action

The empathic imagination Kearney defines as the power of "receptivity" to the other: "It suffers the other to be the other while suffering with (com-patire) the other as other."[16] From a Christian perspective, this empathy or receptivity to others begins with our relationship to God as Other and ends not in the feeling of empathy but in its expressed action through mission to others. We are able to love or empathize with others because God first loved us. The empathetic imagination begins then, in speaking of God's action.

In preaching we do well to remember that the opposite of a God of love is not a God of anger but a passive God. This passive God is the ineffective God whom we too easily proclaim for fear of putting our faith on the line. This passive God is similar to Luther's "unpreached" God—an abstract, hidden God who refuses to become flesh and known.

The passive God is the one whom we say *knows* our pain, is *near us* in our need, who *hears us* when we cry, who *sees* what happens to us, and who *cares* from a distance. We have no need of a couch-potato God who could as easily be watching another channel and might rather flip stations than become involved. Instead, we need the kind of God our God actually is—a God who acts, who chooses to be known through the act of preaching, who intervenes in history, even now, who enters the place of suffering, who brings good out of evil and justice out of

141

oppression, who embraces rather than shuns the enemy, and who in Christ is willing to die on a cross.

Every preacher, in turning to the Bible, has the primary responsibility for discerning not just the action required of the people in the biblical text but also the action of God in and behind the events in the text on behalf of God's people. To preach what the disciples did or what one of the apostles did is simply not enough. They are not our source of hope. To stop short of naming what God was doing is to foreclose the theological venture.

It is one thing to talk about what God was doing in the past. It is yet another thing to talk about what God is doing in the present. We are tempted here to be timid, and with good reason. We neither want to be presumptuous about God, nor do we want to identify our own limited perception of good and evil as God's. It is appropriate, therefore, that we be cautious in claiming with too great a precision what God is actually doing in a particular contemporary situation.

Here are some homiletical strategies using empathetic imagination:

(a) The movement of the sermon may be conceived in a variety of ways. Historically, particularly within the Protestant sphere, the most consistent overall movement has been the movement from law to gospel.[17] This may be understood as a movement from the cross to the Resurrection or from judgment to grace or from demand to privilege or from despair to hope or from bondage to freedom or from the fallenness of this world to the redemptive promise of the future that meets us even in the present. This is *not* a movement from Old Testament to New Testament: Law and gospel are two aspects of God's Word, in both testaments.

(b) Most of us have time in our sermons only for one movement, from law to gospel. It has only been in the present century that Protestant sermons have moved substantially away from the earlier normal length of an hour. If preachers have an hour, it is possible to move several times, back and forth, into law and gospel. Within the present shorter time frame, however, only one movement from law to gospel is generally possible if each is going to be uttered with some expression of fullness. In the first half of the sermon, move to heighten the effect of the law, both in the text and in our situation. In the second half, move to heighten the effect of the gospel (good news). By the end, the two—rather than neutralizing each other—exist in tension with each other. They at times seem contradictory but both are true, the reconciliation of which is an act of faith and is to be understood as an expression of God's love.

(c) Choose words that emphasize the action of God, particularly in the second half. This means removal to the first half of such phrases as "we must," and "we have to," for they put the burden of responsibility upon us. This also means possibly omitting from the gospel section phrases such as "God challenges us to . . . "; "God calls us to . . . "; or "God tells us to. . . ." While these do emphasize an action of God, they quickly turn the responsibility back to us. Rather, we are looking for ways to indicate what difference the Christ event has already made and is currently making for the world. Even the phrase, "God invites us to . . ." is weak; an invitation given is not an invitation accepted. Try instead phrases such as, "God has pushed aside the barriers that prevent us . . . ;" or, "Christ has already overcome the powers of death that we face."

(d) Pick as the central idea of your sermon a pair of concerns (a concern of the text along with a concern of the sermon) that focus on God's action (i.e., a gospel statement not a law statement). Otherwise law will predominate; our action will be stressed; God will tend to be passive and remote; and the hope that is our responsibility to proclaim and that can be rooted only in God's action will remain abstract. This action should be phrased in the present tense, not the future, otherwise the gospel may seem like mere pie in the sky.

(e) When developing a concern of the text as an explicit theme of one or more paragraphs, we can use material from our three sources to support our claims; the biblical text itself, the commentaries, and our own background knowledge accumulated from a variety of sources. When developing a concern of the sermon, use contemporary experience interpreted through the lenses of our theological tradition.

(3) Utopian (Realm of God) Imagination and Mystery

Utopian (*u-topos* = no place) imagination, which for us may be better understood as imagination that perceives the realm of God, is the "ability to disclose the possible in the actual, the other in the same, the new in the old . . . [that discerns] the *dissimilar in the similar* . . . [and] the *similar in the dissimilar*. . . ."[18] It is this, Kearney says, that allows for a "sense of identity in and through temporal differences (by synthesizing our past, present and future horizons of experience . . .)"; personal identity and commonality with others; and shared goals to guide historical actions. As Christians, we understand this movement toward God's intention for the world to be connected with prophecy that moves toward fulfillment. We refuse to condone a future that is foreclosed by anything but God's love as it has been expressed for us through Jesus Christ. This opening of the future, rather than shutting it through human limitation, may be understood, in preaching terms, as an enhancement of the mystery of God.

As Paul Tillich said, that which is essentially mysterious does not lose its mystery in being revealed. It is nonetheless possible in preaching to talk about the mystery of God—and of ourselves in relationship to God and others—in such a way that our representation dispenses with any mystery. Too often the result of preaching is that God is explained, reduced, made safe, and also—an equal heresy—made an object primarily about which we decide rather than being the One who decides about us. Thought rigidifies, clichés flourish, categories are assumed, and expression and behavior become codified. The wonder of the salvation event is reduced to formulaic doctrine and theological jargon that is simply repeated, dry phrases that once bore truth but may now only truly bore. All of our attempts to limit God are doomed, whether we choose to limit God to a particular moral, creed, doctrine, story, time, place, people, person, or practice. We want to re-examine the words of our faith, and to restore them with new meaning.

Frederick Buechner said it well when he said that at its best, preaching "puts a frame around the mystery." Preaching is not an explanation of God as much as it is an invitation to faith and promise. Most of our central doctrines can be formulated as

144

contradictions or paradoxes that enhance mystery and demand faith. For instance, God, who is almighty, in taking human form chose to become mighty only in weakness. Jesus, who lived his life as a servant to others even to the point of suffering death on a cross, is now the servant ruling in love and power over all. The One who was dead is now alive. Our death now means eternal life. Such formulations do not make logical sense. By logic alone we can never arrive at faith. Faith is a matter of imaginative discernment of truth through paradox and contradiction in addition to logical discernment. The *nonsensical* truth that is discerned in faith can in fact *make sense* of all the despair and anguish we may feel in this troubled life. This is part of the mystery we seek to preserve in proclamation. It is preserved in large part, whether the preaching emphasis is primarily on logic or on imagination, by enhancing those contradictions that are necessary to communicate the meaning of and point toward the Christ event.

Here are some homiletical strategies using utopian (realm of God) imagination:

(a) Preaching does not seek to create mystery but to disclose it. Most of life, even with all of our science, is mystery. The mystery at the center of it all and the object of our preaching is the mystery of a God who created everything out of nothing and who in Christ became human and accepted death in order that each of us might have life. This mystery is experienced on a personal level for each of the hearers when they find that their social masks are removed, when the spoken words reflect the darkness that is in them and that they are in, and when, alongside that reflection, is juxtaposed the transformed reflection of who they are already in Jesus Christ.

(b) The mystery of God is further honored when, alongside our own individual reflections, are juxtaposed the reflections of people we do not know from all places on the globe. We recognize them not as strangers but as brothers and sisters in Christ. We recognize them not as dehumanized "issues" but as people with faces, feelings, and families. Each person is loved with the same love that we experience. One of the primary faults of North American preaching, which not surprisingly is also found in our media, is a disproportionate preoccupation with our own culture. This stands as a denial of the validity of the gospel, the good news which has implications for all people everywhere.

As a church we prayed for many years for the end of the Iron Curtain, for freedom of peoples of the East, and for the reduced threat of war. God was struggling for freedom all of those years. And yet, when peace finally came, first with the parties atop the Berlin wall and then with the rise of the new Commonwealth, many of us did not bother to acknowledge God's doing. Yes, there is ongoing suffering, but yes, in its midst we see ongoing signs of God's actions of love, peace, reconciliation, and mercy. Such mystery needs to be proclaimed.

(c) The mystery of God's love is enhanced if we empathize with the worst person that we mention in the sermon, whether from the biblical text or our situation. Someone in the congregation is likely to identify with this person. This does not mean that we condone evil or fail to denounce it. But we do struggle to understand what might drive a person to do evil. This is the ministry of compassion. It prevents us from taking "cheap shots" at individuals (e.g., politicians) or at groups of people (e.g., the rich).

(d) The proclamation of the mystery of God's action in the past and present is a necessary prerequisite if we are to proclaim the mystery of God's future. We move from what we know to what we know only through faith. Out of our knowledge and ongoing encounter with God, we dare to name what are God's dreams for this world. This future we already taste in our celebration of Holy Communion. Prophecy may concern the life of just one person or of many nations. Perhaps this is what Henry Ward Beecher meant when he defined imagination as "the power of conceiving as definite the things which are invisible to the senses."[19] Even in our uttering these dreams, God's Word goes forth that they may be accomplished, not as the never-yet of the philosopher's "utopia," but as the not-yet of the Christian's "Realm of God."

146

CHAPTER EIGHT

TEXTS SHAPING SERMONS
David L. Bartlett

A lmost by definition, homiletics is a field that lacks classic secondary texts. Our concern is always that the Bible speaks to this world in the light of the best critical and theological insight we can bring, and *this* world keeps shifting on us, as of course do criticism and theology.

Nonetheless I venture to guess that Fred Craddock's book *As One Without Authority,* now twenty-two years old, will come as close to a homiletical classic as anyone dare wish. At the very least, anyone writing the history of preaching and of teaching preaching in the latter half of this century will need to attend to Craddock's plea for inductive preaching and to his book's influence on our work.

Introducing his memorable sermon "Doxology" at the end of the book, Craddock writes lines that have helped provide inspiration for a number of preachers and theoreticians in recent years:

> Since the text is a doxology, a burst of praise in the midst of a theological discourse, so is the sermon. To have converted the text into a syllogism, or a polemic, or an exhortation, or a defense of a proposition would have been a literary, hermeneutical, aesthetic, and practical violation without excuse. Let doxologies be shared doxologically, narratives narratively, polemics polemically, poems poetically, and parables parabolically. In other words, biblical preaching ought to be biblical.[1]

In many and various ways preachers and homileticians have sought to obey Craddock's mandate, none of us wanting to be without excuse.

Craddock's enthusiasm for his own exhortation has been perhaps somewhat tempered. In the chapters leading up to the sermon on doxology, Craddock argues for the effectiveness of inductive preaching. While inductive preaching does pay attention to the form of a biblical text, it also pays particular attention to the experience of the preacher in shaping the sermon and to the congregation's experience on which the preacher wishes to draw. Inductive preaching is also open-ended preaching, leaving the congregation to complete the work of the sermon in their own reflection and practice. This is presumably true whether the text for the sermon is open-ended (like the story of the elder brother and the prodigal son in Luke 15:11-32) or straightforwardly parenetic (like James 2:1-7).[2]

In his more recent textbook, *Preaching*, Craddock further modifies his enthusiasm for requiring that the form of the text determine the form of the sermon and leaves perhaps a modicum of excuse for those whose sermons are shaped in other ways.

> The values of permitting the biblical text to instruct the sermon on form as well as content are evident. All the benefits of variety in form as mentioned above are provided in this procedure as well. In addition, there is more assurance of integrity in the sermon if both design and substance come from the same source rather than having a message from one source and the form for its delivery from another. This is not to say that the shape of the sermon *must* come from the text: a text that is a prayer does not necessitate a sermon in prayer form, . . . and so forth. Sometimes the shape of the text will carry over into the sermon quite well. . . . However, more important is attending to the form of the text to discern what it achieves—praise, correction, judgment, encouragement, defense, reconciliation, instruction—and then asking if the sermon is designed with that in mind.[3]

One of the strengths of the textbook is that it provides clues for a great variety of sermonic forms, some of them quite different from the forms of the texts they are intended to interpret.[4]

In his book, *Preaching and the Literary Forms of the Bible,* Thomas Long seems to do precisely what Craddock recommends in *Preaching.* Long provides very helpful discussions of the rhetorical strategies of a variety of biblical genres, and for the most part, instead of insisting that our sermons should somehow follow the same form, he asks what rhetorical purposes the form suggests and then asks how our sermons might accomplish something of those same purposes.[5]

Craddock's cautionary reminder that the rhetorical purpose of the text is a more crucial control on the form of the sermon than the text's genre and structure seems absolutely right, and Long's book shows the success of just that strategy. Not every powerful sermon on a parable will be narrative in form, and some sermons on fairly discursive passages by Paul will be full of story.

Nonetheless one appropriate strategy for preaching a text is to ask how the text might shape the form of the sermon as well as its content and rhetorical purpose. We will not always want to preach hymnically on Psalms or hortatorily on Pauline parenesis, but we will want to ask week after week whether the decision to shape the form of the sermon after the form of the text may not be appropriate to our theological and pastoral purposes.

An anecdote may help. A friend was still mumbling on Monday morning about the sermon his pastor had preached on Sunday. The text for the sermon was the Beatitudes from the Sermon on the Mount:

> "Blessed are the poor in spirit, for theirs is the kingdom of heaven.
> "Blessed are those who mourn, for they will be comforted." (Matthew 5:3-4)

The preacher had turned blessing into exhortation, promise into imperative. "You must be poor in spirit," said the preacher, or perhaps, "We must be poor in spirit." The inclusive first person would not much have helped the sermon. My friend, hearing the text, waited for blessing to be pronounced. Instead he got a pep talk on spiritual fitness.

Of course blessing might have been pronounced in any number of ways. The escape from the form of the text did not itself dictate that gift would turn into demand. But to have stuck to the beatitude—to paraphrase, repeat, specify, delineate the blessing would have been one good way to let the text function as Matthew's Gospel shaped it to function.

We want to avoid a kind of formal fundamentalism. We will not want to damn sermons that are shaped by considerations other than the shape of the text. But we will want to hear sermons on Psalms that lead to song; sermons on parables that attend to plot and character, then and now; sermons on Paul that sound like a real discussion between an exasperated Christian leader and probably equally exasperated Christian church people.

This essay provides an experiment. We ask what shape several different genres of biblical literature take. We ask what a sermon shaped in very much the same way might look like. Of course, like our colleagues, we will waffle a bit on the line between form and content and a great deal on the line between form and rhetorical function. Nonetheless we try to ask formal questions of text and sermon alike. Our suggestions belong in that middle place between text and sermon, not dictating how we are to preach, but suggesting one way worth considering from time to time.[6]

PREACHING ON THE PARABLES

Parables are extended metaphors. Parables are stories. Some parables are more obviously metaphoric and compact. Some stretch toward the short story. Yet the most compact carries a touch of the narrative, and the most extended draws at least implicit metaphorical comparison.

John Donahue reminds us that the root of parable is *para ballein,* to throw alongside of: "Etymologically parable means that one thing is understood in juxtaposition or comparison with

150

another."[7] Most often in the New Testament parables, something fairly familiar (a seed, a woman seeking for a coin) is thrown up against something less familiar (the kingdom of God, God's rejoicing love for sinners).

The richest parables, like the richest metaphors, defy easy translation, especially translation into propositional prose. The apocryphal story says that when the poet was told to explain his poem he simply read it again. Were we to take that cautionary story too seriously we would only read parables, never preach them. Nonetheless the caution is well-taken. Every good parable like every strong metaphor is richer than our explanations; explanations help, but they do not contain the power of the comparison.

More than that, the richest parables—like the richest metaphors—have power in part because they take on new meanings in new generations. It is probably an exercise in homiletical futility to urge urban American congregations, for instance, to place themselves among first-century rural Palestinians. But the picture of the farmer who plants his seed and cannot do a thing except keep on keeping on until suddenly(!) crisis, and he acts or all is lost—that picture translates into new places and new occupations gaining power precisely by its allusiveness (see Mark 4:26-29). That element of inductive preaching that Craddock commends for its open-endedness and ability to involve the listener in reaching any conclusions fits most appropriately those most open-ended and participatory of texts, the parables.[8]

This understanding of parable as almost inexhaustible metaphor cuts directly against the old first rule of parable preaching: Find out *the* point and preach it. Parables move us in certain directions but often they do not make a point or even several points. They leave us understanding but wishing to understand more.

Parable is also story. The ones we know the best are perhaps the most storylike: the good Samaritan (was goodness the issue?); the prodigal son (is he the real protagonist?). Especially with the longer parables it is not only appropriate but vital to look at the same aspects one would with any story: character, plot, conflict, climax, resolution.

As with metaphor so with story. The best of them cannot be reduced to any moral or theological point. If Jesus had really just wanted to say, "God is merciful to sinners," he had the vocabulary and the conviction. Why this complicated story of family conflict, reconciliation, and—what? What is that brother doing out there in the fields? What will he do the next minute? After our story ends, is his father still standing there puzzled and inviting? We all know that the college outline study of a Hawthorne story is not the thing itself, and neither is the blurb that tells us what Eudora Welty surely means by telling us about those people in that predicament. Of course, a sermon on the parable is not the thing itself, but most days it ought to excite us, involve us—not distance us from the characters and their dilemmas.

Very often the parables are surprising metaphors and subversive stories. I do not mean this politically, though there is no way to limit what implications a good parable might have. I mean rather that they either make us really look at what has always been there or make us see something astonishingly new, or they help us see the world from some angle that our limited vision had always denied. When the wounded man looked up from the side of the Jericho road, whom did he see? When the Samaritan bent down, whom did he think to help? Sometimes the parables just confound our expectations altogether. Christian people still get angry when they hear about that vineyard owner paying the one-hour workers as much as those who slaved all day (Matthew 20:1-16). And what about the steward who is clearly cheating someone, though we're not sure whom (Luke 16:1-9).

How do we preach the parables parabolically? There is not one meaning to a parable; there is not one way to preach parabolically. Here are some options, each of them sometimes effective.

Trust the image or the metaphor. Find images or metaphors that shed enough light on the original metaphor that you can play one against another. Small things grow great enough to shelter the birds of the air. Treasure sometimes sought earnestly, sometimes stumbled upon almost accidentally. What treasure did you stumble on in your life this week? What do your people value so much that they would sell all their conventional securities to touch it for a day?

Tell parables on the parable. Of course you are not saying exactly the same thing. You are telling stories that help illumine Jesus' story; Jesus' story illumines the stories you tell. One year Martin Luther King Sunday and the lectionary listing of the parable of the mustard seed came together. When Rosa Parks refused to move to the back of the bus, the preacher gave a theological reading to her courage. She said she was tired. Her opponents said that she was planted. Her refusal was planted, like a seed. Such a small thing. Immeasurable.

Tell the story of the parable in modern dress. Some excellent teachers of preaching just hate this device: too much drama and not enough proclamation, too much attention to the preacher and too little to the text. Of course the act of preaching itself calls attention to the preacher. Standing up there in an odd costume and waving your hands calls attention to the preacher. The lines are fuzzy and not absolute and differ from preacher to preacher and people to people. Some of us have emerged from dramas sacred or secular as touched by the Word as we are when we emerge from most sanctuaries on Sunday morning. These are stories after all. Don't do it every week, but sometimes the retelling does make it come alive as what it is: story. Not proposition. Not theorem. Not command. Not dogma. Story.

Or tell the story as if you were back there, watching or participating or remembering. But tell it with the concerns and questions of your people in your mind (how could you do it otherwise?). Sometimes excellent preaching doesn't say, "Here's what this might mean for us." When I hear your telling of the story, I am beginning already to think what it might mean for me.

Usually tell the story from one perspective only. The prodigal son provides a host of possibilities: father, younger son, older son, perhaps even the servants or the pig-sty owner, though I am old-fashioned enough to want the sermon's story to stay close to the center of Jesus' story. You can tell the story of the good Samaritan from the view of the Samaritan, the lawyer, the man in the ditch.

We are being encouraged to remember all the people of God in worship, especially the children. Parables retold can touch children who still love to hear, "Once upon a time" or, "There was a man who had two sons."

PREACHING ON THE PSALMS

Psalms present their own problems and opportunities for preaching. It is obvious to all that they belong in the hymnody and prayers of the church; it is perhaps less clear that they are appropriate texts for preaching.

The psalms are poetry, not poetry as we think of it, marked by rhyme and meter, but poetry marked above all by parallelism, where one line repeats or counters or builds on the line before.[9] This is not simple dull repetition. Whichever kind of parallelism the psalmist uses, each line enriches the other; new meanings emerge:

> Bless the LORD, O my soul,
>   and all that is within me
>   bless his holy name.
> Bless the LORD, O my soul,
>   and do not forget all his benefits. (Ps. 103:1-2)

The second half of the stanza parallels the first but does more. Blessing is remembering. God is holy not only because of God's holiness (the holy name), but also because of God's goodness (the benefits):

> who forgives all your iniquity,
>   who heals all your diseases,
> who redeems your life from the Pit,
>   who crowns you with steadfast love and mercy,
> who satisfies you with good as long as you live
>   so that your youth is renewed like the eagle's. (Ps. 103:3-5)

Each line recapitulates the last, reinforces it, but moves beyond it, giving further nuance. The psalmist remembers not only redemption from sin but from disease, not only from disease but from desolation and death. Then turn it around: not what are we rescued from but what are we redeemed for? To know God's love and mercy, to know God's benefits, again. And then the final line toward which the stanza drives: youth renewed, life lifted up on eagle's wings. Artur Weiser puts the hymn in canonical context. In God's mercy, says the psalmist, we are daily born again.[10]

Robert Alter reminds us that the psalms are not only poetry that works by repetition and reinforcement, they are conventional poetry. That is to say the images are drawn from a kind of common treasure house of appropriate images for the prayers and the songs of the people:

> Such a reliance on the conventional is perfectly understandable. For a text that is to be chanted by pilgrims in procession on their way up the Temple mount, or recited by a suppliant at the altar or by someone recovered from grave illness offering a thanksgiving sacrifice, you don't want a lot of fancy footwork in the imagery and syntax; you want, in fact, an eloquent rehearsal of traditional materials and even traditional ways of ordering those materials in a certain sequence.[11]

This suggests that from early on the psalms have functioned as they often function for us now, as a kind of memory bank of images that have illumined and strengthened us in the past and that therefore can illumine and strengthen us today. Not surprisingly when crisis comes, people of active or latent faith find themselves humming familiar hymns. Not surprisingly at the great "conventional" moments of our lives, moments when custom and ceremony meet—like baptism, marriage, funeral—we turn again and again to the psalms, not because they provide a brand new word from the Lord but because they revive the words that have sustained us in the past. They are in that sense conventional.

Yet the power of the conventional rests in part in the nuance that makes possible new meanings on new hearings of even the most familiar words. Even the best known texts may make a twist that surprises us. Take Psalm 23, for example.

When we have specified the meaning of "the Lord is my shepherd" new possibilities will still emerge. The poetry itself provides considerable specificity to the metaphor (he makes me lie down; he leads me; he restores my soul). The qualifications qualify but do not limit the possibilities of interpretation.

Images have double meanings, or triple, or more. "He leads me in the right paths" means both that the Lord leads us in the correct path and in the path of righteousness. Sometimes righteousness is just a matter of knowing whether to turn left or right at the intersection. The Hebrew probably does not say "the valley of the shadow of death," but interpretation is conversation and in English this term in the conversation is three hundred years old. Valley of the shadow of death, the shadow death casts before itself: the valley of fear. The shadow death casts after itself: the shadow of grief.

The "person" of the verb forms shifts halfway through. We begin in the third person ("the Lord is my shepherd"), and we move to second person: "Even though I walk through the darkest valley I will fear no evil, for you are with me." We cannot praise God in the third person for long. Speaking of God in the presence of God we turn to God in gratitude and prayer.[12]

How do we preach these conventional images with their unconventional shifts and surprises? We honor imagery as appropriate to preaching. For many faithful people, images precede both theology and doctrine. Preaching the psalms, we will let the imagery be central to our enterprise, repeating the familiar, finding other images that illumine and reinforce the old.[13]

Some preachers are poets and find in the repetitions and reinforcements of Hebrew poetry a model for their own preaching. All of us can find ways to reinforce a theme or an image by repetition that both underlines and expands what has gone before.[14]

The poetry of our preaching (and the poems we quote in preaching) will probably draw on familiar images more than on astonishing leaps appropriate to the "metaphysical" poets. We have a better model for preaching in Robert Frost than in John Donne or T. S. Eliot. The difference between Robert Frost and much other popular verse is, of course, that Frost both surprises us with the nuances he discovers in conventional images and rigorously avoids sentimentality. We will do likewise.

We cannot separate rhetorical form from rhetorical function. Preaching on the psalms will usually not convey new information or end with imperatives: "So the psalm teaches us that God is trustworthy." "In the light of the psalm let us repent our sins." Preaching on the psalms will end with praise or with repentance. Praise or repentance will well up among the people in the presence of God. We will not need to enjoin what the psalm will induce.

PREACHING ON PAUL'S EPISTLES

Paul is a preacher who takes pride in his preaching, but what we have in the canon are not his sermons (except those that may be presented and shaped in Acts). What we have in the canon are his letters.

Paul's letters are a substitute for his presence. In many of the epistles Paul clearly sends the letter and its messenger though he wishes hc himself could be there. The letter therefore partakes of his apostolic authority: It is the unique word he *is* speaking to that church, though he be far away.

Yet he is far away. The letter provides special opportunities and special problems. On the one hand, Paul may be more persuasive, clear, and effective in a letter than he is in person:

> For [my opponents] say, "His letters are weighty and strong, but his bodily presence is weak, and his speech contemptible." Let all people understand that what we say by letter when absent, we will also do when present. (II Corinthians 10:10-11)

Here it seems clear that, far from feeling that Paul's letters are a poor substitute for his presence, some competing apostles have argued that his presence is a poor substitute for his epistles.

157

On the other hand, Paul writes his letters in response to information that is inevitably secondhand, incomplete, and biased. He writes I Corinthians with information both from an oral report by Chloe's people and from a letter sent perhaps by people with quite different interests and agendas. He writes Romans to introduce himself to a church he doesn't know, but he seems to have some very strong suspicions about what's going on. The form of a letter is the form of direct speech, but its power and its problems derive from its necessary indirection.

Closely related to this is the fact that all the letters, except perhaps Romans, represent one side of a conversation, and the only side we get to hear. Reading Paul is a little like hearing one end of a telephone conversation. "You foolish Galatians!" he says, but we're not quite sure what they said or did to provoke that outburst, and we are quite sure that foolish is not how they would describe themselves (See Galatians 3:1).

We see a third characteristic of Paul's epistles. On the whole in the structure of his argument "law" follows "gospel." Or to use categories less loaded with theological freight, obedience follows faith. Paul's great claim is that the gospel brings about the "obedience of faith," but the order is: faith/obedience (Romans 1:5). The structure of Romans is perhaps the clearest example of this move from declaring God's goodness, calling for our response of faith, and then exhorting us to live out the practical implications of God's gift and our faithfulness.

Fourth, when Paul does move to exhortation he typically begins his appeal with the Greek verb *parakalo,* "I exhort, I beseech, I beg, I urge." The term takes on not only the tone of a teacher with a student but of a parent with a child, friend with friend, almost of a lover with the beloved. When Paul beseeches, his life is so bound up in the lives of those besought that everything is at stake for him—as for them. We note a striking lack of professional or professorial distance (See, for instance, Romans 12:1; I Corinthians 1:10; I Thessalonians, where we have already had "gospel" in vss. 2-9; II Corinthians 10:1; I Thessalonians 4:10).

Fifth, Paul finds appropriate ways to bring his own experience to bear on the gospel he preaches. In Galatians, the story of his call and his conflict with Peter establish both his apostolic authority and his claim for a gospel unbound by obedience to laws regarding (at least) circumcision (Galatians 1:11–2:21).[15] In II Corinthians Paul speaks of the ways in which his own ministry has taken on the cruciform shape of the gospel, and in Philippians he tells the congregation that Christ crucified and risen has caused him to count all previously cherished goods as nothing more than dung (II Corinthians 4:7-12; Philippians 3:4-11).

Finally Paul takes into account the experience of his congregations. What he sees around is evidence for the meaning of the gospel as is his interpretation of Scripture. In Galatians he reminds the Galatians that their use of the term "Abba," "Father" in their worship is a sign of the freedom of the Spirit. In I Corinthians he argues that too much reliance on glossalalia in worship tends to drive outsiders away (Galatians 4:6-7, similarly Galatians 3:5, and I Corinthians 14:23).

How do we preach if the form of our sermons is shaped or influenced by the form of Paul's letters?

First, we acknowledge that while we preach from Paul we are not Paul. Many a sermon dies when the preacher instantly identifies with the wise apostle and identifies the congregation with the foolish Galatians. Most often we receive the letters as if all of us, pastor and people alike, were listening to the apostle, not speaking for him.

Second, iffy as it is, there is no way out of making informed guesses about the situation of the churches to which Paul writes and letting the sermon reflect both sides of the conversation. One of the joys of preaching Paul, if you are concerned for the life of a congregation, is that he is, too. Some attention to the social implications of his gospel helps us speak socially to our own people, in their communal context.

Third, Paul teaches us to start with good news and move to exhortation, not to start with exhortation and throw in a little cheery good news at the end. "I know this sounds impossibly difficult but fortunately Jesus died for you and the Spirit is with you. Let us pray." Preaching Pauline sermons, we start with "Jesus died for you, and the Spirit is with you," and we move from there.

Fourth, when we do exhort we are as involved in the outcome of our exhortation as was Paul. We do not give out orders from above but share gospel imperatives beside our people. At our best our authority is not his authority, but our passion for God's people can, however poorly, mirror his passion. When we exhort it will be clear that we love those whom we are exhorting and usually that it is exhortation we also need to hear. "I beseech" is much stronger than "I order" or "you must" or "we ought" or, even, "let us remember."

Fifth, Paul gives us permission to use ourselves as part of the story of the gospel. We will probably not ask our people to imitate us as we imitate Christ, but our testimony is a legitimate part of our claim to preach the gospel—as is the testimony of every other Christian person. Our preaching will attend to other testimonies gladly, but if Paul's letters are our model, we need not simply disappear into impersonal theological claims.[16]

Sixth, Paul lets us talk about the way we see the world. We may be wrong about it, but interpretation of the times is part of the preaching of the gospel, and it is a risk worth taking. What does it mean that we worship this way, or work this way, or raise our families this way? Are questions of sexual morality only questions about biblical interpretation or are they in part based on judgments about the real consequences of real decisions? Paul lets us sneak a little cultural analysis into our sermons somewhere between the discussion of the text and the final appeal.

In the legitimate enthusiasm for narrative preaching, we sometimes undervalue Paul. In some ways his letters are more immediate than even the liveliest of biblical narratives. There he is, warts and all, grace and all. Not too deeply hidden are all those other first-century Christians trying to put together the real gospel and their own diverse and confusing world. Just like us.[17]

160

PREACHING ON THE GOSPELS

Those of us who learned criticism under the reigning influence of the form critics and the renewal of biblical preaching have an enduring infatuation with the pericope as the proper unit for preaching. For reasons both theological and practical, we do well to preach one parable or one miracle story or one conflict narrative on any given Sunday. Yet our early confidence that each pericope contained the gospel in minia-ture, like a mustard seed containing the tree, was perhaps a little extreme. Each pericope carries the gospel only if we read the pericope in the light of the gospel, which is just what our preaching sometimes needs to do.[18]

Of the discussion of gospel genre there is no end.[19] And for the problem of genre there is no clear solution. We can safely say this. The gospel drives forward toward the crucifixion and looks backward from the Resurrection.

This is most evident in the Gospel of Mark, which may not be exactly a passion story with an extended introduction, but which does drive us, in pericope after pericope, toward the inescapable cross and Jesus' cry of abandonment. At the beginning the reader is told that Jesus is the Son of God; at the end, watching Jesus' anguish, the centurion acknowledges the truth toward which the prescript already directed us. So, too, the cryptic conclusion of the Gospel, which directs the women to Galilee and ends in silence, may well send us, the readers, back to the Galilean section of the book, to find there in those stories of miracle and controversy and conspiracy not just the reminiscences of Jesus before his crucifixion but the evidences of the way Christ risen is still present among his people.[20]

The other Gospels may not be so clear or so subtle in the way they move us constantly forward and back, but each does it.

For Matthew, the authority grudgingly acknowledged in the early chapters of the Gospel is claimed triumphantly by Jesus in the final verses. The temptations portrayed in chapter 4 come around again in chapter 27:

161

"If you are the Son of God, throw yourself down" (Matthew 4:6).
"If you are the Son of God, come down from the cross" (Matthew 27:40).

The last temptation is not unlike the first; the final courage and sacrifice were foreshadowed all along.

Luke's foreshadowing and remembering are more complicated still. Jesus' rejection at the synagogue in Luke 4 points to his rejection on the cross, which also points beyond itself to Stephen martyred in Acts 7. Like Jesus, Stephen forgives his tormentors for their ignorance. At Emmaus, the risen Jesus opens meaning of the Scripture. His resurrection also opens the meaning of the narrative Luke tells.

In John's Gospel, Thomas sees the wounds of the crucified and risen one and says, "My Lord and my God," which is what the poem said at the beginning—that the Word was God and dwelt among us and we did not receive him. Jesus keeps talking of being lifted up, pointing us to the astonishing triumph of the end which is simultaneously crucifixion and victory. Cryptic as John's Gospel is, it is less cryptic if we remember that from 1:1 on we have had hints that this one who does signs and speaks puzzles is also triumphant, crucified.

Of course, we won't preach the whole Gospel every time we preach a gospel passage. But more than we have often allowed, the shape of our sermons will include foreshadowings and rememberings. We will not pretend that we do not know the end of the story when we are right there in the middle. We cannot tell a healing story without remembering the brokenness of the healer when the gospel draws to its close. We cannot interpret Jesus' teaching without remembering the faith of the evangelists that the teacher teaches still. Preaching his words is not nostalgia; it is recognition, obedience, discipleship.

Preaching in a liturgical context helps us remember the whole movement of the Gospels. In many churches the most narrowly defined pericope and carefully limited sermon still move the people toward the table where cross is remembered and resurrection is declared. Even for those churches who celebrate eucharist less frequently, hymns, prayers, anthems, other readings, and architecture hold up the larger story of the gospel as we attend the story for this week.

Nonetheless our preaching any Gospel text will make the gospel always visible just at the edges of our exposition or as the subtext for our more obvious text. And in this essay for this occasion it is perhaps permissible to remember the day when an astonished friend returned from a sermon I was not able to hear: "Basically Craddock just told the story of St. Mark's Gospel. It took my breath away."

PART III
TURNING TO THE LISTENER

CHAPTER NINE

AND HOW SHALL THEY HEAR? THE LISTENER IN CONTEMPORARY PREACHING

Thomas G. Long

WHAT IS YOUR IMPRESSION?

In the spring of 1874, an exhibition of paintings in Felix Tournachon's studio in Paris sent convulsions of shock through the self-confident and mercilessly judgmental world of French high culture. Those who attended the showing of nearly two hundred paintings by such artists as Monet, Cézanne, Pissarro, Renoir, and Degas found, instead of the prevailing academic style of painting with its dramatic subjects, solid objects, and reliable tints, a bold and heretical display of light and color. Swirls, dots, and blobs interacted on the canvasses to create the sensation of movement and shimmering light.

The critics were, for the most part, outraged by this new art. "Amateurish" and "incompetent" they sniffed. The label that stuck, however, came from one offended critic who, mocking the title of one of Monet's works on display, sneered that the artists were mere "impressionists."[1] The general public reaction to these "mere impressionists" was as strong and adverse as that of the critics. When the works went on sale after the exhibition, the crowd became so unruly the police had to be called to restore order.

It is difficult today to grasp such widespread and deep public fury over what was, after all, simply an art exhibition. With the possible exception of the stir created in recent years by the showing of the works of Robert Mapplethorpe, nothing in our present experience comes near this dramatic reaction to the impressionist painters. What was it about these "mere impressionists" that provoked this measure of wrath and indignation? What was so threatening to the prevailing taste and sensibility about these painters and their works? It was certainly not simply their unconventional technique, nor was it only their surprising choice of subject matter (quite ordinary, even mundane themes—a Sunday picnic, a couple in a café, a woman playing the piano).

What was deemed to be dangerously radical about these new painters was how every aspect of their artistic approach—vision, style, and subject matter—worked together implicitly to undermine traditional artistic authority. These artists appeared, in fact, to do what no respectable artist of the day should have done, to abdicate their artistic authority in favor of the viewer, to shift the responsibility for the creation of meaning from the one who painted the work to those who gazed upon it. Thus, instead of presenting to the viewers a set of motifs and claims all worked out and ready for consumption, they invited the viewers into the sacred and once-forbidden sanctuary of creativity where only the artists themselves had previously been allowed. There was, notes art historian David Sweetman:

> a concern that an Impressionist work represented something dangerously radical, something beyond a mere revolution in style. In typical Salon work each element was as solid as its subject was weighty, the high degree of polish showed that the painter had mastered his craft and had earned his wages like a good craftsman should. By contrast, the shifting, impermanent colors and lighthearted subjects of these newcomers *seemed to be inviting the spectator to participate instead of imposing a single authoritarian view. They were subversively democratic.*[2]

What caused a thunderclap of outrage in the French art world—the shift of attention from the artist's imposed meaning to the viewer's participation in the creation of meaning—finds a quieter and somewhat surprising echo a century later in North American preaching. Fred Craddock's groundbreaking 1971 book, revealingly titled *As One Without Authority,*[3] both named the turn toward listener-oriented preaching that was already in motion and gave added and articulate encouragement to it. The preacher, Craddock maintained, "should recognize [the listeners] as the people of God and realize that the message is theirs also. He speaks not only to them but for them and *seeks to activate their meanings in relation to what he is saying.*"[4] What Craddock was calling for—sermons intentionally constructed out of the awareness of the listeners' role in preaching—had dramatic implications for the placement of authority in the event of preaching. Preachers, Craddock went on to say in a fascinating paragraph, should resist "imperialism" and, instead, be "good artists":

> The good artist is able to [resist the imperialism of thought and feeling.] A work of art does not exist totally of itself but is completed by the viewer. Nothing is more disgusting than some religious art that is so exhaustively complete, so overwhelmingly obvious, that the viewer has no room to respond. It is this room to respond that also marks a good drama. Edward Albee the playwright said in a television interview that anyone who bought a ticket to see one of his plays had to assume some of the responsibility for the play.[5]

Notice Craddock's assumption about art. "A work of art," he states offhandedly, on the way to claiming something else, "does not exist totally of itself but is completed by the viewer." Contemporary readers of this sentence will, presumably, shrug their shoulders and, without a ripple of concern, reply, "But of course. Art is completed by the viewer." Amazingly, what in 1874 generated riots in the streets of Paris has now become an accepted rule of interpretation, a matter of course, perhaps even a truism: The viewer completes the work. The hearer completes the sermon. But of course.

Moreover, there is abundant evidence that many contemporary preachers have tried, at least, to be "good artists," in Craddock's sense of the term, and have invited the hearers to share the responsibility for completing sermons. What are the signs of this shift in authority in preaching? Compare the typical sermon in a North American pulpit today with its counterpart a hundred—or even fifty—years ago, and one will discern that the locus of authority of the sermon has moved noticeably away from the preacher and toward the listeners. The older sermon, even if preached by a popular and accomplished preacher, will often seem to contemporary ears to be overly long, heavy, and ornate, full of excessive rhetorical flourishes and moral exhortations. Today's sermon, by contrast, is often less theologically and conceptually weighty, more dialogical and conversational in tone, less linear in structure, and more open-ended. The contemporary sermon will typically display far greater reliance upon image, narrative, and evocative phrase, and it will be focused upon ordinary, everyday events and how it is that they are the environment for the experience of the gospel, rather than upon heroic subjects and well-defined dramatic themes. In short, today's sermons tend to be more "impressionistic," inviting the listener to get in on the act and to join with the preacher in the creation of meaning.

THE MUTED TRUMPET

What has caused this shift in contemporary preaching? Perhaps it is simply that preaching has felt the same forces that are at work on other forms of communication in popular culture. Wilbur Schramm, who has written extensively on the history of communication, notes:

> The most dramatic change in general communication theory during the last forty years has been the gradual abandonment of the idea of a passive audience, and its replacement by the concept of a highly active, highly selective audience, manipulating rather than being manipulated by a message.[6]

Everywhere there is the presence of the receiver, the consumer of communication. In education one finds an emphasis upon the student, in literature upon the reader; in

170

journalism the accent often falls more upon the experiences of the journalist-participant and less upon any presumed objectivity of the event being reported. The plots of current movies are often nonlinear and impressionistic, their characters hazily drawn and their dramatic themes understated. As for television, McLuhan taught us that it is a "cool," interactive, viewer-involving medium. This can be graphically seen by a recent round of television commercials, highly debated in the advertising industry, that endorsed a new make of automobile by flashing on the screen images of foaming surf and rolling meadows, undergirded by lilting background music, but *never showing the car itself*, never displaying the very object being advertised. The viewer was given the complete responsibility to supply that essential piece. It may be, then, that contemporary preaching participates in a general trend in contemporary communication when it relies upon the hearers to exercise their authority as listeners and to supply at least some of what preachers of an earlier era felt quite obliged to provide entirely for them: the meanings of the sermon.

Some have claimed, though—however much this shift in sermonic authority is simply the result of a larger cultural movement in communication—that aspects of it are peculiar to preaching, an indication of the timidity of the church and evidence of a broad and deep deterioration in the importance of religious life in the culture. Some critics of the "softer" sermon say emphatically that the shift in authority from the preacher to the hearer is a particularly bad sign for the church, an indication of declining confidence in and clarity about the gospel itself.[7] Faced with the corrosive effects of secularism outside the community of faith and an uneasy pluralism within, preachers, it is claimed, have begun to blow their trumpets unconvincingly, emitting a meeker, less distinct sound. In this view, preachers no longer sure of the gospel themselves construct sermons that sound like "new age" music, all process and devoid of intellectual ideas—pleasant sounds with a fill-in-the-blank content. Preaching flings out loose bits and pieces from a center that can no longer hold. Congregations are served Etch-a-Sketch sermons:

171

You turn the knobs; you make your own picture. To preach "as one without authority," then, is not a virtue; it is an epitaph.

Most homileticians have disagreed and taken a much more positive view of the hearer-oriented sermon, both on rhetorical and theological grounds. Especially since Craddock's remarkable book, there have been many who have either followed his lead or advanced similar views, and it has virtually become a canon law of contemporary homiletics that sermons aimed explicitly at involving the listeners in the active and mutual creation of meaning are not only communicationally and psychologically more effective, but they are also theologically and exegetically more faithful to the character of the gospel itself. One after another, homileticians have joined the choir, eager to sing the anthem that listener-oriented sermons are called for by the rhetoric of the kergyma itself.

But is this true? Is it true that listener-driven approaches to preaching are more faithful to the essential character of gospel communication? And when homileticians make such assertions, do they know what they are talking about? Are they speaking anything like a common language when they affirm the value of hearer-oriented sermons? Well, yes and no. In order to get some clarity about this emphasis upon the hearer's role in preaching and to untangle some of the complex theological issues—in other words, to sift the wheat from the chaff—we need to trace a bit of the history of homiletics' interest in the listener. Herein lies a story.

WHAT WE HAVE HERE IS A PROBLEM OF COMMUNICATION

Once upon a time, homiletics (the theological study of preaching) and rhetoric (the art of effective speaking) were a happily married couple. From Augustine's *On Christian Doctrine* (perhaps the earliest homiletical treatise in Christian literature) all the way to the big, systematic homiletical textbooks in vogue in the nineteenth century, Christian homiletics looked to the Bible and to theology for the *content* of sermons and then to the rules and fashions of classical rhetoric for the *form* and *style* of sermons. It was a mixed marriage—homiletics being Jewish and rabbinical in background, and thus religious; rhetoric being Greek, gentile, and ideologically neutral—and it was a marriage of convenience, but it worked well. Homileticians knew what preachers were supposed to say, and rhetoricians knew how they were to say it, so that listeners could hear it and be persuaded by it. On some occasions theological homiletics took the lead role in the marriage, and on other occasions rhetoric was the governing force, but working together, aiming to "be fruitful and multiply," homiletics and rhetoric set out to produce sermons that were both faithful to the gospel and adapted to the capacities of the hearers.

The marriage, alas, was doomed. First, there was illness. Rhetoric became sick, sick unto death. Every practical theological field involves a marriage between a theological discipline and some human science. Christian education pairs theology and education theory; pastoral theology marries theology to psychology; church administration joins theology and organizational theory, and so on. At the turn of this century, every practical theological field, except homiletics, was beginning to find new life in its marriage and a burst of energy from its partner. All of the partner disciplines, save rhetoric, were experiencing a Copernican revolution in theoretical development. Think, for example, of the impact upon psychology of the work of Freud, the advancement of dream theories, and the discovery of the unconscious and the impetus these developments gave to pastoral theology. Rhetoric, however, was experiencing no such revolution and, in fact, was beginning to falter with age and to develop senility.

Indeed, as the twentieth century dawned, interest in rhetoric as an academic discipline waned drastically; active research all but ceased; courses in the subject were stripped from university catalogs. It is ironic that, just as the other practical theological disciplines were maturing, gaining energy and focus from their partner disciplines, homiletics was placing its aging spouse on a respirator.

Then, Karl Barth unplugged the respirator.

RHETORIC SUFFERS A BARTH ATTACK

How and why Barth and his theological program served, in some circles, to eliminate rhetoric as a partner for homiletics can best be seen in the light of his well-known public conflict in the early 1930s with fellow theologian Emil Brunner. It was largely a dispute between allies, since Barth and Brunner, both representatives of the dialectical movement in European theology, were united in the struggle against the reigning liberalism of the German theological academy. As such, they were in agreement on the essential contours of the Christian faith and the crucial character of the doctrine of the Word of God.

Hope for humanity, they concurred, lay not within the human condition, but utterly beyond it. That which commands our preaching—the saving Word of God, revelation—does not spring from any human capacity, not even from humanity's deepest impulse to be "religious," but comes to humanity as an utterly free act of God, as crisis, as promise, and as gift. On this much, Barth and Brunner were agreed.

But there was one urgent point of disagreement. Brunner was troubled by Barth's strong insistence on the complete discontinuity between the Word of God and the existing human condition. Barth was scrupulous to speak of the Word of God as something completely outside of the human possibility, as an event of and from God and not at all dependent upon anything on the human side.

Yes, Brunner acknowledged, it is true that the Word of God comes to humanity unilaterally and from beyond, but surely it must touch the human situation at *some* point. If not, the doctrine of revelation is simply an abstraction and rendered unintelligible. Brunner was persuaded that even a dialectical theologian must take up the homiletic question, "What does it mean to say the Word of God to a human being?"[8] But what is this point at which the Word of God touches the human condition? What is this "point of contact" between the Word of God and human beings?

Brunner's response to this is complex (Barth would say confused). Human beings, Brunner began, are created in the image of God. Thus, by virtue of the *imago Dei,* the question of God is definitive of human existence, and there is a quest to know God built into the very fabric of human nature. In broad terms, then, Brunner had already named the answer to his question. The point of contact between the Word of God and humanity is the *imago Dei* found in all human beings. But Brunner knew that there were problems with this answer. Hasn't the *imago Dei* been shattered by human sin? Hasn't humanity's quest to know God become hopelessly corrupt? Isn't the loss of the *imago Dei* the theological center of the doctrines of the Fall and redemption of humanity?

Yes and no, replied Brunner. The *imago Dei,* as a theological category, can be divided into two parts: formal and material. The formal *imago Dei* is simply the capacity to be human and to know and to respond to God. The material *imago Dei* consists of the content of a true knowledge of and relationship to God. It was the material *imago Dei,* Brunner argued, that was lost in the Fall; the formal *imago Dei* persists intact and, indeed, serves as the "point of contact" for the Word of God. "Eureka," cried Brunner. He had found the elusive "point of contact": the formal aspect of the *imago Dei.*

To Barth, this was all a shell game. In his reply to Brunner (unambiguously titled *No!*), Barth charged that Brunner was innocently placing on the table a seemingly neutral category called the "formal *imago Dei*" only to smuggle into it a great quantity of the "material *imago Dei*" by sleight of hand. Brunner's " 'formal *imago Dei,* ' " wrote Barth, "has now, as it were, openly become 'what the natural man knows of God, of the law, and of his own dependence upon God.' . . . Evidently the 'formal *imago Dei*' meant that man can 'somehow' and 'to some extent' know and do the will of God without revelation."

To elucidate what he perceived to be the flaw in Brunner's argument, Barth compared God's saving of humanity to the experience of a person who has been saved from drowning by a strong and competent swimmer. Now what, Barth wondered, would Brunner say about this drowning person's "capacity for being saved"? Perhaps, Barth suggested, Brunner would say that the person had a formal, but not a material, capacity to be

175

saved. But what could that mean? Maybe it would mean that the person's formal capacity to be a "person who is saved" is that he is drowning and that he is a person (as opposed to a lump of lead or a tortoise), in which case the whole matter is true, perhaps, but trivial. Or maybe it means that the person actually helped the rescuer by beating a few strokes in the water. "Can Brunner mean that?" Barth asked. "Surely not, for we have heard of 'man of himself can do nothing for his salvation.' And according to Brunner, 'the possibility of doing . . . that which is good in the sight of God' is also lost."[9]

So, Barth claimed, either Brunner means something true, but trifling ("In order for God to save a human being, that human being must be a lost human being") or he means something theologically outrageous: Human beings assist God in their own salvation. *Nein!* No! Absolutely not, thundered an aggrieved Karl Barth to that idea.

THE MERRY WIDOW'S WALTZ

This argument between Brunner and Barth spills over into homiletics precisely on the matter of the relationship of homiletics to rhetoric. What rhetoric has traditionally done for homiletics is to provide practical advice about structuring and phrasing sermons. The preacher should design the sermon this way, should engineer this sort of language, should use this sort of example, should employ these sorts of phrases—these are the kinds of matters about which rhetoric offers its advice.

These rhetorical helps and hints, however, are not formulated in a corner. They are built upon elaborate theories of human communication, formulations of how people listen. If you will do such and such in your sermon, rhetoric claims, people will hear it more effectively because people listen in particular and predictable ways to messages. Put in terms of homiletical theology, this is tantamount to the claim that sermons can be more effective conveyers of the gospel if they obey the rules of communication and are tailored to certain specific traits and capacities of the hearers. In other words, prior to the proclamation of the gospel, there is the rhetorical situation, and the preaching of the gospel must, to some degree, conform to it. If the preacher does not heed the rhetorical needs and capacities of the hearers, the sermon will miss the mark. On the other hand, if the sermon does obey the rhetorical rules and is shaped according to the hearers' patterns of listening, then it will connect to the hearers and communicate more successfully. Or, to use Barth's image, the drowning swimmer still has the ability to help the rescuer by beating a few strokes in the rhetorical waters.

Barth would have none of this. He was methodologically pure on this matter, and it is not too strong to say that Barth recommended that the preacher essentially factor concern about the hearers' situation out of the preaching equation. Rhetorical issues were not merely secondary concerns to Barth; they were to be eliminated from homiletical method for epistemological reasons. The listener does not shape the sermon—the gospel does, the Bible does:

> I have the impression that my sermons reach and "interest" my audience most when I least rely on anything to "correspond" to the Word of God already "being there," when I least rely on the "possibility" of proclaiming this Word, when I least rely on my ability to "reach" people by my rhetoric, when on the contrary I *allow* my language to be formed and shaped and adapted as much as possible by what the text seems to be saying.[10]

Barth gladly drove a stake into the heart of rhetoric and called upon the newly widowed homiletics not to mourn but to dance on the grave. Barth remained true to this theological method in his own homiletical thought, even in the most pragmatic areas. For example, David Buttrick, in his foreword to Barth's *Homiletics,* notes that Barth took the peculiar position of forbidding sermon introductions. Given Barth's overall views, however, it makes perfectly good sense to disallow sermon introductions, since, as Buttrick notes, they can so often be rhetorical strategies to establish contact with the hearers on grounds other than the gospel itself. Classical introductions betray an assumption on the part of the preacher that there is

177

something already "out there" in the hearer that can be summoned as a point of contact for the gospel, and establishing such contact with the hearers is precisely what Barth was convinced cannot be done and must not be attempted.[11]

In the 1950s and 60s, a number of homileticians picked up on Barth's lead, attempting to develop a fully theological, non-rhetorical approach to preaching, and their influence became a powerful one in American homiletics. For them, the emphasis fell upon the message of the Bible, biblical theology, and away from concern about the listener. "It is not the business of the preacher," wrote one Barthian-styled homiletician, "to try to force [the sermon's] result or even to speculate about it."[12]

Such approaches to homiletics, noble in their efforts to be clean regarding theological method, finally crashed against the wall of practice. Preachers cannot really avoid rhetorical concerns. There is a scandalous fleshiness to preaching, and while sermons may be "pure" theology all the way through Saturday night, on Sunday morning they are inescapably embodied and, thus, rhetorical. The sermon must have some structure; some language must be spoken; the hearers in all their concreteness are out there demanding to be factored into the equation; choices have to be made on some basis. With their careful and studied avoidance of the topic of rhetoric, the Barthianesque homileticians and their students did what Barth himself almost never did: ignored the art of imaginative communication and bored people in the pulpit.[13] Left on theological grounds without guidance, they often made poor rhetorical choices and fell into the trap of producing overly abstract and didactic sermons.

One can understand how this could happen. If the preacher is to pay heed only to the Bible and the Bible is seen to be teaching theological ideas, then the sermon could simply become an elaboration of those ideas, and in the most direct and propositional fashion. The result, however, is the sermon as blunt object and the hearer as victim. "On the one hand," noted Heinz Zahrnt, "without [Barth's theology] present-day preaching would not be so pure, so biblical, so concerned with central issues, but on the other hand, it would also not be so alarmingly correct, boringly precise, and remote from the world."[14]

Small wonder, then, that Craddock's monograph, *As One Without Authority*, struck such a responsive chord. In a homiletical world starved of excitement, a world that denied a place to rhetorical and communicational concern while often choosing, by default, the blandest and clumsiest forms of communication, the attention Craddock paid to the hearers and to their communicational needs blossomed on the gray landscape like the flowers of spring. Moreover, Craddock, and others like him, took advantage of the fact that rhetoric itself appears to have made a remarkable, even miraculous, recovery. Comatose for decades, rhetoric suddenly rose clear-eyed and lucid from the death bed, sporting some fancy new names like hermeneutics, narratology, communication science, and reader-response criticism. So, homiletics, led by Craddock and others, has headed off on a long second honeymoon, full of new strength and restored vision.

But a nagging question remains: Is Craddock simply Brunner *redux*? Barth had carefully constructed a seemingly impregnable wall between theological homiletics and rhetoric. What about Craddock and the others who have brought a rhetorical concern for the listener back into the homiletical arena? Have they successfully dismantled Barth's wall, or have they merely created a burst of interest by scrambling recklessly over it?

THREADING THE NEEDLE

The approaches of Craddock and other contemporary homileticians can thus be more clearly seen and accurately assessed against the backdrop of the debate between Barth and Brunner. For the most part they constitute a collection of efforts to thread the methodological needle, to push through the narrow opening between Barth and Brunner. The Barth-Brunner debate left theology, homiletics included, with an impossible dilemma, what Garrett Green has termed "a devil's choice" between positivism and reductionism:

Seizing the first horn of the dilemma leads to an accommodating modernism, the "neo-Protestant" heresy attacked by Barth, whose chief identifying mark is "natural theology" by whatever name it may be called. Choosing the other alternative, however, threatens to land theology in an isolated dogmatic purism in which revelation is protected from anthropological reduction at the price of refusing to speak of it in any but self-referential terms. The theologian is left speaking a language whose conceptuality is internally coherent but powerless to communicate its content because it is unrelated to all nontheological discourse. This alternative can be described as a "positivism of revelation," borrowing the phrase sometimes used by critics of Barth.[15]

Green acknowledges that Barth was essentially right about the argument. In the debate with Brunner, Barth's logic was unassailable, but, even so, Brunner's point cannot be lightly dismissed. He posed the correct and inescapable question, one that Barth finally could not answer and one that must still be addressed. What does it mean to *say* the Word of God to a human being? What is the point of contact on the human side for divine revelation? Contemporary homiletics can best be understood as a series of attempts to address that question anew, to find a middle way between positivism on the one side and reductionism on the other.

We can see the range of possibilities for threading the needle and, at the same time, survey the diverse ways in which the role of the listener is factored into contemporary views of preaching by exploring the positions of several representative homiletical theorists. In recent years, the homiletical literature has become much more diverse, methodologically sophisticated, and rich in theory. Thus a number of homiletical theories could be fruitfully examined, but we must be content to look briefly at the work of only four scholars: Garrett Green, a systematic theologican whose thought has profound implications for homiletics; David Buttrick, whose massive text *Homiletic: Moves and Structures*[16] represents the most dramatic and thorough return to rhetoric among American homileticians; Christine Smith, a pioneer in feminist homiletics who relies upon a strong listener-oriented approach; and Fred Craddock, an innovator in listener-driven homiletics and one whose thought continues to serve as a compass for other homileticians.

1. Garrett Green

Though not himself a homiletician, Green provides a very provocative and homiletically interesting answer to Brunner's question. "Imagination," Green maintains, "is the anthropological point of contact for divine revelation." Imagination is a basic human ability; the exercise of imagination is something that all people do in the normal course of living in the world. Unlike Brunner's notion of the "formal *imago Dei*," which turned out under scrutiny to contain some smuggled content, imagination, argues Green, is truely and purely formal. Imagination can imagine good things and bad things; it is neutral regarding content and value. Apart from revelation, human imagination knows nothing of God and can know nothing on its own. Indeed, left to its own devices, imagination becomes a factory of idols, and only when imagination is seized by revelation can human beings truly "imagine God."

There is a nascent homiletics in Green's thesis. He writes:

Proclamation . . . can be described as an appeal to the imagination of the hearers through the images of scripture. The preacher's task is to mediate and facilitate that encounter by engaging his or her own imagination, which becomes the link between scripture and congregation. The preacher must pay particular attention to the imagery of the biblical text, seeking to present it with such clarity and force that it will be seen and heard by the congregation. To save sinners, God seizes them by the imagination: the preacher places himself at the service of this saving act by the obedient and lucid engagement of his own imagination.[17]

So, according to Green, what is happening in the listener's head? The hearers of sermons are essentially imagining creatures. Their imaginations are like muscles, flexing and producing this or that image at random. The task of preaching, therefore, is to summon the imagination to grasp the gospel, to appeal to this basic human ability by imaginatively presenting to it the crucial biblical images. Thus, Green threads the needle. He balances the rhetorical side of preaching (concern with imagination, images, metaphors, etc.) with a vigorous understanding of revelation. Only when human imagination is given what it could not produce for itself, the true images from Scripture, can it in faith imagine God rightly.

One problem with Green's approach, however, is that it presents an exclusively imagistic and, thus, narrowly poetic understanding of the task of preaching. Preaching, to be sure, employs images and explores them imaginatively with the hearers. But preaching also tells stories, explains doctrines, explores ethical dilemmas, gives instruction, erupts in praise, and engages in many other forms of discourse. The history of Christian preaching demonstrates that listeners have more needs than the formal imagination can embrace, and that, humanity does not live by images alone, but by every word that comes from the Word of God.

2. David Buttrick

David Buttrick is quite aware of the issues involved in the Barth-Brunner debate, but he refuses to accept its sharply defined and discrete categories. Theologically, of course, there is the action of God on the one side and the response of the hearers on the other, but Buttrick positions preaching at the busy and intellectually messy intersection where they merge. So Buttrick describes the work of preaching in two-fold fashion, as a "double-hermeneutic": "We interpret revelation in light of being-saved, and we grasp being-saved in view of revelation."[18] By this, he wishes to acknowledge the two sides of the preaching transaction—revelation and the human situation—but he also wishes, and helpfully so, to blur the boundary between them and to show their dialectical relationship.

This can be observed by exploring Buttrick's view of the hearers. There they are in the pews, obviously connected

182

somehow, loosely or firmly, to the community of faith. But they are also parts of other groups ("labor communities, political blocs, social groupings, family, neighborhood, nation, and so on"[19]). Thus they are a mixture and, to be candid, something of an emotional and spiritual mélange. They are troubled by the presence of evil and by capricious suffering, aware of the capacity for disordered sexuality in themselves and others, know the possibility of madness, and experience many other ambiguities in human experience.[20] They are also aware of Christ being formed in their consciousness in many different ways. They are part faith and part fear, bound to the Christian community, but tethered by other loyalties as well. In sum, they are both-and, betwixt and between; they are "being saved" and they are "in the world." They are "being saved in the world."

This is a very promising beginning, but when Buttrick comes around to describing the practice of preaching, he is brilliant and provocative, but he begins to miss the bull's-eye. Having pictured the Sunday preaching environment in all of its richness and ambiguity, he then, puzzlingly, steps out the church window into thin air to build a homiletic. Instead of wondering about how language operates in this context of a people who are doubly defined (being saved and being in the world), he moves to a rarefied notion of how language forms in consciousness generally—in everybody, everywhere, always.

In the nuts and bolts section of his homiletical textbook, Buttrick seems to assume that each and every hearer is essentially alike. In terms of receiving language and allowing it to form in one's consciousness, every hearer operates basically just like the next one. A certain sermon illustration, for example, will form in the consciousness of Fred Murphy in precisely the same way that it forms in the consciousness of Ethel Kim in the next pew. This being the case, Buttrick is able to make unbendable rules about sermons: "A personal illustration will *always* split consciousness"; "long prose quotes . . . do not function . . . "; "multiple illustrations will always . . . make understanding more difficult," and so on. Indeed, the responses of the hearers are so uniform, predictable, and subject to the influence of the sermon that Buttrick is able to assert that "when congregations drift off into wanderings of mind, it is *always* the fault of the speaker."

This is obviously not true. In fact, so many of Buttrick's rules are clearly exaggerations that one suspects him at times of winking slyly at the reader, employing hyperbole as a playful strategy to force the reader to reconsider unchallenged assumptions. Actually, when one takes Buttrick's homiletical suggestions with a sense of humor and proportion, all of them are stimulating and most of them are quite helpful. What should be seen, though, is that the practical dimensions of his homiletic do not fully match his theological understanding of the preaching situation. On the one hand, Buttrick has this fertile theological notion of the people of God as "being saved in the world," a rich and raucous admixture of faith and folly. On the other hand, he builds his practical homiletic on a comparatively sterile base, the idea of people in the pews as a loosely hooked up collection of computer clones, all processing the same information in the same predictable ways. A potentially exciting conversation between homiletical theology and rhetoric has been largely overcome, then, by a quasi-technological monologue in which rhetoric does most of the talking while homiletics takes notes.

3. Christine Smith

Not all contemporary homileticians are eager to maintain the balance between revelation and the human context. For example, in the explicitly global-feminist homiletical theory of Christine Smith we find one of the more radically listener-oriented approaches to preaching available. "When one understands," she writes, "the goal of preaching to be the creation of solidarity, we must trust each person to do her or his own searching, struggling, celebrating, and naming."[21] She approves of an understanding of preaching that "does not tell people what to believe [but assumes] . . . that people have the power to discover their own truths and faith."[22]

What, if anything, assists the hearers in this discovery? The focus remains consistently upon the community of hearers. No source of revelation or assistance that purports to come from outside this community is easily admitted. Preaching is a kind of "faith sharing" in which the preaching honors, expresses, and seeks out truths that are already intrinsically present within the community.[23] Moreover, "Christian feminists," she states, "no longer assume that the Bible has ultimate authority,"[24] and even God "is not a far-removed, eternally benevolent being, but a sacred presence among us and within us, more than we are but intricately interwoven with all human activity."[25] Brunner's "point of contact" has been broadened and transformed, in Smith's work, to become a field of emergence encompassing virtually all experiences of human mutuality, especially those of women, which she privileges on liberationist and feminist grounds.

Where Garrett Green calls for the preacher to move from the biblical images toward the experience of hearers through the imagination, Smith reverses the process: Women begin "with their own female lives and experiences for the naming and imaging of God. . . . "[26] Not surprisingly, then, "salvation is not that which happens to us when we are 'saved' from ourselves by a mediating savior; rather salvation is something we do with each other in community."[27] In Smith's view, what Barth's famous swimmer needs is not a rescuer from the river bank, but rather just some assistance from the others struggling in the water.

The virtue of Smith's approach is her strong emphasis upon the community of faith, her insistence upon the dignity of hearers, and her awareness of suffering as a crucial context for theological discourse. For all of her language about community and solidarity, however, there remains an aching loneliness in this approach to preaching. The category of revelation is absorbed into koinonia. There is no saving Word from outside, and the community is, in the end, basically abandoned, left essentially to its own thoughts and emotions, finally able to talk meaningfully only to and about itself.

4. Fred Craddock

Craddock's understanding of the preaching situation, the rhetorical context of proclamation, has been subtly evolving over the years. In his early work, when he was developing the inductive approach to preaching, he relied upon a broadly optimistic anthropology. "It is theologically basic to the inductive method," he wrote, "that . . . the listener not be viewed as totally alien to God and devoid of Godwardness."[28] Craddock did not overlook human sinfulness, but he constructed his homiletic on the enduring "*imago Dei,* however distorted it may be."[29] The listener, claimed Craddock:

> has a "memory" of his true destiny but his ability to achieve it is perverted. Because of man's perverted self-understanding he does come into conflict with the Word of God, but a point of conflict is also a point of contact. Even a perverted relationship is a relationship; were there no relationship there would be no conflict. The inductive method operates on this assumption, that man does ask the question of his own being and of his relation to Ultimate Reality.[30]

This is, indeed, Brunner *redux,* and, as such, Craddock's view at this early stage asks the right question but provides an answer that is subject to the fierce methodological critique of Barth.

In his textbook *Preaching,* published a decade and a half after *As One Without Authority,* a somewhat different picture of the listeners emerges. Now, instead of individuals wandering "east of Eden," nostalgic for the garden and searching, however misguidedly, for God, we have a congregation of the faithful whose memory has been built upon through years of liturgical practice. In short, we have the *church* as a major theme, and Craddock has allowed his ecclesiology to shape his homiletics:

> Preaching is not only *to* but *for* the people. . . . Preaching is like prayer not only in the sense that God is the audience, but also in the sense that God is the church's; it did not arrive in town with the pastor but was already there. Unspoken at times, yes; confused and inchoate at times, yes; but there, as surely as the Bible was there, as faith was there, as need was there, as hope was there, as a sense of mission in the world was there.[31]

The congregation of the faithful says to the preacher not only, "Pray for us," but also, "Preach for us, we do not know how to speak as we ought." It is precisely at this point that revelation enters the equation. Craddock understands revelation to be a certain way of speaking, a breaking of the silence that enters into the life of the church, teaching it how to speak. Preaching, he says, is "making present and appropriate to the hearers the revelation of God."[32] By revelation, Craddock does not mean content alone (though content is not absent), but rather *mode* of communication. "If preaching is in any way a continuation into the present of God's revelation, then what we are doing and how we are doing it should be harmonious with our understanding of the mode of revelation."[33] In sum, revelation is God teaching the preacher, and then the church, how to talk. "At the risk of sounding presumptuous, it can be said that we are learning our method of communicating from God. . . . That is, the way of God's Word in the world is the way of the sermon in the world."[34]

BEGINNING IN THE MIDDLE

Once again, then, Fred Craddock is pointing homiletics toward a new and promising pathway. Preachers who stand up to preach need to recognize that they are speaking in the middle of a conversation, the church's conversation. Preachers need to learn how to speak as those who weave their speech into the fabric of what is there already spoken, sometimes extending the design, sometimes altering it, but always mindful of it.

To recognize that preaching is an act of speech in the midst of the church's life and in the middle of the church's ongoing conversation moves us in several helpful directions. First, however, many of the sorts of issues Barth and Brunner debated are important for theological methodology, they turn out not to be the starting ones, or perhaps even the primary ones for preaching. Preaching enters into the middle of the conversation, and people are out there in the pews (and in the world) already wondering about God and talking about God. Where did they get this God consciousness? Is it a remnant of the *imago Dei*—a memory of Eden built into the human frame, as Brunner suggested? Who knows? Preachers can remain conveniently agnostic about the origins of people's curiosity about God, but they cannot remain neutral about the fact that it is out there.

In this sense, preachers today are in the situation of Paul. Whether he was preaching in a house church, a synagogue, or out in the open on Mars Hill, Paul was giving expression to the gospel in the middle of an ongoing theological conversation, in a place where curiosity about and talk of God were already present. Preachers continue to enter into this conversation called to speak the gospel—God's talk—which is both a source and a resource for reinforcing, adding to, enhancing, and correcting the talk that is already out there.

Therefore, homiletics must now give major attention to that which has been only a minor motif in the past: ecclesiology. The doctrine of the church, as the speech community of God, will provide the framework for any truly pertinent homiletic. One can already see this emerging in the work of David Buttrick, Christine Smith, John McClure, Charles Rice, and others. Homiletics must still take into account general conditions of communication, and much of value can be learned from nontheological rhetoric. Homiletics becomes truly interesting, however, when it moves beyond general theories of communication to the particular phenomenon of speech within the Christian community. Then it begins to explore how the sermon can serve as a paradigmatic act of Christian speech, encouraging and informing other acts of gospel speech: education, pastoral care, ethical guidance, evangelistic witness.

The Sunday congregation is a talkative bunch. They pray, and they sing; they gossip, and they lament; they confess their faith, and they confess their doubt; they teach their children the faith, and they announce that faith to the world. In the middle of this buzz of conversation, the preacher stands up to speak. The hum of words gradually grows silent, and all eyes turn toward the pulpit. "Is there," they wonder, "a word from the Lord?" Life depends upon the answer to that question.

CHAPTER TEN

WHO IS LISTENING?
David Buttrick

A church in New Orleans has a series of pictures. The pictures line a hallway. Ever since the turn of the century when the church was founded, photographers have taken formal pictures of the congregation seated in church. Costumes change: long skirts and bowler hats disappear and are replaced by blown dry hair and, even on Sunday, mini-skirts. But, all in all, the pictures seem remarkably similar. There are always folk growing old, proud young couples, and a usual quota of pleasantly impudent-looking children. Though Christian congregations in America may well be different, economically varied or distinguished by various racial or ethnic mixes, the human "picture" may be more alike than we guess. Who is a congregation? Sermons are not monologues; good sermons are remarkably interactive with an audience. Who are the people who listen?

Obviously congregations are patched together from individuals who are unfailingly social. Human beings are natural-born relaters. Thus the primary mode of being human is not individual but rather *relationship;* we are who we are in relating.

Nevertheless, when we try to describe congregations, initially we tend to depict individuals. Years after leaving a pastorate, a preacher can wander through an empty church and, looking at the pews, recall the faces once addressed. The man who sat square in his staunchness—was his rear bent at ninety degrees? Remember how his wife was always leaning forward birdlike, her lips pursed, as if eager for every sermonic morsel. Over to one side, recall the high school girl, ogled in church by adolescent admirers, how she sat serenely self-possessed with her arms folded under her breasts. Or what of the wonderful old lady whose amiable raucousness seemed so out of sync with her white hair and wise wrinkled face; she was a bright, unsuspected angel to many others. The up-and-comers, the nosy, the chronically hurt, the excessive, the sweet-but-frightened, the take-chargers, the alone, the lorn, the unloved—many of the same faces fill every congregation. Congregations are the sum total of an astonishing pattern of individuals who relate in one body of faith.

PACKAGES OF UNIQUENESS

Each person in a congregation brings to church a package of uniqueness, but always within the constants of being human at a particular time and place. People are different. They display different family-formed patterns of behavior, which frequently they seem to reenact. They belong to different groupings in the wider community, not only informal groups defined by economics, age, sex, or employment, but formal affiliations as well; they are members of unions, Boy Scout troops, the DAR, the VFW, political parties, bridge clubs, service organizations, Little League, country clubs, and so on. They define themselves by playing different social roles.

Of course, they are also embodied. Along with other animals, they must eat and drink, sleep and defecate. Moreover, they must manage their bodily appetites in appropriate ways, which, in an age of advertised desires, is no easy trick. As embodied, they are aware of themselves aging as they pass through strange, often quite startling stages. Furthermore, people are sexual; though "good sex" may be an overstated and elusive goal, sex, full of untidy human pleasure, fantasy, sweetness, and confusion is going on in every congregation with passion and astonishing variety.[1] Our embodiedness is also vulnerable. From day one, we are in a way beginning to die; we inherit predispositions to illness in our genes. Though we may revel in the sweat of heady youth, most of us are soon aware that bodily strengths may be temporary; age enfeebles and illness can destroy quite without warning. We are fragile creatures.

Unfortunately, congregations are made up of sinners. Not only do our bodily urgings frequently lead us into deadly forms of self-abuse, not to mention injury to others, but our anxieties, our profound desire for security and the preserving of identity, can lead us into disastrous idolatries. Thus people in congregations are those who, like all people everywhere, seek to secure themselves against the tragic character of finitude and, at the same time, satisfy the insatiable inner sense of longing that characterizes humanness. Preachers preach with sinful lips to sinful people.

GETTING TO KNOW YOU

Preachers live in congregations and, as unwitting symbols of the Holy, are frequently shown the hidden interior of congregational faces. There is a kind of day-to-day "coming to know you" involved in being a pastor to people, but there are also moments of *extremis* when ministers are called out in the middle of the night to shouting kitchen-table marital conflicts or oxygen-tent hospital bedsides or police stations and, if a minister is at all approachable, sometimes night after night. Thus do people's lives get built into a minister's soul.

Strangely enough, it is difficult to describe how pastoral intimacy orders our preaching.[2] Obviously, ministers do *not* think of each and every parishioner during the preparation of sermons; we do not speak to individuals with individual problems from the pulpit in spite of Harry Emerson Fosdick's urging.[3] Do we speak on death whenever someone dies in the congregation? Or do we offer pulpit marriage counseling every time we listen to an adultery confessed? No, for the sake of sanity, happily we do not. But obviously pastoral work will tell on us; we feel with the sorrowing, we are anxious over the terminally ill, and we are endlessly moved by the courage of ordinary people undergoing extraordinary trials. They hand us faith! So if we are at all thoughtful and have even some slight sense of the dramatic, mysterious, tragic, or farcical in human life, pastoral interaction, though draining, may deepen us as preachers. The late Edward Lewis Wallant wrote a wonderful novel titled *The Tenants of Moonbloom* about a rent collector, Norman Moonbloom, who lived remotely in himself like an incubating egg. Through a series of strange encounters, Norman is baptized into humanness. His eggshell cracks and he is somehow open to his tenants in a new way; he begins to listen to them and, in clumsy ways, he begins to serve them. He attends an excited woman, herself an orphan, about to have her own first child. He listens to a drunk spin dreams of being free. He marvels as a loving old man honors his slatternly daughter as if she were pure as snow. In every apartment, Norman finds strange human wonder: "Ohh," he cries, marveling at the astonishing range of humanness, "Ohh, Ohh, Ohh!"[4] Pastors marvel in much the same way over the raunchy, sweet, profound presentments of humanness within their congregations and, if reflective, internalize their people into a kind of world before God in consciousness. Nevertheless, we do not address people's pastoral problems individually in preaching; they are, after all, a congregation.

Of course, pastorally we do learn a kind of tender respect for the sheer complexity of human life that may well show up in sermons. We get to know the man who struggles for some sort of freedom in his alcoholism. Therefore, we do not engage in wholesale attacks on drinkers from our pulpit. Or we listen to a sensitive woman explain how she dearly loves her husband and yet can't seem to break away from a lover's rumpled bed. We listen, and thus will not harshly castigate sexual sins in our sermons. We learn how intricate, ambiguous, glorious, and sinful we human beings are. We are not proposing an easy tolerance that so revels in "humanness" it goes along with anything and loses moral fervor. Pastoral work doesn't necessarily breed naive tolerance—everything is emphatically *not* okay—but it does deepen insight into the common weaknesses of our shared humanity. Our Lord loved sinners and, indeed, died for sinners; censoriousness is seldom an appropriate pulpit posture.

Now a crucial truth: Our people are generally religious. Their religion, however, is *not* a separate facet of themselves; instead, religion is tangled up with the total mix of their humanity. It is never neatly compartmentalized for purposes of discussion like the monument at Chautauqua with four sides: art, education, recreation, and religion. Most people in our strange, strained secular age have difficulty articulating their religiousness. As a result, some of us may suppose that we clergy are peculiarly religious, whereas people in our congregations are not. No, we preachers are not unique; our people have the same religious affections and random religious thoughts as we do. In fact, our people may be more helpfully religious than we. They crave meaning. When young they, too, dreamed of living their lives bravely for God. They, too, have wondered what will befall them in dying. They can be morally anguished and may earnestly seek to live useful, loving lives for others. In churches, we preach to religious people and not to the unconverted. They have been baptized, and we should take their incorporation into Christ seriously.[5]

PERSONAL RELIGIOUS EXPERIENCE

Are there constants in religious experience we can address? Are there kinds of religious problems that virtually all people discover within their self-awareness? Yes, there are. At the outset, there is the issue of self-justification. While human beings in the twentieth century do not cringe guiltily before the throne of God as did folk in earlier ages, they still struggle with themselves.[6] Even if, bypassing Freud, we work from a simpler model of the self, surely we recognize that persons can suffer profound inner alienation. To say the least, relationships between the "me" and the "myself" can be strained. The "me," as George Herbert Mead suggests, is a voluntary, acting, speaking self, while the "myself" is a social creation, formed by the way in which people speak and act toward us.[7] The problem, and surely it is a common human problem and not a pathology, is how the "me" can embrace the "myself" with even a semblance of

193

arm-in-arm approval. Because the "myself" is a social product, most people try to ease inner estrangement by earning some form of public approval. If others admire us, or even like us, why, then, perhaps we can approve ourselves. The strategy is of course exhausting simply because social justification is a stern "god" indeed! The gospel message of justification by God's loving grace obviously addresses the problem of inner alienation.

In addition to everyone's search for inner reconciliation, many people struggle with a more intense sense of disapprobation. All of us are badly brought up, for all of us internalize more law than grace, even in a permissive age when parents seem to be circumspect about inducing guilt in their young. Therefore, we condemn ourselves under some sort of inner "ought," even if it is only the tyranny of "I ought not to feel guilty" or "I ought to be more like others." Some sense of indiscriminate, often undefined, guilt is in most human beings, unless they are pathologically exempt. Often, it appears as nothing more than a nagging sense of moral disappointment. At other times, particularly with religious insight, the sense of sin can enlarge; we can become aware of the distortion in our lives before God. Nowadays, such a profound sense of sinfulness may be dimmed. We are, after all, secular people. Nevertheless, lurking, if undefined, guilt is a human phenomenon and probably must be considered a religious fact of life.

Can we isolate other religious impulses that seem native to us all, impulses to be discovered in one-to-one conversations with ourselves? Yes. Perhaps we can single out a kind of aloneness that lives in most of us. Though we have grown up in groups, and though we rub human fur with human fur day-by-day, nonetheless we may be ontologically lonely. Though we are with people, their secret center selves are somehow inaccessible. Other people are profoundly mysterious. Not only are others remote, but so are we, even to ourselves. We can count the twigs and leaves that float up from within our dark pool selves, or be startled by sudden anxieties, but we do not seem to have clear access to our own souls. Is there no one who can know us and through whom we can be known? There may be a kind of longing for an Other within our lives, an Other with whom we can be known, yet loved. The gospel of God's love can address the self in self-awareness.

IT'S STORY TIME

In addition, let us take note of religious structures that are connected with our sense of personal narrative. In an off-Broadway musical a few years ago, one of the characters sang a plaintive song: "Why am I here? Where am I going?" Human beings seem to have some awareness of destiny. The sense of destiny may be connected with both memory and anticipation. Though we live in presence, nonetheless we can think back through our storied past and we can look forward, dreaming a future. We seem to sense that our human stories, like most stories, have some sort of plotted meaning and, more a *telos*—some kind of implied conclusion. Notice we are not describing a notion of self-fulfillment. Self-actualization does not lend itself to narrative meaning; ultimately its only conclusion is a looking glass. No, most people have an odd sense that there is some purpose for their being born. Most people crave meaning.[8]

The trouble, of course, is that our personal stories are not meaning enough. We sense our stories are woven into some larger story simply because we are relational creatures. Thus human beings tend to find the meaning of their lives in some kind of narration that is larger than their own personal *curriculum vitae*. We find meaning in communities that, in turn, have historical stories—the nation, the race, the church, the corporation, the university, and so on. Belonging to such groups can give us some sense of permanent value and identity. They may also become idolatries. Nevertheless, the search for meaning in a wider social "story" may be a kind of religious longing.

What we have argued is that human beings have religious dimensions that, rightly, preachers awaken and address. In so arguing, we are separating ourselves from a Barthian denial of

195

"point of contact."[9] Our point of contact is in religious longing, which, ever unsatisfied, can easily turn into idolatry. Nevertheless our religious longings do serve to give some general if inchoate meaning to the word *God*.

Now, please underscore once more the fact that religious impulses are seldom separated from common experience. Religion cannot be compartmentalized, but is a consciousness that happens in connection with our full humanity. According to legend, Luther was conscious of God while seated in a "two-holer." So, we can be religiously aware while laughing ourselves silly over an off-color joke, or chattering at a cocktail party, in a swaying subway train, or, miraculously, even in a classroom. If preaching attempts to address the inner estrangements of people, it must reckon with the scandal of our religious pervasiveness.

THE SHARED WORLD

Let us turn now and look beyond structures of self-awareness. Human beings have a world. The lived-world is not an objective world "out there" beyond consciousness. No, the world is built-in and shared in consciousness. The world is *built-in* because, ever since Kant, we have been forced to realize that matters of shape, dimension, color, and so on are products of human perception; we live in what can best be described as a phenomenal world in consciousness. The world is *shared* as we relate to one another. Through language and convention, the world is given meaning; thus a hammer will be named "hammer" by English speaking people, and the name will include an understanding of how hammers function in conventional activity.[10] Thus the world is structured as a shared-in-common world in human consciousness.

We live in a complex *human* world. To borrow a term from Richard Niebuhr, we are "radial" people.[11] We internalize a shared social world in consciousness, a valued world drawn into consciousness by language, images, advertising, slogans, customs, rituals, and so on. In such a shared phenomenal world we live together. The idea of a constructed human world is explicated by Peter Berger and Thomas Luckmann in *The Social Construction of Reality*.[12] In their thought, the social world is a kind of projection. The customs, ideas, rituals, values, and the like of human society project a structured world, a divinized "sacred canopy" of myth and meaning that in turn conditions, and indeed may coerce, human behavior. The world construct is not exactly what we live in so much as a world that lives in and among us. No wonder that Berger in his *Invitation to Sociology* can refer to "man [sic] in society" and then, in a subsequent chapter, to "Society in Man."[13] We live in a phenomenal world that is shaped in consciousness.

The social world in which we live is a world that can be dominated by what the Bible terms "principalities and powers." In terms of social phenomenology, the "powers" can be identified with those social attitudes, faiths, loyalties, and the like that can easily take over the way we think and live.[14] In Scripture, not only must human beings in their self-awareness be redeemed, but the "powers that be" must also be tamed and transformed by the work of Christ.[15] Christ is the herald of God's new order, a sociopolitical reality that will necessarily disrupt our "world" and the powers of our world. Salvation in Scripture is not only personal liberation, it is the transformation of the human social world.

Unlike the so-called "social gospel" preachers of the late-nineteenth and early-twentieth centuries, we do not preach about a world "out there." No, somehow we must find a homiletical way to address the social world as it is formed in the shared consciousness of a congregation—a world of images, slogans, attitudes, values that can be quite resilient to the gospel. In recent years, therapeutic preaching has attempted to address the self in existential self-awareness. As a result, we have produced a host of pleasant, heart-felt Jesus people who have socially supported the most appalling economic and political cruelties. We have failed to address the structured world in consciousness where the principalities and powers reign. Sin, in the Bible, is not so much an inner indisposition as a form of social captivity from which we must be set free. Salvation surely includes the transformation of the shared human world in consciousness.

THE WHOLE STORY

Of course, just as persons have a sense of narrative history, so also does the social world. The world we live in would appear to be dominated by myths and meanings, those transsocial patterns we have labeled "powers that be," and some of the myths and meanings have narrative shape. Though personally we may recall our own lives as a story, we read our stories within larger narratives: stories of nation and race and, yes, of humanity. Almost all societies have myths of origin and destiny.[16] Though human beings may think vertically, measuring their lives against cultural symbols of ideal humanity, they also think horizontally, seeing themselves within larger narratives that give meaning to their lives. Such large scale stories may or may not be religious. Certainly, the dialectical Marxist story that concluded in something like a proletarian "heaven on earth" did not feature God or gods. But, to be truthful, most cosmic stories do tend to be religious; they are stories of origin (e.g., Genesis 1–11) and conclusion (e.g., Revelation 21, 22) under some sort of divinity. Can we admit that these less than cosmic stories may tend to be idolatrous? Stories of nation or race or religious tradition (such as Christianity) are usually identity stories; that is to say, they tell us who we are within social groupings. Such stories may be sinfully important to us insofar as they secure our identity and, in fact, seem to preserve identity.[17] By contrast, the narrative structure of the Hebrew/Christian tradition is a sweeping story of God and humanity that, though it scarcely offers security, does give meaning and wonderful import to our lives.

Inevitably, the world in which narrativity unfolds is some sort of modeled "cosmology." Not only are we capable of seeing ourselves in a universe, but we are able to locate the universe "under" God. Actually we use terms such as *under* or *above* to indicate God's transcendence in relation to our world-in-consciousness. The social world we share in common is a world "under" symbols of God. Human consciousness models God and world and, within the model, unfolds a story of God and humanity.

THE SHAPE OF CONTEMPORARY CONSCIOUSNESS

Some special features of contemporary consciousness must be mentioned. We can enumerate them briefly:

(1) *Secularity:* That we live in a secular age is by now a truism.[18] In everyday life, almost no one, even officially religious people such as clergy, regards life as "under God." We simply do not think of the world as crammed with signs and beckonings from God. If medieval persons saw a cross, immediately they thought of the cross on which Christ was crucified. Perhaps they might also associate the sign of the cross with the power of salvation. But, nowadays, people see a cross and assume it is advertising a church. Our associations are no longer sacred. Ever since Proust likened the eucharistic host on the tongue to a French kiss, sacred metaphor has been sliding from common consciousness. In fact, religious symbolism seems strangely archaic to most people from Western cultures; it is a collection of "holy pictures" left over from a superstitious past. Our language has been demystified by the denotative precision of descriptive sciences as well as read-between-the-lines clinical analysis from the social and psychological fields. We are secular. Even in religiousness, we are secular in style. When we preach, we speak a common secular language because, for public speaking, there simply isn't anything else.[19]

(2) *Transience:* Is it any secret to say we live "between the ages"? Quite obviously, we do. The term "postmodern," though ill defined, has floated into public speech. For some it is a polemic ("postliberal") Barthian banner under which they intend to march proudly backward into a stubbornly retained neoorthodoxy. For others, it means that once-upon-a-time "modernism" is now regarded as a temporary step toward a more radically different cultural "mind." What is obvious even to nonacademic laity is that a sense of cultural stasis has broken down and that we are now flooded by change. If Western history can be divided into epochs—a Greco-Roman world, a medieval synthesis, and the Enlightenment (also sometimes called "The Protestant Era")—we are now in transition.[20] The mind of Enlightenment, characterized by a correspondence between human rationality

and divine reason, is now past tense.[21] Perhaps the intellectual model of "Western culture" is also gone. We know from history that transitional ages can last a hundred years or more. Meanwhile, where are we going? Why are we going so fast? What can we hold on to? People these days live in a sense of ending, but in America, a reactionary land, they are not yet gripped by any enthusiasm for future renewal.

(3) *Relativity:* In cultural high periods, fixed truths are fashionable not only in the pulpit but in the common mind. Our age is now radically aware of relativity.[22] We see relativism in the rise of hermeneutic suspicion. Is truth feminist or African or a province of the poor?[23] Must we deconstruct to see what aspects of truth have been carefully tucked out of sight and, therefore, out of our cultural mind? Communities seem to interpret reality; so is truth to be spelled with a small "t" according to who does the interpreting? Is interpretation governed by who's in charge?

A sense of relativity may be more culturally profound than we guess. If we trace our way back through an art gallery of the past, we can notice the changes. In Giotto's time, paintings depicted a world without depth, a flat world lacking dimension. Yet in Giotto's paintings we find an odd mix of figures, human and divine: The angels and demons are often painted in greater detail than the human figures. Giotto's world, though flat, was crowded with disclosures. Two hundred and fifty years later, paintings were very different indeed. They were objectively detailed, particularly in their natural backgrounds (people were sometimes strangely artificial), and frequently featured a somewhat "fenced" composition. There were no more supernatural beings, unless they were hidden behind the compositional "fence!" What marked eighteenth-century art was dimension; every painting was painted from the same third-person dimensional viewpoint. Nowadays, our sense of reality has changed again. We paint not only what might appear to an objective viewer but also crowd our canvasses with the unseen—images of memory, fantasy figures, daydreams, because they are also reality *in consciousness.* In addition, what is obvious in the arts and in film is a use of multiple perspectives as if human consciousness were angled by some moving epistemological camera boom coming at reality from very different positions.[24] Our age is marked by an acknowledged relativism.

What is preaching trying to do? Presumably preaching is attempting to form, or better to transform, the listener's world in a number of ways. Obviously preaching wants to constitute the modeled world in consciousness as God's world and to replot the several entwined stories in which we live into a larger God's story. Both of these intentions deserve comment.

RETELLING A STORY

We have noted that people live within some narrative sense of life's unfolding movement. Actually, most of us rewrite our stories as we go through life, reinterpreting the past from new, and sometimes suddenly altered, situations. (Psychoanalysis, for example, constitutes a fairly radical mode of editing our lives.) Likewise, our life stories take place within larger histories— stories of family, of churches, of political parties, of race, of nations, and others. These stories, like Israel's story, also get rewritten again and again in view of "paradigmatic events."[25] In the Jewish/Christian tradition we come across a story, God and Israel, set within a cosmic framework of creation and eschaton. Such is the task of preaching. In preaching we must set human stories within a cosmic/mythic framework—creation, fall, redemption, and eschaton. Without a cosmic framework, Israel's story would be reduced to a tedious human/divine "interaction ritual." What we are suggesting is that by setting all our stories within creation and eschaton, we bring meaning to life. Creation tells of God's choosing humanity and eschaton offers images of what God has in mind for redeemed humanity. The story of the Fall (along with the awesome account of Cain and Abel) provides a profound "symbolism of evil," while the wonderful tale of Noah counters the Fall with a promise of God's patient grace. Stories interact with and can transform connecting stories. If stories tend to provide identity, preaching changes our sense of who we are by reforming the narratives in which we live.

201

A special word about eschatological vision: All societies portend visions of their own fulfillment. Of course, in times of transition, societies may become disillusioned. Quite literally they may give up dreaming. Obviously Jesus announced a soon-to-arrive social order, a "kingdom of God." The kingdom was a compelling vision of the future, which led true believers to repent and change. Some vision of the end of a story can fill existence with both energy and celebrative anticipation. If, however, eschatological vision separates from narrativity and becomes a vertical dream, it can become "pie in the sky" and earn the now famous Marxist rebuke. However, as a conclusion to our story, a conclusion depicting God and a redeemed humanity, eschatological vision can be ethically motivating. Surely in sermons we can portray a world free from racism, from sexist dominations, from "we're number one!" patriotisms. Such vision may assist our world toward social transformation while we struggle "between the ages."

RENAMING GOD'S WORLD

We have argued that in preaching we address a phenomenal "world" structured in intersubjective congregational consciousness. We do. We speak to a world internalized from all kinds of cultural presentments. What preaching does is to constitute the world "under" God or, at least, in relation to God. In some traditions, preachers will seek to convey a sacramental universe in which God is regarded as a ubiquitous presence hiding in, through, and with all things. In other more Calvinist traditions, following Augustine, preachers may portray God as separate from, yet related to, creation. These are theological options, each producing a somewhat different and distinctive rhetoric. The important thing is not the two options but that each renames the world in relation to God; they constitute a God-world. God was at the start; God will be in on the conclusion; God is ever in relationship to humanity in the world.

To constitute the world as God's world means that *all* things and events must be redefined in relation to God. In effect, preaching renames reality in view of God. In recent years, therapeutic preaching has linked psychological self-awareness to God. Preaching these days must go much further. The glory of the Hebrew scriptures is that they unfold all human events—Ahab's ill-advised military excursions, for example—in relation to God. Perhaps, because we have been afraid of Protestant political conservatism, most preachers have failed to interpret public events in the light of God's eschatological purposes. At a time when people long for meaning in both social affairs and political history, the pulpit must not fail to speak. God has created a good world. God will redeem humanity; even now the "Holy City seen of John" is descending![26]

ON PREACHING THE CROSS

Now let us add particular comment with regard to Jesus Christ. Christian preaching not only reconstructs our world and transforms human stories in relation to God, Christian faith also interprets God through the figure of Christ, crucified and risen. Obviously, all religious speaking redefines life in relation to a God or to gods. The question is, What kind of God and, therefore, what kind of world? God, in most religious thinking, is an absolute dominator, infinite and eternal. In Christian faith, the absolute is disclosed via the image of Christ crucified, who is both impotent and foolish according to St. Paul.[27] Can compassionate self-giving love seem to be anything else? Therefore Christian preaching, while it must never be christologically idolatrous, does interpret God and world through the cross. The creation is a display of awesome intelligence and power, but both must be redefined by God's "modest" self-giving love. As for eschatology, must we not conceive of God's judgment as something other than a sorting out of sheep and goats with goats at risk, in view of a Christ who, while we were sinners, died for us? Christian preachers set the figure of Christ before the mystery of God and, in view of the cross, redefine the human world.

203

Of course it is "in Christ" that preaching addresses the religious longings, fears, and guilts of self-aware humanity. Is not the message of a self-giving God the basis for "justification through grace"? And surely news of God's cross-displayed love is encouragement for all guilty, hurt humanity stumbling in loneliness toward the mystery of dying. The gospel is assuredly good news addressed to persons in congregation.

SIDE COMMENTS ABOUT LISTENERS

(1) There is a popular notion fostered by some communication studies that the obtuse biases of individual listeners will prevent hearing. The thesis: *People hear what they wish to hear and "bleep" what they don't want to hear.*

As far as we have been able to discern, well-spoken language forms in consciousness in much the same way, no matter who may be the audience. Now, admittedly, people may not wish to hear certain messages. They may become irate and, subsequently, may reject what they have heard, but, if language is properly designed, persons in an audience *will* hear. We must claim such because, quite obviously, for many folk the gospel may be a message "from death to death" that they do not wish to hear.[28] The gospel, in its prophetic power, clearly runs counter to all-American cultural values, so that people may *not* want to receive the message we preach. Nevertheless, adequately formed language will be heard and will probably not be twisted into other meanings by listeners. Baldly, if preachers preach well, people will hear. Most of the "static" in receiving a message may be caused by careless homiletics rather than by the social or political inhibitions of a listening audience. Yes, only about 60 to 70 percent of public-speaking language is retained by listeners at best.[29] If, however, the major structural meanings are well-established, people will hear. They may not be happy over a message, but they *will* hear.

(2) There is another notion, equally pervasive. The thesis: *Different social groups hear differently—the young, the old, the rich, the poor, women, men, black, white, and so on.*

204

Yes, there are conventions connected with the African-American preaching tradition that are distinctive; black audiences are familiar with these various repertoires. There are similar conventions that seem to govern Asian sermons. But such special conventions do not contradict a general statement: Language *forms* in consciousness in much the same way with any congregation. A much more important matter relates to the hermeneutic of the gospel in different communities.[30] A hermeneutic of the oppressed may function critically with regard to sermons and, therefore, is a matter of huge homiletic concern. Nevertheless, language forms in consciousness again in a rather constant way.

(3) There is another caveat. The thesis: *Faithful biblical preaching will take cues from Scripture and bypass secular rhetoric which, at best, is a clever sophistry.*

The notion we have stressed seems to be a left-over reaction from the biblical theology movement. Biblical theology tended to overdraw a comparison between Hebrew and Greek thought; Hebrew thought was honest, humane, and even earthy, while Greek thought was speculative, abstract, and philosophically suspect. Because rhetoric has roots in classical Greek thought, it was singularly suspect. But rhetoric is actually a kind of cultural awareness; it helps us to see how the people to whom we speak think, understand, visualize, and believe.[31] Good rhetoric works from the common, everyday language that ordinary people use and, of course, such is the language of preaching.

So preachers once more must become rhetorically aware. If the language of the gospel is to form in consciousness, it must be imaged so as to align with the images of the phenomenal world already in consciousness. These days, rationalism is in collapse, so that people seem to be thinking through images. If so, preachers must weigh images with rhetorical care and theological precision. Likewise, because people are viewing life from different perspectives within themselves, preachers will have to design sermons with variable points of view; a third-person objective language can no longer suffice. As for the structural design of sermons, they should not be static, categorical systems of "points." While people do think in categories when writing out grocery lists or doing accounts, the profound moments in life are seldom grasped categorically; usually we think about ourselves in some sort of movement of thought or narration. All these matters are the stuff of a contemporary rhetoric to which preachers must attend. We are building a faith world in congregational consciousness, which is nothing less than a matter for theological reflection and rhetorical savvy.

Who are our listeners? Above all, they are people whom, in God's grace, we love. Ultimately, preaching is an act of neighbor love. We care enough to find out how our congregational neighbors think and speak. We love enough to set ourselves aside and form language as a gift for them. Preaching isn't an art or a piety. Perhaps preaching is merely a learned craft. In love preachers apply homiletic craft in order to wrap the gospel as a gift for their neighbors.

CHAPTER ELEVEN

PREACHING THE BODY

Barbara Brown Taylor

Those of us who preach in mainline denominations know that we have a language problem in the church. Some of our best words have decayed from long use and rough treatment. Others have been kidnapped by strangers and yet others institutionalized by so-called friends. *Charity* is more likely to mean a tax-deductible donation to us than anything having to do with the heart, *mission* is something every corporate business has, and *stewardship* is a dreary season in the fall. Other words have been used as weapons for so long that no one will go near them anymore. *Repentance* has come to mean "sorry" and *sin* to mean "wrong," although both words possess far more promise than that.

The language of faith is like soil that has been farmed too hard for too long. Remembering the past years of plenty, we plant our sermons in it and wait with our chins in our hands, but the yield is not what it used to be. We preach in a diluted and disillusioned land, where language is used to conceal the truth, not to tell it, and words are distrusted by those who have been bullied and betrayed by them. Our congregations are made up of people who have learned to protect themselves from words, especially words that want things from them. They have been promised the good life in exchange for their votes, their money, their hard work, and they are tired of waiting for returns that never arrive. They come to church searching for a different kind of discourse, but few of them are able to check their wariness at the door. They listen to us with the same ears they listen to all the other public voices in their lives—politely but cautiously, reserving the right to decide for themselves what is true and what is not, based on their own experience.

One of our problems in addressing them is that their experience is so diverse. On any given Sunday, we speak to people who were raised in the church and those who have just come through the door. Some believe in a God of grace and others in a God of law; their own creeds are a collage of bits and pieces culled from memory, culture, and personal preference. Most have been influenced by popular religion and few know the difference between a Gospel and an Epistle, although they would be happy for someone to teach them. Their experience of a believing community is, in most cases, limited to an hour on Sunday mornings. When it is over they scatter in a hundred different directions, each of them left to his or her own devices.

It is not surprising, then, that we cannot be sure what they hear when they listen to us, or—more accurately—what they see. I say "God" and the pale young woman in the last pew sees an angry, imperious boss while the first-grade boy sitting in front of her sees the beaming face of his grandfather. Someone else imagines a wheel of light radiating heat and someone else a large pair of hands cradling the earth. I say "sin" and the red-faced man in the too-tight suit sees last year's income tax return with a few misleading figures on it, while the middle-aged couple to his right see their daughter living with her boyfriend, and someone else sees a human arrow that has strayed miles from its mark.

The language of faith is fluid, not solid. Words like *grace, judgment,* and *redemption* are not abstract ideas but names for certain experiences. When we preachers pronounce them, we speak from our own experience and the experience of the church into the experience of our listeners, and it is like tossing nets into deep water. However carefully we choose our words and however well we aim them, we cannot predict what they will encounter on the way down. There are snags we cannot see and currents we cannot control, but it is all part of a day's work. We are fishers, not engineers. We tend our nets and cast them as best we can, giving ourselves to the task without knowing how it will all turn out in the end. Our success, like our lives, rests in other hands.

When we forget that, we use the words of faith as if they were steel girders instead of the finest filaments of meaning. We use them as if everyone understood what they involve, when the truth is that they involve everyone who hears them in different ways. What, then, is a preacher to do? Learn to speak a dozen different languages or insist that the congregation learn to speak the same one? Revive the language of faith or invent a new one to take its place?

In practice, many preachers have tried to resolve the dilemma by resorting to language that substitutes explanation for experience. They teach from the pulpit, explaining that grace means this and salvation means that, and that people of faith have traditionally done this but not that. They clarify biblical texts, distilling their main points and suggesting appropriate congregational responses to them. In doing so they do valuable work, orienting their listeners to the wisdom of the church, but the result is often *beliefs* and not *belief*—mental assent to the information that has been given them and not a vital experience of the living God.

"There is no lack of information in a Christian land"; says Fred Craddock, quoting Søren Kierkegaard, "something else is lacking, and this is a something which the one man cannot directly communicate to the other."[1] Much of our direct communication from the pulpit is like a travelogue to someplace our listeners have never been. We may do a masterful job of telling them about the various points of interest in God's country—the architecture, the museums, the geography, the politics—but when it is all over and the lights go up, they have been on our trip, not their own. What is still lacking is something we cannot give them directly, which is a sense of having been there for themselves.

It may be enough simply to get their wanderlust going, but there is another possibility, and that is to learn how to describe God's country so that people recognize it as their own country; not as a foreign land they may visit some day but as the place where they live right now in the presence and providence of God. Such knowledge is not a matter of information but of revelation, and it cannot be taught. It may, however, be evoked by those who are willing to stand in the synapse between heaven and earth and tell others what happens to them when they do. Preachers who do this form a human bridge. Linking their experience to the experience of their listeners at one end and linking it to their experience of God at the other, they become live wires through which holy current may pass, illuminating the ordinary with God's extraordinary brightness.

THE AUTHORITY OF EXPERIENCE

This emphasis on human experience has obvious disadvantages. Our wiring can be faulty (indeed, some say it is innately so). We can short out and shock those we meant to light up. We can flip the wrong switches and train our beams on the wrong things. We can mistake what is lit for the light itself and lead others to trip over the cords we have left lying around. But there are both practical and theological advantages as well. The most practical one is that we can no longer rely on the authority of Scripture and dogma to sanction our speech. For many of those who listen to us, the Bible and the creeds of the church are ancient artifacts of questionable value. They no longer make us worth listening to; on the contrary, it is often up to us to make them worth listening to, by breathing recognizable life into their historical forms. For better or worse, the authority of our age is the authority of experience. If we want to speak meaningfully to people, we will speak to them about the real lives in which they experience meaning, meaning that is felt as well as thought and intuited as well as perceived. We will speak out of our own experience, reviving the language of faith by recovering the live connection between words and events, between nouns and verbs, between the names of things and the things themselves.

This is the work of incarnation, which is the best theological reason for speaking from experience. As Christians, we are believers in the word made flesh. We believe that God's truth was embodied in a human being, who surrendered his life for the life of the world, whose risen body is still at work in the world in our own bodies, the body of the church. Given such a heritage, it makes perfect sense that those of us who preach it should use what I want to call *body language,* following our leader by speaking in ways that reveal the word made flesh—not only in the body of Jesus but also in the body of the world.

Long before Jesus came along, our God was a God who used material things to reach out to us: floods, rainbows, burning bushes, pillars of cloud and of fire, ravens and heavenly manna. God was present in them all, guiding and providing for us in tangible, visible ways. When we lost our ways, God sent flesh and blood prophets to point them out to us again, people whose very lives became enacted dramas of God's word.

Then the angel Gabriel was sent by God to a city of Galilee named Nazareth, and God was no longer interested in flesh and blood but invested in it, smuggled into the world inside the body of a young woman in order to receive a body of his own. With that decisive act, God became incarnate and there was no going back. From that point on, the distinction between the sacred and the secular was blurred forever. Nothing was too humble to contain the holy: not a manger, not a stable, not the sweet-smelling body of a Hebrew boy child. The door between heaven and earth was blown off its hinges, and nothing was ever the same again.

The child became a man and the man became a preacher whose sermons were full of commonplace things: seeds and nets, coins and fishes, lilies of the field, and birds of the air. Wherever he was, he had a knack for looking around him and weaving what he saw into his sermons, whether it was sparrows for sale in the marketplace, laborers lining up for their pay, or a woman glimpsed through a doorway kneading her family's bread. He told everyday stories about everyday people, only he told them with a twist.

"The kingdom of heaven is like this," he said over and over again, comparing things they knew about with something they knew nothing about and all of a sudden what they knew had cracks in it, cracks they had never noticed before, through which they glimpsed bright and sometimes frightening new realities. As they listened to Jesus, it became clear that nothing was simply what it seemed. Every created thing was fraught with divine possibility; wasn't that what he was telling them? Every ho-hum detail of their days was a bread crumb leading them into the presence of God, if they would just pick up the trail and follow. In his preaching as well as in his life, Jesus spoke body language—physical, sensory language his hearers could see and hear and touch. The Incarnate Word preached an incarnate word, so that no one who stood in his presence could miss his point: that God is very present, that the kingdom is very near, that the most ordinary things in the world may speak the extraordinary language of God.

To hear these words, it is necessary to hold them lightly—never just literally, but liberally—turning them over and over in your hand, looking at them from every possible angle, considering the ways in which a mustard seed may speak of faith, or a new wineskin of hope, or a little child of love. Is that field of wheat just a field of wheat, or is it the field of the world, which God has planted and God will reap, separating the grain from the chaff? Is that lamp just a lamp on a stand, or is it everyone who is willing to burn with the light of Christ? Is that stranger just another hungry stranger, or is it the Lord holding out his hands to be fed?

Body language describes faith as process, not content; disciples are not those who believe certain things but those who live in a certain way. Body language is the primary language of story, short on concepts and long on pictures. It seizes the listener at the levels of emotion and intuition, appealing to those centers of religious meaning that the secondary language of creed cannot touch.

A REVOLUTION OF IMAGES

True creativity speaks both languages, and preachers who wish to proclaim a lively word will become proficient in both. They will be fluent not only in the language of theology but also in the language of image, learning to paint pictures and tell stories as effectively as they compare ideas and organize thoughts. This is no new development in homiletics. Before there was Christian doctrine there was Christian story. The revolution begun in the New Testament is a revolution of images, in which the invisible God becomes human, servants become friends, losers become winners, and death becomes life. These are not propositions to discuss but pictures to choose between. Conversion to Christian faith means conversion from one set of images to another, with radical changes in how we see ourselves, our neighbors, our world, and our God as a result. Our response to these changed images is not "I agree" or "I disagree," but "I will" or "I won't," which makes our appropriation of the Christian life an imaginative and not simply an intellectual exercise.

"Faith is the enduring ability to imagine life in a certain way," writes James Whitehead.[2] In this context, imagination is not to be confused with science fiction or fantasy. It is, instead, a willingness to accept and sustain particular images of what it means to be human, even when there is precious little payoff for doing so. It is a rarefied kind of make-believe, in which one acts "as if" certain things were true and, in the acting, discovers that they are. Imagination is the meeting place of God and humankind, the chamber between heaven and earth where the sacred and the commonplace mingle and flow in unexpected ways. It is the place of revelation where Moses saw his bush and Jacob his ladder, the place where Mary was when she said yes to the angel, and the place Simon Peter and Andrew decided to go when they left their nets to follow a stranger. Imagination is where all sacraments take place, as ordinary things like bread and wine and water and oil take on holy significance, becoming God's tools in human hands.

For preachers, imagination is the ability to form images in the minds of their listeners that are not physically present to their senses, so that they find themselves in a wider world with new choices about who and how they will be. Further, it is the ability to make connections between two different frames of reference so that a spark is struck at the point where they intersect, illuminating a new possibility. When Albert Einstein made a connection between the two frames of reference called "time" and "space," it was an imaginative act. When Dante Alighieri described the central pit of hell as a river in which sinners are frozen alive, it was an imaginative act. His connection between the two frames of reference called "hell" and "ice" is enough to set anyone's teeth chattering. When Jesus said, "I am the good shepherd," it was an imaginative act, in which he connected his own ministry to that of a herdsman so that *messiah* took on new and unexpected meaning.

In these examples and countless others, imagination does its work by attending to things that are known in order to discover things that are not. It is the work of analogy or metaphor, and it relies heavily on the evocative power of images to move the mind and heart. While few of us are aware of it, our lives are governed less by our deep convictions than by our deep images. The pictures we carry inside of us—pictures of ourselves and those we love, pictures of God and of the future—these are visual catalogs of the meaning we make of our lives. They are the engines that make us go, or fail to make us go. They speak the language of our souls, and language from the pulpit that connects with them holds far more promise than language that does not.

Those of us who preach have been given a healing word to proclaim, but "much of our preaching," wrote Phillips Brooks in 1907, "is like delivering lectures on medicine to sick people."[3] The enduring question for those of us entrusted with the potent balm of the gospel is how to administer it so that what we offer those who listen to us is not talk but health. At least part of the answer lies in the use of body language, language rich in the images that spark the human imagination and drive the human soul, language steeped in the mystery of incarnation by which the shape of God is revealed in the world. While there are no grammar books on this language, I want to suggest several rules of usage for the preacher.

SEVERAL RULES OF USAGE

Show, Don't Tell

The first is a maxim of creative writing teachers everywhere: "Show, don't tell." The difference between the two is largely the difference between experience and explanation. A sermon that tells a truth offers the congregation an explanation they may accept or reject: God is love, Jesus is Lord, the Kingdom is very near. The effectiveness of such a sermon depends almost entirely on the congregation's relationship with the one who delivers it. If the preacher is deemed trustworthy, the congregation may decide to take his or her word for it, but without that trust the preacher is simply one more authority figure claiming something that may or may not be true. In either case, a sermon that tells its truth requires little from its listeners beyond their assent to what is being proposed.

A sermon that shows its truth wants more than that. The preacher who chooses this longer and less direct route offers the congregation an experience they may explore. The truth itself may be the same as that of a sermon that proceeds by explanation, but in this case the preacher is as concerned with *how* it is known as *that* it is known. The sermon will be more like a map than a destination, and the preacher will ask the congregation to go to all the trouble of walking through the territory instead of flying over it, but when they arrive, they will arrive at a truth they have discerned from their own experience.

In his book *Ministry and Imagination,* Urban Holmes suggests that revelation moves along a continuum that begins with experience and moves from there to image to concept to judgment to action.[4] Clearly, a great deal of traditional preaching concentrates on the righthand side of the continuum, explaining theological concepts that dictate certain judgments and require certain actions. In churches where it is the custom to end the sermon with a call to response, a preacher often has no choice but to work the action end of the scale, but preachers who are free from that ritual are not necessarily free from its attraction. A sermon that ends with a rallying cry has a way of sounding more sincere than one that does not, and preachers who fail to sound one may worry (or worse yet, be told by their congregations) that they have not done their jobs.

This is a pity, because it assumes that the important work of faith takes place in the bright-lit arenas of explanation and action instead of further down the scale, in the lifelike shadows

215

of experience and image. If Holmes is right, then faith is not only at work there but is born and reborn there, where the primary encounter with the holy takes place.

So the first rule of usage for body language is to trust human experience, not because it is necessarily praiseworthy but because it is the place where God acts. God comes to us in our own bodies, in the bodies of our neighbors, and in the body of the world. God's word is an incarnate word, and the language of experience is a language we can all speak, even when we no longer share a common religious language. Preachers who stick close to human experience do not have to impose God's truth on life; they may evoke it instead, calling forth their congregation's own wisdom about what is true and what is not. "Is not life more than food, and the body more than clothing?" (Matthew 6:25). "Can a blind person guide a blind person? Will not both fall into a pit?" (Luke 6:39). "Is there anyone among you who, if your child asks for bread, will give a stone?" (Matthew 7:9).

Jesus spent a lot of time teaching people how to learn from their own experience. When they asked him for explanations he gave them stories instead, leading them to discover the truth for themselves so that what they finally found was theirs, not his. He seemed to believe they had it in them. He seemed intent on showing them that the kingdom was not a far off place where someone else would have to lead them but that it lay in the very ground under their feet—like buried treasure, like leaven in a lump, like a pearl of great price—and that they were capable of doing the digging, the kneading, the searching required to make it their own.

God Is in the Details

A second rule of usage is to pay attention to life. If God is in the world, then every detail of this life is worth attending to. "All tactile things are doors to the infinite," writes the poet Charles Wright. "Poems are made up of details; good poems are made up of good details; great poems are made up of luminous details."[5] Body language is full of such details. It is sensory, even

216

sensual, language that appeals to the eye, the nose, the tongue, and the skin as well as to the ear. It has weight and scent to it, texture and temperature. It is concrete language that speaks in particular terms and never in general ones because it believes that for some unknown reason, God rewards keen attention to this world with glimpses of another.

"If you desire God, hold fast to the world," Dietrich Bonhoeffer advised his preaching students. "We can neither understand nor preach the gospel tangibly enough. A truly evangelical sermon must be like offering a child a beautiful red apple or holding out a glass of water to a thirsty man and asking, 'Wouldn't you like it?' "[6] Preachers who wish to experience what Bonhoeffer is talking about may pause here to imagine a lemon, exploring it with all five senses in the mind. Go over every detail of it in your imagination, noticing the color, the dimpled rind, the smell of the oil. Imagine slicing it in half so that the juice drips down your hand and then lick your fingers. If you salivate, then you have experienced the power of your imagination, which is strong enough to evoke a physical response to something not physically present to the senses. It does its work through attention to detail, relying on association instead of argument.

For most preachers, attention to detail is not a natural gift but an acquired skill. It is something we learn by doing, setting aside a day or part of a day to take a seat somewhere in the world and do nothing but notice: notice the way people dress and walk and act toward one another, notice the shape of their hands and the sound of their voices. Notice the difference between a Chinese face and a Japanese one, a Boston accent and a New Orleans one. Notice the way ferns unfurl toward the light, the way a flock of starlings in flight all turn at the same time. Notice the difference between a zinnia and a marigold, between the smell of a magnolia and a pine. Notice how hard it is simply to notice, without judging or interfering. Notice how much more there is to see than was apparent at first glance.

"The world is charged with the grandeur of God," wrote Gerard Manley Hopkins, who was both priest and poet, and no

one was better than he at noticing it. His journal is full of
luminous details, like these from May 3, 1866:

> Meadows skirting seven-bridge road voluptuous green. Some
> oaks are out in small leaf. Ashes not out, only tufted with their
> fringy blooms. Hedges springing richly. Elms in small leaf, with
> more or less opacity. White poplars most beautiful in small grey
> crisp spray-like leaf. Cowslips capriciously colouring meadows in
> creamy drifts. Bluebells, purple orchids. Over the green water of
> the river passing the slums of the town and under its bridges
> swallows shooting, blue and purple above and shewing their
> amber-tinged breasts reflected in the water, their flight unsteady
> with wagging wings and leaning first to one side then the other.
> Peewits flying.[7]

On one hand, they are useless details. Who cares what color a
swallow is? Unless, as for Hopkins (and not only Hopkins), a bird
becomes the embodiment of the Holy Ghost, who "over the bent
World broods with warm breast and with ah! bright wings."[8]

Learning to see God at work in the world may be as simple and
as strenuous as learning to see—not what we want to see, and not
what we think we are supposed to see—but what, by the grace of
God, is. We may start with birds, we may start with buildings, we
may start with anything we choose. The point is to attend to the
details of everyday life, peering into them for evidence of the
giver of all life. This is God's world and God is busy in it. Can you
see? Look hard, and then look again. Go for the deeper meaning
this time, the holiness hidden just beneath the everyday surface
of things. Is that a sapling breaking through the asphalt or is it a
picture of life that is stronger than death? Is that a street person
lying in the bushes or a piece of the broken body of God? Keep
an eye out for the living parables that are always taking place
around you—at the grocery store, the doctor's office, the
shopping mall—all the dramas of everyday life where meaning is
being made, or sought, or rejected. Pay attention to your
own part in those dramas. What is your role? Are you a
bystander or a principal player? What truth do people see when
they look at you?

218

Striking Sparks of Kinship

A third rule of usage for body language is to suggest connections—between the body of Christ and the body of the world, between the bodies of individual believers and the body of the church—so that those who recognize themselves in the words we speak recognize themselves in relationship. It is not enough to describe their experience well. While there is real comfort in hearing one's life rendered with insight and care, the moment of revelation is a moment in which one life glimpses its kinship with other lives. The truth about bodies is that none of them exists in isolation. On visible and invisible levels, we are all knit together—human beings and stars and barn swallows and sea kelp—all of us caught and held in the trembling web of creation.

If, as I suggested earlier, imagination is not only the ability to make pictures in the mind but also to make connections between two different frames of reference so that a spark is struck at their intersection, then preachers have limitless resources at hand. On the most obvious level, there are connections to be made between the world of the Bible and the world of the listener, so that here and now intersect with there and then in illuminating ways, but that is only the beginning. There are also connections to be made between the wisdom of the church and the wisdom of the world, between the faith of the past and the perplexities of the present. Modern believers live their lives in the vacuum between disparate frames of reference, and they need all the help they can get finding the points of intersection: between heaven and earth, between self-transcendence and self-interest, between unity and fracture, between a flat, disenchanted world and a world stacked with layers of meaning.

"The fundamental issue in ministry today," writes Urban Holmes, "is the recovery of a sense of enchantment and the ability to be enchanting."[9] For the preacher, that is often a matter of making unexpected connections—between a bird and the holy spirit, between a stranger and an angel, between the life of the world and the life of God—so that listeners who overhear those connections week after week learn how to make them, too.

When that happens, imagination is no longer the individual act of a preacher but the communal work of the people of God.

This cannot happen, however, if preachers insist on pouring the connections they make in cement. Revelation does not work that way. When it happens, it is like standing in the arc of an electric current that leaps between two charged poles. For a moment everything is lit, and then it is not, although what has been glimpsed in that moment is not soon forgotten. To force the connection is to lose it: Try to weld the two poles together and the whole system shorts out. The challenge for the preacher is to learn how to bend the two poles toward each other so that the connection is set up but not complete, leaving an opening for listeners to enter into on their own.

The poet Charles Wright, whom we have heard from before, calls this "working in the synapse." Art, he says (and I include preaching), tends toward the certainty of making connections. It is the artist's job to hold the ends of the junction apart, he says, to preserve the tension and keep it alive so that those who enter into it experience the spark of the synapse for themselves.[10] The problem with this, for many preachers, is that we do not trust our listeners to negotiate the process on their own. We are afraid they might not get it *right,* so we pour a concrete bridge for them to walk across and the live synapse becomes a dead end. When we reduce stories to morals and turn parables into allegories, that is what we are doing. We are back into the old, old business of flattening out experience so that we can write advice all over it, making God and all creation yawn.

The alternative is to trust the power of the images we evoke and to trust our listeners' responses to them, knowing that we are not in charge of the whole process but only a part of it. Our part is, in the words of Eudora Welty, to stay on the lookout for "the continuous thread of God's revelation"[11] and to pick up that thread with language that is as vivid and alive as what it means to describe. Our part is to deliver sermons in which the gospel is experienced anew, so that our listeners begin to suspect that faith is process instead of content, an ongoing discussion with God about the Word made flesh. Every time we stand up to preach, we continue that discussion, telling God about our incarnation as God tells us about God's own. Every sermon is a contribution to the third testament of Christ's body in the world, in which we make our small donations to the living, growing canon of God's word.

But our part is always dependent on the Holy Spirit's part. Once we have done all we know how to do, tending our sermons and casting them upon the waters to the best of our ability, it is up to God to provide the increase—or not—so that we never forget whose word it is we preach. It is enough for us to learn how to speak that word, not only with our lips but in our lives on earth, where God consents to meet us again and again.

CHAPTER TWELVE

THE HEARER'S EXPERIENCE
OF THE WORD
Henry Mitchell

I t is far more than mere good manners to pause and reflect on the contributions of great teachers; to fail to appreciate the product of their genius is actually to fail to be benefited to the full—an enormous and sinful waste. Thus I find this exercise of gratitude to be more for my own good than that of our honoree, Fred B. Craddock.

My topic, "The Hearer's Experience of the Word" was assigned by the editors, but it is hardly a mystery why they did so. My latest work is titled *Celebration and Experience in Preaching* (1990). So, the task immediately before us is to determine how to deal appropriately with the *experience* of the Word or sermon. Emphasis on this topic is found both in Dr. Craddock's writings and in my own.

I propose first to discuss briefly a history of the relation between Dr. Craddock's writings on the topic and my own commitment to it. Then I will explore and expand on our joint corpus of insights on the theme.

THE MEETING OF MINDS: A BIT OF HISTORY

My involvement in homiletics started out in isolation, and found its way to collegiality with other homileticians, like Fred Craddock, over a period of some fifteen plus years. In 1966, I completed a master's thesis in linguistics titled "The Genius of Negro Preaching." It was, so far as I could tell, an unprecedented effort to define and codify the principles governing the best of the African-American preaching tradition. The homiletics departments at accredited seminaries had been indecisive about the African-American tradition. Some admired this powerful idiom, but made no effort to comprehend or copy this gift. Others went so far as methodically to suppress it. Black graduates of white seminaries were thus forced out of touch with their own constituents' culture.

Strangely enough, my thesis was not a conscious effort to address this need. However, what started as an academic exercise launched a powerful process of awareness and ferment. This thesis and its fall-out were destined to exceed by far any vision I might have had at the beginning.

Soon the findings of my research cried for further elaboration, and a book called *Black Preaching* (1970) was written. The folk culture of African Americans was carefully examined, and, as never before, I saw phenomenal power and effective method worthy of the admiration and use of all ethnic groups. The book became a kind of rationale and working apologetic for the tradition, giving African American preachers needed self-confidence and a fresh self-esteem concerning their ethnic preaching heritage.

In 1974, my ethnic explorations were shared with the wider world as the Lyman Beecher Lectures at Yale. One of these lectures was titled "Preaching as Meaningful Personal Experience." It also appeared later as a chapter in my book, *The Recovery of Preaching* (1977). As late as this, however, there were no footnotes referring to other homileticians. I had scrupulously avoided reading other sermons and books on homiletics. I insisted that my role was to mine the rich vein of my own ethnic ancestors. Both of my grandfathers were black Baptist preachers named Henry, and my title at Colgate Rochester Divinity School was Professor of Black Church Studies. I shunned the very appearance of any dependence whatsoever on some other tradition, whether for insight or for legitimization.

It was already obvious, however, that such isolation could not endure any longer. My Beecher lectures had been delivered to a virtually all white audience, and these lectures soon appeared as chapters in my book in the Harper's Ministers Paperback

Library. My efforts in ethnic isolation had served their definitive purpose; it was time for cross-cultural exchange.

I looked first for compatible spirits, and to my delighted surprise they were not hard to find. The very first that I encountered was Fred B. Craddock, first as author of *Overhearing the Gospel* and then as author of his earlier *As One Without Authority*. His ways of dealing with abstract reason and experiential encounter were much like what I myself believed, but he stated the issues in different terms and images.

It was interesting to learn that he, too, had been a kind of loner during his earlier writing, and that the audience he finally gained came quite unexpectedly. He was "overheard," at last, and I was among the overhearers. In my case, I learned that I had well-thought-out and well-stated company in my homiletical findings. He had vivid ways of saying things closely related to what I had been saying about the experience of the gospel. His word about the parables of Jesus in *Overhearing the Gospel* was unforgettable:

> The parables of Jesus were told to be overheard. "There was a certain man": anonymous, past tense, somewhere else—nothing here addressed to me. Relax and enjoy the story. And then it happens; I am inside the story, and the door closes behind me.[1]

As the years wore on, I met him in person and even lectured in his classes, but the main interaction was the reading of his work. I continued to insist, as one had to, that there was a pristine independence about my work, but it was no small comfort to know that my once-thought-original declarations were paralleled by Fred Craddock. I had been saying things equivalent to, but not as striking as, such Craddock comments as:

> Long after a man's head has consented to the preacher's idea, the old images may still hang in the heart. . . . The longest trip a person takes is from head to heart.[2]
>
> However, there are clear and welcome signs in recent years that we have learned anew that the presence of a full set of emotions is no evidence of the absence of intelligence, nor is the ability to feel strongly about a matter to be interpreted as lack of maturity.

225

Effective preaching reflects the minister's open receptivity to those life scenes which are noticeably emotional in flavor but which constitute memorable and important stations along the way most people travel.[3]

Have you ever noticed how much of *what* we experience is shaped by the anticipation of *how* we will share it with someone? . . . You did not coax your daughter into her very first step, . . . and then sometime later think of communicating the experience. Were you not at the very time of the experience searching for words, phrases, analogies to go into the journal, the letter, the phone call? . . . There is no surgery—literary, logical, or experiential—by which *what* and *how* can be severed.[4]

In addition to these ideas held in common, and perhaps without Professor Craddock's specific awareness, there was another bridge which provided a kind of dialogue with him. One of his prize-winning student homileticians at Candler School of Theology turned out, through cross registration, to be one of my very best students at the Interdenominational Theological Center, also in Atlanta. Her manifestly superior grasp of my own less traditional concepts and methods was undoubtedly enhanced by her prior work with Craddock, which she often mentioned. As she effectively assisted her classmates, she was bound to arouse in any professor a hope that one day she, too, would become an instructor of homiletics. Craddock no doubt shared this vision concerning Martha J. Simmons, now of San Francisco.

It was in dialogue with the now Reverend Dr. Simmons that my dialogue with Craddock was moved from a relatively low-key interaction to a more detailed encounter and correlation of ideas. The results are interwoven in the discussion that follows concerning the crucially important process of helping the hearer to *experience* the sermon and not just understand it.

ESSENTIALS OF EXPERIENCING THE GOSPEL

Fred Craddock insists that "as for the sermon itself, the most consistently effective delivery is by reexperiencing the message as it is being spoken."[5] What he says of the preacher is equally true of the audience. The most effective hearing is that which involves the whole person in the sermon as a meaningful experience, rather than just a set of abstract ideas. While this approach for both the preacher and the hearer may sound simple enough, the fact is that centuries of tradition have viewed preaching as primarily the expounding of great ideas, not as vital encounter with life-transforming implications. So there is much to be re-thought, starting with what preaching does to generate experiences of the Word.

1. Preaching as "Depth-to-Depth" Communication

The first essential of sermons that generate experiences of the gospel is that they come holistically from the *inner depths of the preacher* and involve the issues of life that stir those depths in others, the hearers. It is futile to expect a sermon on peripheral issues to draw hearers into experiences of deep encounter. There has to be an intimate and personal identification with the issue at hand. The catalyst for this hearer identification is the preacher's own genuine identification with the issue and with the scriptural remedy. Fred Craddock has paraphrased Kierkegaard on this subject with refreshing accuracy:

Rather he [Kierkegaard] is saying that the way to understand and to communicate the Christian Faith is through disciplined participation in that faith. This is not an option for the communicator. How does one become qualified to talk of forgiveness, of penitence, of the death of Christ—read a good book on the subject? It is by obedience and sacrifice. Appropriation of the gospel is the minimum condition for approaching pulpit or podium. From the standpoint of the hearers, the qualities of the teller affect the response to the story. The decision that a message is worth listening to is a decision that the teller is worth listening to. If the speaker is not in his [sic] speaking, if his absence is evidenced by an overage of clichés, quotations, and secondary sources, the hearers feel deceived and deprived. Anyone could have said it. When we respond we respond to someone.[6]

It might seem clear enough that a preacher should be in the sermon, sharing from her or his deepest concerns, but it is all too often not so. Preachers frequently speak because they have to say *some*thing, rather than because there is something in their depths that cries out to be said. I once asked a class of ten to compile a group list of their ten most important issues in living the Christian life. Their near unanimity was grounds for expecting that in each preacher's hundred sermons for the year, these issues would surface with regularity. Imagine my surprise when there were only two such sermons in a total of roughly a thousand. Little wonder that congregations were bored and hungry when the preachers were not preaching on issues that they themselves were deeply concerned about.

There is no substitute for personal involvement of the preacher in the sermon itself, and that involvement is best drawn from the issues that most concern and often perplex the preacher. Preaching with power is from the "gut," as we say, and that which comes from the preacher's depths communicates with the depths of the hearer.

2. Preaching as Communication in the Concrete

A second prerequisite of sermons generating experiences of the gospel is that the materials of the sermon be expressed in *concrete terms and images*—not in glittering abstractions, but in day-to-day details and dynamics—the sights, sounds, smells, tastes, and textures. I have it on good authority that Fred Craddock considers these so important that he requires beginning students of preaching to launch their studies of every pericope with a listing of all its sounds, tastes, colors, and so on.

The gospel does not consist primarily of abstractions; it consists of the specific/concrete details of the life, death, and resurrection of Jesus. The Incarnation could be described as God communicating such an abstraction as divine love in concreteness, produced in living color, with all the fascination and fatigue of true mortals like us.

The record of Jesus' ministry includes many details of very human emotion, such as when he felt compelled to reveal to the

228

crowd that his major purpose was to be their spiritual bread, not their physical food. This disappointed the crowd. They said, "This is some hard talk. Who wants to hear such stuff?" From that point, a great many of them left. This suddenly deserted prophet/preacher felt wounded and frustrated. One hears it in his wistful query, "Do you also wish to go away?" (John 6:67).

No doctrinal formulation is equal to the task of describing such love by God. We can only say that it is *like* what we see in the concrete, historical person, Jesus. We experience his gospel best in tangible, colorful, gripping detail.

3. Preaching as the Revisitation of the Familiar

Even more to the point is our third prerequisite; that the details be *familiar*. This applies to both the details of the story, so to speak, and to the familiarity of the biblical base and common belief system. Let us deal with the last of these first.

Craddock uses the word *recognition* to apply to the biblical base and general belief system, so that one is never too far from the conventional frame of reference. Whatever new image is offered, it is only an opening up and fulfillment of that with which we were familiar and to which we were committed already. Craddock says, that "the nod of recognition precedes the shock of recognition."[7]

Jesus used the same approach when he said that he had come not to destroy the law, but to fulfill it (Matthew 5:17). Craddock finds many instances of this approach in both the Old and New Testaments. When the prophet Nathan told David, "You are the man" (II Samuel 12:1-15), this was the process of moving from easy recognition to fresh insight recognition.

This use of the familiar images and traditional literature of the status quo must not be avoided for fear of passive affirmation of the world as it is. In typically effective phrase, Fred Craddock explains this use of the familiar: It avoids giving the hearer an overload of new insight and/or information, lest the ear be overwhelmed and then closed in self defense.[8] Use of the familiar is in fact the best way to motivate and empower hearers to deal actively with the evils that beset them and their world. No authentic prophet dares not to cry out in the mother tongue and homespun "visual aids" of the people to whom she or he preaches.

The writer of Ephesians is often understood to side with the oppressors of women (5:22) and children (6:1-2). But if one reads the full contexts in Scripture, one finds good basis for suspecting that his true intent is quite the opposite. In each case, the sentence affirming the status quo is an introductory bit, gaining the recognition and attention of the hearer. But this passage is only introductory, as can be seen by the explosive final admonition in each case.

The word to wives is preceded by a statement of equality, and the passage ends with a startling, unprecedented obligation of husbands to wives (Ephesians 5:21, 25, 27-28). No matter how powerless children were considered to be in Greek and Hebrew society, the writer tells parents not to abuse them (6:4). Such demanding words needed this recognition/familiarity as an introduction.

So, Paul's use of the familiar is essential to the exegesis of these often misunderstood passages. It shows shrewd understanding of the traditions of his day and validates activist strategy. Holy wisdom and established belief systems are best changed from within, not from external attack. The prophet needs underlying logic, but hearers are moved to change only when claim can be made to loyalty to the belief system that has brought a culture to its present level of development. In addition to all this, recognition begets openness to new, transforming experience.

Familiarity is also essential in the details of the story, as we have mentioned above. The hold of many an effective sermon is so great because, in its story or stories, one has thought, seen, heard, and smelled the same things hundreds of times. The hearer has so much in common that he or she slips unresisting into the very scenes and lines of the gospel, to emerge only after a profound encounter and, possibly, a life-changing experience.

It was just such an approach that Jesus used. When he told of lost coins and sheep and sons, he was speaking of things that were so familiar as to attract little attention to themselves. This left the hearer free to deal with the message as a whole and as an experience. It may well be that such things as sheep are not that familiar to today's urban audiences, but something is. And that something can be painted into the picture or read into the gospel experience in such a way that hearers easily see their own plight and find themselves in the problem and then in the remedy offered in the message.

We hear the Apostle Paul say that he is forgetting the things that are behind him and pressing for the mark (Philippians 3:14). He is well trained in abstract thinking, but he knows that anyone hearing this letter read would identify with him and his idea more completely by visualizing the mark metaphorically related to as the finish line in a race. Who wouldn't identify easily, even those without legs, with the image of the competitor on the track, not looking back and pressing ahead to reach the finish line? It is a clear and provocative image.

Thus do we see an example of the great impact and potential for focus in the revisitation of the familiar. This is what is meant when we say that the hearer slips unresisting into the very scenes and lines of the message.

4. Hearing as Spontaneous Self-recognition

A final essential emerges here, for this slipping into the very scenes and lines is the result of *self-recognition*. The listeners see and hear so much of themselves in the sermon that, before they know it, they are in the story and, as Fred Craddock puts it, the door is already shut behind them.

In Isaiah 6, the prophet, recently bereaved by the death of his hero, good King Uzziah, entered the Temple. He was empty and open, and the very atmosphere of the Temple, with its lofty ceiling, helped him to sense the presence of the Lord, high and lifted up. It was an awesome experience; he envisioned angels and all the accoutrements of the heavenly throne room. He was excited, but not very proud of himself in the midst of his blessed experience. In fact, he felt so small and impure in the presence of the majestic and holy God that he cried out that he felt undone.

But his sense of being undone did not last long. God sent an angel to relieve his distress. Graphically he envisioned an angel taking a hot coal from the altar and touching and cleansing his lips. This was a symbol for his total cleansing and acceptability to God. God then called, asking, "Whom shall I send, and who will go for us?" The relieved Isaiah gladly answered, "Here am I, send me."

There is probably no more detailed and graphic account of the inner feelings of a person in the whole of the Bible, with the exception of the words of our Lord on the cross. When this story is retold with feeling, the hearer can hardly avoid the same sense of initial awe, the sense of being undone, and then the relief and joy of being forgiven and even called by God. Such is the power of spontaneous self-recognition.

These are the four essentials or prerequisites: depth-to-depth communication, concrete terms and images, revisitation of the familiar, and self-recognition. They constitute a means whereby the whole person is addressed and drawn into encounter with the gospel. But there is still much to be determined as to the kind of format in which these essentials shall be employed. We turn, then, to what Fred Craddock refers to as the form of a sermon,[9] and what I have long called "vehicles of encounter."

SERMON FORMS, OR VEHICLES FOR EXPERIENTIAL ENCOUNTER

We have gone as far as one can go with principles of the experiencing of the Word. We now need to deal with the specifics of the format in which the experience occurs. There is no single form or vehicle that all must use, but there can never be an experience of the Word in a shapeless vacuum or without a choice of form. Fred Craddock says, "Form shapes the listener's experience of the material."[10] Indeed, once the scriptural text, behavioral purpose, and literary form have been determined, the sermon should virtually write itself.

Craddock may be said to lead the growing list of homileticians who now insist that this form should come from the biblical text whenever a form is at all manifest in the text and/or its pericope. To select a form or vehicle different from the one inherent in a given text is to do violence to its divinely intended meaning, since meaning and form are inseparable. Thus a narrative parable text demands a narrative sermon form, and the purpose of the sermon should be the purpose of the text. To extract abstract theological points from the parable of the prodigal son, and then to preach those points, would border on the sacrilegious abuse of Scripture.

To understand further how these forms or vehicles of encounter are used to generate experience of the Word, it is necessary to classify them by genre, and then to look at how each functions. In effect, we will look at Craddock's "forms" and my "vehicles" and other sources, and establish a listing of each under a genre. It is understood that the related types under each genre will demand varying degrees of hearer involvement. But all within a given genre will foster experience by means of the inner dynamics typical of that grouping.

Before we do this, however, there is need to foresee and deal with the fact that many forms may fit more than one genre's definition. It is also possible for one form to be used within another form. So it has to be clear that the important thing is not the ability to make an unambiguous assignment of genre, but to use whatever the genre might be for a powerful experience of the Word.

1. Narrative Genre

Far and away the most familiar genre is the narrative, the story of an occurrence, real or imaginary (e.g., parable). The story generates experience by means of the familiar details mentioned above, which draw the hearer in by spontaneous identification. The usual and most specific identification is with the protagonist of the story. The hearer also easily identifies with the conflict in the plot, and so engages vicariously in the movement or action in the narrative. When the protagonist gains the resolution of the conflict, the hearer feels the same way and is not only ready to be glad and celebrate, but also to commit himself or herself to the

233

action necessary to the resolution. This would include whatever this resolution or victory might cost. The experience of the Word is just this compelling; it achieves the purpose for which it is revealed.

One of my most unforgettable experiences of the Word occurred one clear summer evening on a hilltop in the foothills of the Sierra Nevada Mountains in California. It was a vesper service for a church-sponsored youth camp. As the elderly preacher spoke, the high-school youth, as well as we counselors, were led to sense ourselves as being at the very foot of the cross.

This veteran pastor and college president had a knack for the kinds of details you could almost literally see. We sat enthralled as we envisioned the muscles in the centurion's arms, and learned that he had to be able to subdue all one hundred of his men. He was the top sergeant over these hated troops of occupation, with all the size, gruffness, and brutality that this often implied. I'll never forget the hobnail boots this soldier wore, and the mockery drawn from the Jews by the sound of these boots as these arrogant legionnaires marched down the cobblestone streets.

This was a career soldier, and he had officiated at many an execution. His continued standing as a centurion and his career in the legion were at stake as he began to feel disturbing inner reactions to this candidate for execution. He had never seen a man take the pain of the blows and the cruel mockery the way this Jesus took it. This centurion tried to shut out these feelings of awe and reverence at the way this man Jesus calmly conquered death, even while nailed to a cross. He tried to hush the cry for justice welling up within his soul. But he couldn't hold his peace. As Jesus "gave up the ghost," the centurion's mouth flew open and he put his entire career on the line as he cried out, "Truly this man was the Son of God!" (Mark 15:39).

One hundred ten campers and some twenty counselors gasped at the sight. The few youth not already committed to Christ joined the sergeant and the rest of us on that hill. We were unanimous in our own cry of, "Truly this man was the Son of God." It was something like forty-five years ago, but the picture is as vivid as if it had happened yesterday. And my recall is likely matched by most, if not all, of the one hundred and thirty who were there. Such is the grip of vivid detail and action, as we are drawn into narrative-type identification with and vicarious experience of the Word.

There are a number of forms or vehicles of encounter that could be said to fall within the definition of the genre called narrative. All of them have protagonists, plot conflicts, and resolutions of the conflict. Thus they have the stuff of which experiences or encounters are made: recognition and identification.

Some forms listed here may or may not have all the standard ingredients, but all have enough of the necessities of narration. Craddock mentions the following narrative forms found in the New Testament: miracle stories, parables, proverbs, resurrection stories, and such accounts as Paul's story of the first communion service.[11] I would add from modern times the conversion story. It is likely the most vivid and moving tale any preacher can tell. It is a model of the way stories should draw hearer identification, and it is also the prize example of another genre called the testimony or monologue. If such a personally experienced event is told in a conversation between two or more persons, it becomes also a member of the genre called dialogue. Many of the other genres that follow will consist of tiny narratives within the sketch or study or parable.

2. Character Sketch Genre

There are, of course, untold texts for which there is no contextual narrative. In many such, however, the writer or speaker is, or becomes, the context within which the text evolves meaning. Thus, the writer's personhood—as revealed in other writings and in such records of his or her life as are available—becomes the basis for interpretation. A vivid, detailed sketch of the writer is painted, and the text's meaning appears in personal context, and, therefore, concrete, moving terms. There may not be a narrative-type suspense level, as it moves toward resolution of the conflict, but the interest and identification may be very intense and effective.

The Bible can hardly be said to provide models of character sketches all in one sequence, but all the necessary details are there. Thus when a non-narrative text is by Peter or Paul, by or about Deborah or David, it is brought to clear visualization by personal data gathered from the Bible and biblical resources. The goal is so to portray the person that her or his words and deeds come to life with meaning and power.

I think, for example, of Acts 18:26b, about the ministry team of Priscilla and Aquila. They expounded the way of God to Apollos "more perfectly." Since Priscilla seems to have been the more vocal one, I would build a sermon around a character sketch of her. It would be based on the six references to her in the New Testament, and on the data I could find about her leaving Rome, and the opportunity she had had to think and talk theology with Paul while they worked on tents. The encounters with the text would end with the joy of Priscilla and her spouse over the improvement in the substance of the preaching of this gifted scholar and orator, Apollos.

3. Group Sketch Genre

The group sketch or study is much like the character sketch, except that the intended audience is a group as such. They may have the same characteristics as an individual, but they see themselves and determine their behavior as a group. It may be a labor union, a branch of the armed services, an extended family, an ethnic group, a social class grouping, or a congregation. Whatever the group, the gospel—as perceived and experienced in concert with others—is more penetrating when it is known that these others share the blame or blessing.

This genre takes on considerable importance when we recall the vast difference between what people will do in a group and what they will do alone, or as individuals. Lynchings are only carried out by mobs; major donations are best solicited from whole groups of rich folk. People do daring things, both good and bad, with the support, spoken or implied, of a group. Can you imagine Christ at Calvary without a crowd-generated cry of "crucify him!"?

Groups are, however, not beyond the positive influence of preaching that is experience centered. It is hard to imagine a greater sin than racial prejudice, and yet I can think of a preacher who effectively tackled that sin with experience-centered preaching. The sermon employed a kind of group-study genre, and moved the group as a body to the higher plain of heaven, which had powerful implications for what the fellowship ought to be like here on earth.

This theologically conservative pastor in an agribusiness town had been ordered by his deacons to choose between resigning and withdrawing his invitation to an African American congregation's youth. They were to cross the tracks, literally, and skate with the host church's youth. The order was given on a Saturday night, and the pastor asked his deacons to give him until the close of worship the next day to tender his reply. I didn't hear or read his sermon for that morning, but several people described it as a kind of group tour to heaven. In the midst of the joy there, the pastor casually reminded the group of biblical passages that declare the place to be fully integrated: every kindred and people and tongue (Revelation 7:9). As for himself and his family, they planned to be there. There was choked emotion in his voice and tears in his eyes as he said he hoped they'd all join him and his family in that great congregation around the throne.

He submitted his resignation, and the congregation refused to accept it. Surprisingly, the vote was apparently unanimous. A very recent addition to the deacon board, from a state in the deep South, came forward and asked to speak. He, too, had tears as he declared that he had been wrong all his life. If God would forgive him, he would never be that way again. Clearly the group had been to heaven vicariously, and the change thus accomplished vastly exceeded anything that might have occurred in response to a pastoral thrashing or an abstract discourse on ideal race relations.

4. Other Genres

The dynamics mentioned in the first three genres are to be found in the others, with which we will not deal in detail. They

237

include the dialogue; the monologue/testimony; and the genre called metaphors, similes, and analogs (parables). This latter genre may not have the personal identification seen in dialogues and monologues, but one sees the same intensity of encounter based on familiar inanimate objects such as salt, light, or sown seeds.

One other genre I have given the label "stream of consciousness." It takes place when one reads a psalm and identifies with the psalmist, rather than just reading the psalm for devotional *ideas*. One shares the frustration and despair of the writer in Psalm 22 when he cries, "My God, my God, why have you forsaken me?" (v. 1). Jesus felt the same way as he saw himself as abandoned on the cross. This twenty-second Psalm said for Jesus just what needed to be said/sung.

The pattern of psalms of complaint, such as the twenty-second, is to move through the pain cathartically and get it out of one's system. Then the psalm moves on to praising the Lord, as in verse 25: "From you comes my praise in the great congregation." One can assume that this is what Jesus did on the cross, even though his loss of strength may have made the rest of his psalm inaudible. This movement in the stream of consciousness, from complaint to praise, is still common in such places as the spirituals, which move from such complaints as feeling like a motherless child to declaring oneself a true believer; from the loneliness of nobody knowing "the trouble I've seen," to "Nobody knows but Jesus." As the psalmists sang and prayed their way to wholeness, so can we. We simply need sermons that help us to move into the stream of consciousness of the psalmists by identifying with them in both complaint and praise.

THE CONCLUSION OF AN EXPERIENCE OF THE WORD

No experience of the Word is complete without a striking and forceful ending. This conclusion must be clearly focused on the original biblical text and behavioral purpose, and it must be carefully timed, moving to maximum impact. Great works of art are, at the same time, experiential encounters, and they move this same way. Symphonies restate the melodic theme in grand crescendo, and then comes the end, the coda. Dramas reach their heights with the powerful resolution of the plot's conflict, then denouement. The Word is best remembered and acted upon when the encounter is concluded in a similar manner, unashamedly involving the whole person, with special attention to the noblest emotions such as faith, love, and commitment. Good sermons also are works of art, not argument; symbol, not syllogism.

Fred Craddock is known to have insisted to students, "Let's *land* this thing." A free translation might be, "Let's not just keep going on and on, and let's not simply peter out." His direct word is, "It gives confidence to the preacher throughout the sermon to have the end, the goal, clearly in view. . . . The sermon, in order to have its own integrity, must have its proper ending."[12]

The definitive essential of concluding an experience of the Word is characteristic of all preaching traditions; it is the need to *review and summarize,* literally or symbolically, the thrust of the sermon. However, the cognitive requirement of summation must be accomplished in a manner consistent with the goal of profound encounter. Thus it may more often be done indirectly and symbolically, as opposed to direct and literal cognitive restatement.

For instance, a sermon on the text where Joshua challenged the Israelites to "choose this day whom you will serve" (Joshua 24:15) would no doubt have a behavioral sermon-purpose of moving hearers to be more decisive about their faith. What better conclusion than James Russell Lowell's poem: "Once to every man and nation comes the moment to decide. . . . And the choice goes by forever, twixt that darkness and that light."[13] This poem sums up Joshua's challenge, and it has the added advantage of having been set to music as a great hymn of the church, to be sung afterwards by the hearers. This provides both the needed focus and concluding experiential impact or climactic utterance, without diluting or polluting the substance of the sermon.

239

Another essential of a good conclusion to an experience of the Word is the artistic quality of *timing of impact*. There is a logic of hearer response, which requires that suspense gradually intensify up to resolution; then, the sermon ends. To go too high and suddenly drop the impact level before the end of the sermon is to signal closure and sever attention, regardless of how much of the sermon is yet to be preached. Professor Craddock calls this the principle of end stress, withholding the point of primary interest until the end.[14] Timing in a sermon is not everything, but a sermon without it is not likely to be a transforming experience. A well-focused, passionately delivered, positive conclusion gives "ecstatic reinforcement" to the whole sermon.

Such intentional dealing with human emotion is problematic if not unethical in the minds of some clergy. They find purposeful appeal to human emotion to be manipulative. But the love and selflessness these clergy seek to spread abroad are also highly emotional, so we must affirm high principled dealing with emotion. We cannot expect love and commitment to increase by the unilateral action of the Holy Spirit, while we deal solely with the cognitive. Good timing, purposefully emotive, is absolutely essential.

The conclusion of the sermon on the Joshua text offered above exemplifies two types of conclusion to an experience of the Word: the penetrating question and heightened rhetoric. Joshua's depth-stirring challenge is for stimulating commitment. It confronts the Hebrews with a haunting reality the claim of which is inescapable. It is not just a clever question. It is no-frills logic. It concerns deserved, sincere loyalty to Jehovah. It delivers high impact.

The second type of conclusion employs the expressive power of poetry and heightened rhetoric. For instance, the words "once to every man and nation comes the moment to decide" have a punch not possible with conversational language. Used only in conclusion, and focused on the purpose of the text, Lowell's poem is an effective summation and reinforcement of the purpose of the whole sermon.

The Apostle Paul offers resources for the use of heightened rhetoric in II Corinthians 4:8-10: "We are afflicted in every way, yet not crushed; perplexed, but not driven to despair; persecuted, but not forsaken; struck down, but not destroyed." It is powerful affirmation and conclusion, either for a sermon on this same text, or for any other sermon on enduring difficulty. One finds such powerful rhetoric from Genesis to Revelation, and, of course, one can craft one's own affirmations.

My favorite type of conclusion is celebration, which also often includes the use of great rhetoric. It is the intentionally emotive process of deep joy and gladness about the deeds of God on our behalf. Celebration may also include our own self-affirming determination to respond appropriately to God. My preference may be culturally conditioned, but I am certain that it could give much to every culture, rich or poor, educated or uneducated. I believe that the healing certitude and empowering transformation of authentic celebration are the most effective influences for spiritual commitment available.

Now the fact that this powerful type of conclusion has been so widely misused would suggest the need for some brief guidelines. The first and most important would be the firm rule that the text and purpose of the sermon must be what is celebrated. Second, celebration always affirms some great biblical truth. One may get heated up but never genuinely joyful about less. Third, one cannot celebrate what one is still struggling to comprehend. So, finally, there should be no new concepts in the celebration. Good celebration is an artistic, powerful restatement of what has already been understood and related to.

These all add up to the fact that no real experience of the Word is possible without carefully designed closure, which must be the artistic resolution and fulfillment of the entire encounter. Mass media communication and cultural pluralism have fortunately exposed the obsoleteness of the old sermon/essay style of Western culture, with primary cognitive goals. The Word preached today dare not be less compelling and holistically engaging than the cultural context.

CONTRIBUTORS LIST

Gail R. O'Day teaches at Candler School of Theology, Emory University, Atlanta, Georgia.

Gene M. Tucker teaches at Candler School of Theology, Emory University, Atlanta, Georgia.

M. Eugene Boring teaches at Brite Divinity School, Texas Christian University, Fort Worth, Texas.

Leander E. Keck teaches at Yale Divinity School, Yale University, New Haven, Connecticut.

Eugene L. Lowry teaches at Saint Paul School of Theology, Kansas City, Missouri.

Richard Lischer teaches at Duke Divinity School, Duke University, Durham, North Carolina.

Paul Scott Wilson teaches at Emmanuel College in the Toronto School of Theology, and the University of Toronto, Ontario, Canada.

David L. Bartlett teaches at Yale Divinity School, Yale University, New Haven, Connecticut.

Thomas G. Long teaches at Princeton Theological Seminary, Princeton, New Jersey.

David Buttrick teaches at Vanderbilt Divinity School, Vanderbilt University, Nashville, Tennessee.

Barbara Brown Taylor is Rector of Grace-Calvary Episcopal Church, Clarkesville, Georgia.

Henry H. Mitchell teaches at the Interdenominational Theological Center in Atlanta, Georgia.

1. TOWARD A BIBLICAL THEOLOGY OF PREACHING

1. Fred B. Craddock, *As One Without Authority* (Nashville: Abingdon Press, 1971), p. 3.
2. Ibid., p. 144.
3. Ibid., p. 153.
4. George A. Lindbeck, *The Nature of Doctrine: Religion and Theology in a Postliberal Age* (Philadelphia: Westminster Press, 1984).
5. Ibid., p. 72.
6. Ibid., p. 118.
7. Wendell Berry, "The Responsibility of the Poet," in *What Are People For?* (San Francisco: North Point Press, 1990), p. 89.
8. See Walter Brueggemann, *Israel's Praise: Doxology Against Idolatry and Ideology* (Philadelphia: Fortress Press, 1988).
9. Claus Westermann's study of this movement from plea to praise, *Praise and Lament in the Psalms* (Atlanta: John Knox Press, 1981), has had decisive influence on the study of psalms of lament.
10. The hypothesis of the place of the answering salvation oracle in the liturgy of the psalms was most fully developed by Joachim Begrich, "Das priesterliche Heilsorakel," *ZAW* 52 (1934): 81-92. This study is now reprinted in *Gesammelte Studien Zum Alten Testament* (Munich: Chr. Kaiser Verlag, 1964), pp. 217-31. There have been some who have contested Begrich's hypothesis, most notably Edgar Conrad ("Second Isaiah and the Priestly Oracle of Salvation [Reply to J. Begrich]," *ZAW* 93 (1981): 234-246); and also his *Fear Not Warrior: A Study of 'al tira' pericopes in the Hebrew Scriptures*

[Chico, Calif.: Scholars Press, 1985]), but by and large Begrich's hypothesis continues as the consensus view.

11. Claus Westermann, *The Praise of God in the Psalms* (Richmond, Va.: John Knox Press, 1965), p. 65.

12. Walter Brueggemann, *The Message of the Psalms* (Minneapolis: Augsburg Press, 1984), p. 57.

13. The designation of Second Isaiah as a poet was first used most decisively by James Muilenburg, "Isaiah 40–66" in *The Interpreter's Bible,* ed. by Nolan B. Harmon (Nashville: Abingdon Press, 1956), vol. V., pp. 381-419, esp. pp. 386-93.

14. Claus Westermann, "Sprache und Struktur der Prophetie Deuterojesajas," in *Forschung am Alten Testament* (Munich: Kaiser Verlag, 1964), p. 118.

15. H. Eberhard von Waldow, "The Message of Deutero-Isaiah," *Interpretation* 22 (1968): 259-88, stresses the oral delivery of Second Isaiah's message.

16. This analysis of Isaiah 41:8-13 follows the form critical categories proposed by Westermann, "Sprach und Struktur," pp. 117-24.

17. Claus Westermann, *The Old Testament and Jesus Christ* (Minneapolis: Augsburg, 1968), p. 27. See also "Alttestamentliche Elemente in Lukas 2, 1-20," in *Tradition und Glaube: Das Frühe Christentum in seiner Umwelt,* ed. G. Jeremias et al. (Göttingen: Vandenhoeck and Ruprecht, 1971), pp. 317-27.

18. Gail R. O'Day, " 'I Have Overcome the World' (John 16:33): Narrative Time in John 13–17," *Semeia* 53 (1991): 153-66.

19. Joseph Sittler, "The Necessity and Embarrassment of Choice," in *Gravity and Grace,* edited by Linda-Marie Delloff (Minneapolis: Augsburg, 1986), pp. 99-107.

20. See Peter Berger and Thomas Luckmann, *The Social Construction of Reality* (Garden City, N.Y.: Doubleday and Company, Inc. 1966) [Anchor Edition, 1967], pp. 135-37, for a discussion of the role of a mother's words of assurance in a child's social construction of reality.

21. Sittler, *Gravity and Grace,* p. 100.

22. Ibid., p. 103.

2. READING AND PREACHING THE OLD TESTAMENT

1. John Barton, *Reading the Old Testament: Method in Biblical Study* (Philadelphia: Westminster Press, 1984), p. 11.

2. Stanley Fish, *Is There a Text in This Class? The Authority of Interpretive Communities* (Cambridge: Harvard University Press, 1980), especially pp. 15-17, 167-73.

3. Hans Walter Wolff has called attention to this in terms of the history of the pentateuchal literature as the Yahwist's interpretation of history: "The Kerygma of the Yahwist," *Interpretation* 20 (1966): 131-58; originally published in German in *Evangelische Theologie* 24 (February, 1964): 73-97; reprinted in Walter Brueggemann and Hans Walter Wolff, *The Vitality of Old Testament Traditions* (Atlanta: John Knox Press, 1975), pp. 41-66.

4. One of the most profound and influential literary interpretations of this story is that of Eric Auerbach, *Mimesis: The Representation of Reality in Western Literature* (Princeton: Princeton University Press, 1953; reprinted Garden City: Doubleday, 1957), pp. 50-55.

5. Tamara Cohn Eskenazi, *In an Age of Prose: A Literary Approach to Ezra–Nehemiah*, Society of Biblical Literature Monograph Series 36 (Atlanta: Scholars Press, 1988).

6. Ibid., p. 97.

7. Thomas W. Overholt, *Channels of Prophecy: The Social Dynamics of Prophetic Activity* (Minneapolis: Fortress Press, 1989), esp. pp. 17-26.

3. RHETORIC, RIGHTEOUSNESS, AND THE SERMON ON THE MOUNT

1. As representative of the spectrum of the many books and articles representing this relatively new discipline in New Testament studies, see, for example, Dan O. Via, "Structure, Christology, and Ethics in Matthew," in *Orientation by Disorientation: Studies in Literary Criticism and Biblical Literary Criticism Presented in Honor of William A. Beardslee* (Pittsburgh: Pickwick Press, 1980) pp. 199-215, and the many works by Beardslee himself; Joanna Dewey, *Markan Public Debate. Literary Technique, Concentric Structure and Theology in Mark 2:1–3:6* (SBL Dissertation Series 48. Chico, Calif.: Scholars Press, 1980); George A. Kennedy, *New Testament Interpretation Through Rhetorical Criticism* (Chapel Hill: University of North Carolina Press, 1984); James D. Hester, "The Rhetorical Structure of Galatians 1:11–2:14" *JBL* 103 (June 1984): 223-33; Wilhelm Wuellner, "Where Is Rhetorical Criticism Taking Us?" *CBQ* 49 (July 1987): 448-63; Barnabas Lindars, "The Rhetorical Structure of Hebrew," *NTS* 35 (July 1989):

382-406; Duane F. Watson, "A Rhetorical Analysis of 2 John according to Greco-Roman Convention," *NTS* 35 (January 1989): 104-30; Frank Witt Hughs, *Early Christian Rhetoric and 2 Thessalonians* (Sheffield: Journal for the Study of the New Testament Press, 1989); Peter Lampe, "Theological Wisdom and the 'Word About the Cross': The Rhetorical Scheme in I Corinthians 1–4," *Interpretation* 44, no. 2 (April 1990): 117-31; Burton L. Mack, *Rhetoric and the New Testament* (Minneapolis: Fortress Press, 1990); Duane F. Watson, ed. *Persuasive Artistry: Studies in New Testament Rhetoric in Honor of George A. Kennedy* (Sheffield: JSNT Press, 1991); and Amos N. Wilder *Early Christian Rhetoric* (Cambridge: Harvard University Press, 1971).

2.

	Matt.	Mark	Luke	John
δίκαιοξ (righteous)	17	2	11	3
δικαιοσύνη (righteousness)	7	0	1	2
δικαίοω (to make righteous)	2	0	5	0
δικαίωμα (righteous ordinance)	0	1	0	0
δίκαιως (righteously)	0	1	0	0

3. It is a defect of many commentaries and surveys of the New Testament that a standard part of the introductory materials is a surface "outline" on the biblical book devised by the scholar and imposed on the text as a set of handles to aid the student in remembering the content of the book. In the better commentaries this outline was discovered as a part of the exegetical process and represents the actual rhetorical structure built into the text by its author, rather than a preemptive strike on the part of the commentator.

4. Fred B. Craddock, "The Gospels as Literature" *Encounter* 49 (1988): 20; cf. *Luke: A Bible Commentary for Preaching and Teaching,* Interpretation (Louisville: Westminster/John Knox, 1990), p. 5.

5. Compare Mark's use of the flashback in 6:14-29, which takes the reader back to a previous event during the time the disciples are on their mission journey, which Mark does not narrate. Luke makes copious use of speeches that tell preceding history, as in Acts 7. Writers often use internal monologue for this purpose.

6. For example, an examination in a synopsis of the chain of ten miracles (in nine miracle stories) of Matthew 8–9 shows that they are placed in a topical, not historical-chronological arrangement, though Matthew has both changed the chronology of his sources and tightened their purported chronological relationships. The tight "chronology" is Matthew's *literary* creation.

7. The idea was popularized by B. W. Bacon, "The 'Five Books' of Matthew Against the Jews," *Expositor* 15 (1918): 56-66 and especially in his *Studies in Matthew* (New York: Henry Holt, 1930) pp. 265-335. This general outline was adopted by many others, then received a baroque typological elaboration by Austin Farrer, *St. Matthew and St. Mark* (London: Dacre, 1954). W. D. Davies, *The Setting of the Sermon on the Mount* (Cambridge: Cambridge University Press, 1964) pp. 14-25, gives an extensive and sympathetic treatment of the theory, with a substantial critique. John P. Meier is perhaps the most significant contemporary advocate of this understanding of the Matthean structure, which he has incorporated into his view of Matthean salvation history *(Matthew* [New Testament Message 3; Wilmington: Michael Glazier, 1980]; *The Vision of Matthew: Christ, Church, and Morality in Matthew's Gospel* [New York: Paulist Press, 1979]).

8. This formula may have been embryonically present in Q; see Luke 7:1 at the conclusion of the "Sermon on the Plain." Matthew does take over Q phrases and sentences and make them into his own favorite expressions, for example, "little faith" (from Q in Matt. 6:30, but then often in Matthean redaction) and "the law and the prophets" (Q in Matt. 11:13, then often redactionally). It is the formulaic elaboration and repetition that is redactional, not the phrase itself.

9. For example, a fairly lengthy speech occurs in chapter 11, a "narrative" section, and the speech against the Pharisees in chapter 23 must, on this theory, be combined with the eschatological discourse of chapters 24 and 25, despite their different topics and change of location.

10. Michael Goulder, *Midrash and Lection in Matthew* (London: SPCK, 1974).

11. For example, David R. Bauer, *The Structure of Matthew's Gospel: A Study in Literary Design*, JSNTS 31, (Sheffield: The Almond Press, 1988), neither refers to Goulder's view in the text nor include his book in the bibliography of almost 300 items.

12. This is not the place for a discussion of the Synoptic problem and the solution affirmed by most scholars and in this study, the two-source theory. For an up-to-date brief discussion affirming the two-source hypothesis and bibliography giving alternative perspectives, see Franz Neirynck, "Synoptic Problem" in Raymond E. Brown, Joseph A. Fitzmyer, and Roland E. Murphy, eds. *The New Jerome Biblical Commentary* (Englewood Cliffs, N.J.: Prentice-Hall, 1990), pp. 587-95.

13. The best explication of this understanding of the setting of Matthew is given in Ulrich Luz, *Matthew 1–7: A Commentary* (Minneapolis: Augsburg, 1989), pp. 73-94. Volumes 2 and 3 of this splendid work are in preparation and translation.

14. Several good synopses of the Gospels are available, but the best and most widely used remains Kurt Aland, *Synopsis of the Four Gospels* (New York: United Bible Societies, 1982), available in inexpensive English, Greek, and Greek-English editions from the American Bible Society. *Synopsis* refers, of course, not to a summary or "harmony," but to an edition of the Gospels in which individual pericopes are printed with their parallel texts from other Gospels on the same page for comparison in wording, order, and structure. An additional convenient tool for the study of Q, which includes parallels to the Gospel of Thomas, has been provided by John S. Kloppenborg, *Q Parallels: Synopsis, Critical Notes, and Concordance* (Sonoma: Polebridge Press, 1988).

15. This does not mean that Matthew is writing fiction. As we shall discuss below, Matthew receives much of the Sermon on the Mount from tradition, some of which certainly goes back to the preaching of the historical Jesus. It is not our task here to pursue the question of just which sayings come from the pre-Easter Jesus of Nazareth. For a clear, reverent, and judiciously critical discussion of method in reconstructuring the life and message of the historical Jesus, see John P. Meier, *A Marginal Jew: Rethinking the Historical Jesus* (New York: Doubleday, 1991). For our present purposes, however, it is important to be clear that the Sermon on the Mount in Matthew 5–7 was never preached on a Galilean hillside, but is "preached" by the character Jesus in the story Matthew has composed.

16. Placing an item first is one of Matthew's structural strategies of registering its importance. Every reader of Matthew notices, for instance, the enhanced importance of Peter in Matthew compared to Mark, for which a comparison of Mark 8:27-30 and Matthew 16:13-20 or Mark 6:45-52 and Matthew 14:22-33 is sufficient reminder. Matthew also points to this by narrating the call of Peter *first*, and not only by naming Peter first in the list of the Twelve in 10:2, but by explicitly labeling Peter as "first." It is thus an interesting question whether Matthew trusted induction as much as Craddock.

17. Although it is easy to count words, "perhaps" is necessary here due to the ambiguity of whether 23–25 is one speech or two in

Matthew's mind. If 23 is included as part of Jesus' final speech, then it is the longest and the Sermon on the Mount is the second longest. In any case, the two longest and in some sense more important speeches are the first and the last, and preachers hardly need to be reminded of the cruciality of beginnings and endings.

18. I prefer this explanation in terms of Matthew's hermeneutical strategy to that of Goulder, *Midrash,* p. 35, that by chapter 12 editorial fatigue had set in and Matthew rather lazily followed Mark's story line rather than exercising his previous creativity. (Compare Robert H. Gundry, *Matthew: A Commentary on His Literary and Theological Art* [Grand Rapids: Eerdmans, 1982], p. 10).

19. See Robert Funk, *New Gospel Parallels,* The Synoptic Gospels (Philadelphia: Fortress Press, 1985), pp. 3-12.

20. T. Keim in the first volume of his *Geschichte Jesu von Nazara,* published in Zürich in 1867, was apparently the first to propose this outline. After being noticed by a few others, Edgar Krentz, "The Extent of Matthew's Prologue: Toward the Structure of the First Gospel," *JBL* 83 (1964) reintroduced this view to the current discussion. Jack Dean Kingsbury has argued for this view in several works, including *Matthew as Story,* 2nd ed. (Philadelphia: Fortress Press, 1988), from which the above wording is taken. Kingsbury's student David R. Bauer has recently published a monograph supporting this outline, *The Structure of Matthew's Gospel* (see note 11).

21. A thorough history and moderate critique of this view is given by Franz Neirynck, "APO TOTE HRXATO and the Structure of Matthew," *Evangelica II,* BETL 99 (Louvain, Belgium: University Press, 1991), pp. 141-82.

22. The four in parenthesis are sometimes not counted as "formula quotations."

23. See, for example, Krister Stendahl, *The School of St. Matthew and Its Use of the Old Testament* (Philadelphia: Fortress, 1968) and R. H. Gundry, *The Use of the Old Testament in St. Matthew's Gospel* (NovTSup 18; Leiden, The Netherlands: Brill, 1967).

24. Peter F. Ellis, *Matthew: His Mind and His Message* (Collegeville, Minn.: Liturgical Press, 1974), pp. 10-13; C. H. Lohr, "Oral Techniques in the Gospel of Matthew," *CBQ* 23 (1963): 404-27.

25. Luz, *Matthew 1–7,* p. 38, points out that the chiastic arrangement fits even in terms of the length of the speeches, with the first and last being longest, the central one being next, and the shortest occupying the two "B" positions in the ABCBA pattern.

26. W. D. Davies and Dale C. Allison, Jr., *A Critical and Exegetical Commentary on the Gospel According to Saint Matthew*, vol. 1, ICC (Edinburgh: T. & T. Clark, 1988), pp. 66-68. One can perceive that the story line does unfold as a collection of threes and tripartite stories without necessarily agreeing that the rubrics and structuring of their major headings is the most appropriate.

27. The section 2:13-23 is one unit, though broken up by formula quotations. Thus the formula quotations cannot be a structural device *on the same plane* as the triadic pattern.

28. Davies and Allison, *Gospel According to Saint Matthew*, p. 67.

29. Compare Craddock, *Luke*, p. 4, and contrast the case with New Testament epistles, which were direct communication to the first readers, but are still indirect communication to the modern reader. See Fred B. Craddock, *Overhearing the Gospel* (Nashville: Abingdon Press, 1978).

30. See Janice Capel Anderson, "Matthew: Sermon and Story," in David J. Lull, editor, *Society of Biblical Literature 1988 Seminar Papers* (Atlanta: Scholars Press, 1988), pp. 496-507.

31. Ellis, *Mind and Message*, p. 38.

32. See Ellis's detailed argument, *Matthew*, p. 32.

33. Luke 6:24-26, the woes, seems not to have been in Q but were added by the developing tradition between Q and Luke or by Luke himself. See M. Eugene Boring, *The Continuing Voice of Jesus: Christian Prophecy and the Synoptic Tradition* (Louisville: Westminster/John Knox, 1991), p. 258.

34. Davies, *Setting*, p. 307.

35. Aboth 1:2.

36. The contemporary preacher will want to respect the indicative form of the Beatitudes, and not transform them into advice or commands: "How to be happy," or "We must be peacemakers."

37. "Kingdom of Heaven," of course, is the same as "Kingdom and God," Matthew's Jewish respect for the word "God" leading him to express it indirectly.

38. Though not explicated in Matthew 1:20-24, the Matthean community knows that Jesus taught *agape*, love, to be the first and greatest commandment from its repeated hearing of Mark 12:28-34. If the interpreter considers this historical approach which takes into account Matthew's setting to be methodologically unsound, the supremacy of the love commandment would still dawn upon the reader as the justification for Joseph's conduct when Matthew 5:43-48 and especially 22:34-40 were read. In

addition, the point would be sharpened when it was discovered that the landowner of Jesus' parable in 20:1-15, who acts with amazing grace, considers his action to be δίκιος "right/just" (20:4).

39. As in the case of Joseph in Matthew 1:18-25, divorce is an appropriate example for us too. Even contemporary ministers who want to be guided by the biblical witness find themselves, in the name of both justice and love, out of step with some of the biblical precepts concerning divorce, sometimes with varying degrees of guilty conscience.

4. ROMANS IN THE PULPIT

1. See Stanley Kent Stowers, *The Diatribe and Paul's Letter to the Romans.* SBLDS 57 (Chico: Scholars Press, 1981); Stanley E. Porter, "The Argument of Romans 5: Can a Rhetorical Question Make a Difference?" *JBL* 110 (1991): 655-77. Porter argues that Romans 5 also fits the *diatribe*.

2. For an analysis of the role of "By no means!" (*mē genoito*) see Abraham J. Malherbe, *"Mē genoito* in Diatribe and Paul," *HTR* 73 (1980) 231-40.

3. Fred B. Craddock, *Preaching* (Nashville: Abingdon Press, 1985), p. 122.

4. See also Patricia M. McDonald, SHCJ, "Romans 5:1-11 as a Rhetorical Bridge," *JSNT* 40 (1990): 81-90 and Michael R. Cosby, "Paul's Persuasive Language in Romans 5," in *Persuasive Artistry* (G. A. Kennedy Festschrift), Duane F. Watson, ed. JSNTSup 50 (Sheffield: JSOT Press, 1991), p. 213. Cosby quotes *Rhetorica ad Herenium* (attributed to Cicero): *Transitio* "is the name given to the figure which briefly recalls what has been said, and likewise sets forth what is to follow next . . . it reminds the readers of what is to come" (4:26-35).

5. NRSV's "since we are justified by faith" not only fails to express this adequately but can easily be taken as a timeless principle instead of an event that "we" have experienced.

6. Commentators and translators generally agree that although most manuscripts read "let us have peace" *(echōmen)*, the minority reading is to be preferred *(echomen)*. The same variation occurs in v. 3 *(kauchōmetha)*. I do not find Neil Elliott's recent defense of the

majority reading persuasive. *The Rhetoric of Romans. Argumentative Constraint and Strategy and Paul's Dialogue with Judaism.* JSNTSup 45 (Sheffield: JSOT Press, 1990), p. 229. The same is true of Porter, "The Argument of Romans 5," pp. 662-65. This is a clear instance where quite different understandings of Paul depend on a slight difference in the text—a long or a short "o". Craddock's insistence that the preacher should establish the text is particularly important here. See *Preaching*, pp. 107-10.

7. See C. E. B. Cranfield, *Romans.* ICC I, p. 204, where representative traditions are cited.

8. Cosby, "Paul's Persuasive Language," p. 214.

9. "Does not disappoint" is probably a litotes, a deliberate, negated, understatement whose actual point is the opposite; here it means "hope keeps its promise." So also "I am not ashamed of the gospel" (1:16) = "I am proud of the gospel." For a contrary view, see C. K. Barrett, " 'I Am Not Ashamed of the Gospel,' " in his *New Testament Essays* (London: SPCK, 1972), pp. 116-43.

10. See Leander E. Keck, "The Post-Pauline Interpretation of Jesus' Death in Romans 5, 6-7" in *Theologia Crucis—Signum Crucis* (E. Dinkler Festschrift), Carl Andresen & Günter Klein eds. (Tübingen: J. B. C. Mohr [Paul Siebeck], 1979), pp. 237-48.

11. For example, John C. O'Neill, *Paul's Letter to the Romans* (New York: Pelican Books, 1975). Walter Schmithals even argued that Rom. 5:1-11 was not part of this letter at all but originally followed II Thess. 1:12. *Der Römerbrief als historisches Problem* (Gütersloh: Gerd Mohn, 1975), pp. 197-202.

12. In v. 1 Paul speaks of justification "on the basis of faith" because there he views it from the standpoint of the recipient's not earning it (as the preceding discussion of Abraham emphasized); here he speaks of justification "by his blood" because he has in view its basis, Christ's death, as 3:21-26 pointed out.

13. The "how much more" construction *(pollō mallon)* appears here for the first time in Romans. While Paul uses it also in I Cor. 12:22; II Cor. 3:11; Phil. 2:12, in Rom. 5 it is used four times (vv. 9, 10, 15, 17). The expression is not found in the Deutero-Paulines. It is used, however, in Matt. 6:30; 7:11; 10:25; Mark 10:48. Luke's *posō mallon* is its equivalent (Luke 11:13; 12:24, 28; 18:39).

14. One must therefore dissent from the claim that "Paul deliberately distinguishes justification (from sins) and reconciliation," as Neil Elliot claims in *The Rhetoric of Romans,* p. 229.

15. This accentuation is also reflected in "while we were enemies," which is consistent with reconciliation. Justification is the rectification of the relationship to God, the aligning of one's existence to the norm, but reconciliation implies prior alienation or hostility. In other words, the change to "we were reconciled" requires the appropriate shift to "enemies." Both justification and reconciliation express salvation in relational terms.

16. It is true, of course, that in I Thess. 1:10 Paul refers to the coming wrath. But it is also possible that there he is quoting tradition. In any case, the Roman reader had not read I Thessalonians! What they knew of Paul's understanding of God's wrath was what he had just written to them, not what he had written half a dozen years before to someone else.

17. See BAGD, p. 362.

18. For a more detailed discussion in terms of discource analysis, see N. S. L. Fryer, "Reconciliation in Paul's Epistle to the Romans," in *Salvation by Faith: Aspects of Pauline Soteriology in Romans. Neotestamentica* 15 (1981), pp. 34-68.

19. Given the fate of Romans 5:1-11 in the lectionaries, the considerations adduced in this discussion are especially important for those whose preaching follows a lectionary. The Roman Catholic, Episcopal, Lutheran, and Revised Common lectionaries all include Romans 5:1-11 in each of the cycles, but the text appears sometimes whole and sometimes in parts. Of the eight Sundays when Romans 5:1-11 appears in three years, the whole passage in read only three times.

5. THE REVOLUTION OF SERMONIC SHAPE

1. Richard L. Eslinger, *A New Hearing* (Nashville: Abingdon Press, 1987), p. 65.

2. Fred B. Craddock, *As One Without Authority* (Nashville: Abingdon Press, 1971), p. 5.

3. Ibid., p. 7.

4. Ibid., p. 9.

5. Ibid., p. 14.

6. Ibid., p. 1.

7. Ibid.

8. Fred B. Craddock, *Overhearing the Gospel* (Nashville: Abingdon Press, 1978), p. 135.

9. Lucy A. Rose, "Narrative Homiletics: Its Present, Past, and Future," unpublished essay, 1991.
10. John S. McClure, "Narrative and Preaching: Sorting It All Out" in *Journal for Preachers* 15, 1 (Advent 1991): 24-25.
11. Ibid., p. 25.
12. Ibid.
13. Ibid., p. 26.
14. Ibid.
15. Ibid., p. 27
16. Ibid.
17. Ibid.
18. Rose, "Narrative Homiletics," pp. 1-11.
19. Cited in Eslinger, *A New Hearing*, p. 20.
20. Craddock, *Overhearing the Gospel*, p. 137.
21. Craddock, *As One Without Authority*, p. 60.
22. McClure, *Narrative and Preaching*, p. 25.
23. Craddock, *As One Without Authority*, p. 146.
24. David Buttrick, *Homiletic* (Philadelphia: Fortress Press, 1987), pp. 333-63.
25. Ibid., pp. 292-93.
26. Henry H. Mitchell, *The Recovery of Preaching* (San Francisco: Harper & Row, 1977), p. 58.
27. Craddock, *As One Without Authority*, p. 62.
28. Ibid., p. 123.
29. Ibid., p. 125
30. Ibid., p. 62.
31. Ibid., p. 55.
32. Ibid., p. 56.
33. Ilion T. Jones, *Principles and Practice of Preaching* (Nashville: Abingdon Press, 1956), p. 93.
34. H. Grady Davis, *Design for Preaching* (Philadelphia: Fortress Press, 1958), p. 15.
35. Craddock, *As One Without Authority*, p. 54.
36. Ibid.
37. Ibid., p. 56.
38. Buttrick, *Homiletic*, p. 299.
39. Ibid., p. 301.
40. John Killinger, *Fundamentals of Preaching* (Philadelphia: Fortress Press, 1985), p. 108.
41. Ibid., pp. 108-9.

42. Robert E. C. Browne, *The Ministry of the Word* (Philadelphia: Fortress Press, 1976), p. 86.
43. Ibid., p. 87.
44. Ibid., p. 15.
45. Gabriele Lusser Rico, *Writing the Natural Way* (Los Angeles: J. P. Tarcher, 1983), p. 190.
46. Don W. Wardlaw (ed.), *Preaching Biblically* (Philadelphia: The Westminster Press, 1983), p. 11.
47. Ibid., p. 16.
48. H. Richard Niebuhr, *The Meaning of Revelation* (New York: Macmillan, 1941), p. 32.
49. William A. Beardslee, *Literary Criticism of the New Testament* (Philadelphia: Fortress Press, 1970), p. 4.
50. Ibid., p. 2.
51. Ibid., p. 4.
52. Marshall McLuhan, *Understanding Media: The Extensions of Man* (New York: New American Library, 1964), pp. 36-45.
53. Craddock, *As One Without Authority*, pp. 62-63.
54. Craddock, *Overhearing the Gospel*, p. 104.
55. Ibid., p. 137.
56. Fred B. Craddock, *Preaching* (Nashville: Abingdon Press, 1985), p. 160.
57. Ibid., p. 167.
58. Craddock, *As One Without Authority*, p. 45.

6. PREACHING AS THE CHURCH'S LANGUAGE

1. Karl Barth, *Church Dogmatics*, vol. I, part 1 (Edinburgh: T. & T. Clark, 1975), p. 4. Capitals removed.
2. Gerhard Lohfink, *Jesus and Community: The Social Dimension of Christian Faith*, trans. John P. Galvin (Philadelphia: Fortress Press, 1984), pp. 14, 71, 43. Cf. pp. 9-20.
3. Ibid., p. xi.
4. Ibid., pp. 99-100. The list is a mere sampling of passages. In the New Testament other expressions carry the same meaning: *heatos* and *heis ton hena*.
5. Ibid., p. 146 italics omitted.
6. Ibid., p. 168 italics omitted.
7. Barth, *The Preaching of the Gospel*, included in Richard Lischer, *Theories of Preaching: Selected Readings in the Homiletical Tradition* (Durham, N.C.: Labyrinth Press, 1987), p. 343.

8. Lloyd Bitzer writes: "Rhetorical works belong to the class of things which obtain their character from the circumstances of the historic context in which they occur" ("The Rhetorical Situation," in Richard L. Johannesen, ed., *Contemporary Theories of Rhetoric: Selected Readings* [New York: Harper & Row, 1971], p. 384).

9. Kenneth Burke, *A Grammar of Motives* (Berkeley: University of California Press, 1959 [1945]), pp. 3-9.

10. George Lindbeck, *The Nature of Doctrine: Religion and Theology in a Postliberal Age* (Philadelphia: The Westminster Press, 1984), p. 21, where he follows Bernard Lonergan, and pp. 16-17, 31-32.

11. Quoted in Lohfink, *Jesus and Community*, p. 1.

12. Phillips Brooks, *Lectures on Preaching*, in Lischer, *Theories*, pp. 19, 277-78.

13. Charles Grandison Finney, *Lectures on Revivals of Religion* (New York: Fleming H. Revell, 1988), pp. 1-14, 185-212.

14. Robert Bellah, et al., *Habits of the Heart: Individualism and Commitment in American Life* (New York: Harper & Row, 1985), pp. 152-55, 71-75.

15. See Wener Elert, *The Structure of Lutheranism*, Vol. I, trans. Walter A. Hansen (St. Louis: Concordia Publishing House, 1962), p. 81.

16. Barth, *Church Dogmatics* I, 1, p. 117.

17. Ibid., p. 193.

18. Ibid., p. 166. But see his "narrative" interpretation of the "Royal Man" in IV, 2 and David H. Kelsey's interpretation in *The Uses of Scripture in Recent Theology* (Philadelphia: Fortress Press, 1975), pp. 39-50.

19. William Malcomson, *The Preaching Event*, quoted in Thor Hall, *The Future Shape of Preaching* (Philadelphia: Fortress Press, 1971), p. 84.

20. Richard M. Weaver, "The Spaciousness of the Old Rhetoric," in *The Ethics of Rhetoric* (Chicago: Henry Regnery Co., 1953), pp. 178-79.

21. Stanley Hauerwas's work has been suggestive to this essay, especially "The Church as God's New Language" in *Christian Existence Today* (Durham, N.C.: Labyrinth Press, 1988), pp. 59-62.

22. Fred B. Craddock has incorporated this passage into his discussions of the problem of preaching to those who already believe. His is one of the most creative responses to the central question of this chapter: How does the church speak to itself when it has become dulled to its "distinctive talk about God"?

23. See Nicholas Lash, "Performing the Scriptures," in *Theology on the Way to Emmaus* (London: SCM Press, 1986), pp. 37-46. For a fascinating case study, see Stephen E. Fowl and L. Gregory Jones, "Living and Dying in the Word: Dietrich Bonhoeffer as Performer of Scripture" in *Reading in Communion, Scripture and Ethics in Christian Life* (Grand Rapids: William B. Eerdmans, 1991), pp. 135-64.

7. BEYOND NARRATIVE

1. An excellent review of this theory may be found in Eduard R. Riegert, *Imaginative Shock: Preaching and Metaphor* (Burlington, Ontario: Trinity Press, 1990), especially pp. 65ff.
2. See Walter Ong, *Ramus, Method, and the Decay of Dialogue* (Cambridge, Mass.: Harvard University Press, 1958) and Karl L. Wallace, *Francis Bacon on Communication and Rhetoric* (Chapel Hill: University of North Carolina Press, 1943).
3. See Edward P. J. Corbett, *Classical Rhetoric for the Modern Student*, third edition (New York: Oxford University Press, 1990), pp. 557ff.
4. Francis Bacon, *The Advancement of Learning*, cited by Corbett, p. 559.
5. Samuel Taylor Coleridge, *Biographia Literaria*. Chapter XIII, 1817.
6. See, Horace Bushnell, "Our Gospel, a Gift to the Imagination," in Conrad Cherry, ed., *Horace Bushnell: Sermons* (New York: Paulist Press, 1985), pp. 95-117. For a treatment of Bushnell's homiletics see the chapter on him in Paul Scott Wilson, *A Concise History of Preaching* (Nashville: Abingdon Press, 1992).
7. Horace Bushnell, "Preliminary Dissertation on the Nature of Language as Related to Thought and Spirit," in *God in Christ* (Hartford: Brown and Parsons, 1849), p. 55.
8. Urban T. Holmes, *Ministry and Imagination* (New York: Seabury, 1976), pp. 99ff.
9. Riegert, *Imaginative Shock*, p. 121.
10. Richard Kearney, *Poetics of Imagining: From Husserl to Lyotard* (London: HarperCollins Academic, 1991), p. 4.
11. Ibid., p. 225.
12. See John S. McClure, *The Four Codes of Preaching: Rhetorical Strategies* (Minneapolis: Fortress Press, 1991), p. 67.

13. See Thomas H. Troeger, *Imagining a Sermon* (Nashville: Abingdon Press, 1990).
14. These ideas are developed more fully in Paul Scott Wilson, *Imagination of the Heart: New Understandings in Preaching* (Nashville: Abingdon Press, 1988), pp. 32ff.
15. Kearney, p. 225.
16. Ibid., pp. 224-25.
17. See Wilson, *A Concise History of Preaching.*
18. Kearney, pp. 218ff.
19. Henry Ward Beecher, *Lectures on Preaching* (London, 1872), p. 127.

8. TEXTS SHAPING SERMONS

1. Fred B. Craddock, *As One Without Authority* (Nashville: Abingdon, third edition, 1979; first edition, 1971), p. 163.
2. See ibid., pp. 51-76.
3. Fred B. Craddock, *Preaching* (Nashville: Abingdon Press, 1985), p. 178.
4. Craddock, *Preaching,* chapter 9.
5. Thomas G. Long, *Preaching and the Literary Forms of the Bible* (Philadelphia: Fortress Press, 1989). See for instance pp. 50-52, 61-65. David Buttrick's book *Homiletic* raises the question of form from a quite different perspective, but there is an implicit suggestion that some forms are appropriate to one kind of text and some to another. Preaching in the mode of immediacy is particularly useful when preaching narratives; preaching in the reflective mode helps with Paul. David Buttrick, *Homiletic: Moves and Structures* (Philadelphia: Fortress Press, 1987). See especially pp. 333-90.
6. Much of the theological grounding for the formal concerns of this essay are to be found in David L. Bartlett, *The Shape of Scriptural Authority* (Philadelphia: Fortress Press, 1983). That book, in turn, owes a great deal to Paul Ricoeur's essay, "Toward a Hermeneutic of the Idea of Revelation," in Paul Ricoeur, *Essays on Biblical Interpretation,* ed. Lewis S. Mudge (Philadelphia: Fortress Press, 1980), pp. 73-118.
7. John R. Donahue, S. J., *The Gospel in Parable* (Philadelphia: Fortress Press, 1988), p. 5. Donahue goes on to remind us that,

properly speaking, parables—because they are so often similes—are more often metaphoric than metaphor (pp. 6-11).

8. As Craddock's analysis suggests. See *As One Without Authority*, pp. 62-65.

9. For my understanding of the poetry of the Psalms I am deeply indebted to Robert Alter's fine book, *The Art of Biblical Poetry* (New York: Basic Books, 1985). Thomas Long also very helpfully applies Alter's insights on parallelism in *Preaching and the Literary Forms of the Bible*, pp. 48-50.

10. See the fine discussion of the psalm in Artur Weiser, *The Psalms: A Commentary*, trans. Herbert Hartwell (Philadelphia: Westminster, 1962), pp. 655-63.

11. Alter, *The Art of Biblical Poetry*, p. 112.

12. On the move from third to second person discourse, see Paul Ricoeur's essay "Toward a Hermeneutic of the Idea of Revelation," p. 89.

13. There are many fine resources on using imagery in preaching. Among the most helpful are Thomas H. Troeger, *Creating Fresh Images for Preaching: New Rungs for Jacob's Ladder* (Valley Forge: Judson Press, 1982) and Christine Smith, *Weaving the Sermon* (Louisville: Westminster/John Knox Press, 1989).

14. One way of understanding David Buttrick's emphasis on the integrity of "moves" in a sermon is to suggest that a "move" works rather like a stanza of a psalm. One particular theme is presented, repeated, varied, underlined, specified. The next move or stanza may well complement or contrast with the first. See Buttrick, *Homiletic*, p. 37-53.

15. Hans Dieter Betz explores the rhetorical function of this autobiographical section in *Galatians: A Commentary,*. Hermeneia Series (Philadelphia: Fortress Press, 1979), pp. 56-127.

16. I am helped in applying this insight by Richard Thulin's book, *The "I" of the Sermon: Autobiography in the Pulpit* (Minneapolis: Fortress Press, 1989).

17. See Fred Craddock's fine article, "Preaching to Corinthians," in *Interpretation* 45, no. 2 (1990): 158-68.

18. John Donahue has been most helpful in reminding us that the parables are found *in* Gospels, for instance, and not out there floating along one by one. See *The Gospels in Parable*, especially pp. 25-27, 194-216.

19. For a history of the discussion and a proposal see Mary Ann

Tolbert, *Sowing the Gospel: Mark's World in Literary-Historical Perspective* (Minneapolis: Fortress Press, 1989).

20. I first proposed this reading for Mark's odd ending in *Fact and Faith* (Valley Forge: Judson Press, 1975), pp. 103-6. Robert Fowler presents a more nuanced argument in *Let the Reader Understand: Reader-Response Criticism and the Gospel of Mark* (Minneapolis: Fortress Press, 1991), pp. 262-63.

9. AND HOW SHALL THEY HEAR?

1. The description of the Impressionists' controversial debut is drawn from David Sweetman, *Van Gogh: His Life and His Art* (New York: Simon and Schuster, 1990), pp. 60-63.
2. Ibid., p. 62.
3. Fred B. Craddock, *As One Without Authority* (Nashville: Abingdon Press, 1979).
4. Ibid., p. 60. Italics added.
5. Ibid., p. 65.
6. Wilbur Schramm as quoted in Robin R. Meyers, *Preaching as Self-Persuasion: A New Metaphor for the Rhetoric of Faith,* unpublished manuscript, p. 44.
7. See, for example, William H. Willimon, *Peculiar Speech: Preaching to the Baptized* (Grand Rapids: William B. Eerdmans, 1992), especially pp. 47-51.
8. Emil Brunner, "Theologie and Kirche," *Zwischen den Zeiten* 8 (1930), as quoted in Garrett Green, *Imagining God: Theology and the Religious Imagination* (San Francisco: Harper & Row, 1989), p. 31.
9. Karl Barth, "Nein!" in Emil Brunner and Karl Barth, *Natural Theology* (London: The Centenary Press, 1946), pp. 79-80.
10. Ibid., p. 127.
11. David Buttrick, "Foreword" in Karl Barth, *Homiletics* (Louisville: Westminster/John Knox Press, 1991), p. 8.
12. Dietrich Ritschl, *A Theology of Proclamation* (Richmond, Va.: John Knox Press, 1960), pp. 132-33.
13. For a fascinating treatment of the rhetorical creativity of Barth himself and the essential place that rhetorical expression plays in Barth's theology see Stephen H. Webb, *Refiguring Theology: The Rhetoric of Karl Barth* (Albany: State University of New York Press, 1991).

14. Heinz Zahrnt, *The Question of God: Protestant Theology in the Twentieth Century*, trans. R. A. Wilson (New York: Harcourt, Brace & World, 1969), p. 118.
15. Green, *Imagining God*, p. 34.
16. David Buttrick, *Homiletic: Moves and Structures* (Philadelphia: Fortress Press, 1987).
17. Green, *Imagining God*, p. 149.
18. Buttrick, *Homiletic: Moves and Structures*, p. 261.
19. Ibid., p. 258.
20. Ibid., p. 259.
21. Christine M. Smith, *Weaving the Sermon: Preaching in a Feminist Perspective* (Louisville: Westminster/John Knox Press, 1989), p. 57.
22. Ibid., p. 57.
23. Ibid., p. 56.
24. Ibid., p. 94.
25. Ibid., p. 93.
26. Ibid., p. 77.
27. Ibid., p. 87.
28. Craddock, *As One Without Authority*, p. 61.
29. Ibid.
30. Ibid.
31. Fred B. Craddock, *Preaching* (Nashville: Abingdon Press, 1985), p. 44.
32. Ibid., p. 51.
33. Ibid.
34. Ibid., p. 52.

10. WHO IS LISTENING?

1. Many preachers seem to suppose that sexual impulse is a youthful proclivity largely reserved for the Reebok set, but research seems to suggest instead that to be human is to be sexual *life long*. Recommended reading: Robert Penn Warren, *The Cave* (New York: Random House, 1959), chapter 1.
2. The task is difficult for *me*. For a brilliant analysis, see Fred B. Craddock, *Preaching* (Nashville: Abingdon Press, 1985), chapter 5, "Interpretation: The Listeners."
3. Fosdick regarded preaching as a correlate of pastoral counseling: The test of a good sermon was "how many individuals wish to see the preacher alone" for personal counseling (L. Crocker, *Harry*

Emerson Fosdick's Art of Preaching: An Anthology [Springfield, Ill.: Charles C. Thomas, 1975] p. 40). Fosdick also wrote that "even when a preacher speaks to thousands, the preacher speaks to them as individuals and is still a personal counselor." ["Personal Counseling and Preaching," *Pastoral Psychology* 3, no. 22 (March 1952).

4. Edward Lewis Wallant, *The Tenants of Moonbloom* (New York: Harcourt, Brace & World, 1963), pp. 143-48.

5. Here I differ from a fine book by James Sellers, *The Outsider and the Word of God: A Study in Christian Communication* (Nashville: Abingdon Press, 1961). Sellers supposes that congregations must be addressed as "outsiders" because, though baptized, they are still secular people.

6. A rigid law/grace pattern of preaching, which sometimes is pursued in the Lutheran tradition, is difficult to maintain these days and probably cannot be reinstated. If a general sense of the presence of God has evaporated, how can we speak convincingly of a Law of God? We cannot. At best, preachers may be able to work from what Karen Horney once labeled "the tyranny of the should." See Karen Horney, *Neurosis and Human Growth* (New York: W. W. Norton, 1950), chapter 3.

7. George Herbert Mead, *Mind, Self, and Society* (Chicago: University of Chicago Press, 1934), chapter 3.

8. Edward W. Farley, *Good and Evil* (Minneapolis: Fortress Press, 1990), pp. 106-9.

9. For discussion, see Barth's remarks on the subject of sermon introductions in *Homiletics,* trans. G. W. Bromiley and D. E. Daniels (Louisville: Westminster Press, 1991), pp. 121-25.

10. The world in consciousness is scarcely an "objective scientific" world, a world without human meaning. All things are given value by human language or gesture. So, it is incorrect to suggest that things—for example money or guns—have no moral meaning *per se*. The N.R.A. seems to suppose that a gun in and of itself has no moral value because, in use, it may kill animals or be employed in target practice or act as a deterrent in a policeman's holster. No, socially intended, a gun is *for* killing, however it may be used. There are no neutral things. Everything has some sort of social value provided by human convention or language. For a profound analysis, see Alfred Schutz, *The Phenomenology of the Social World,* trans. G. Walsh and F. Lehnert (Evanston: Northwestern

University Press, 1967), chapter 3. More specifically, see Schutz, *The Structure of the Life-World,* vol. I, trans. R. Zaner and T. H. Engelhardt, Jr. (Evanston: Northwestern University Press, 1973), chapter 3.

11. H. Richard Niebuhr, *Experiential Religion* (New York: Harper & Row, 1972), chapter 2.

12. Peter L. Berger and Thomas Luckmann, *The Social Construction of Reality* (Garden City, N.Y.: Doubleday & Company, 1966).

13. Peter L. Berger, *Invitation to Sociology* (Garden City: Doubleday and Company, 1963).

14. For discussion of the "powers" within a social phenomenology, see my *Preaching Jesus Christ* (Philadelphia: Fortress Press, 1988), chapter 4.

15. As in I Corinthians 15:20-28, see my *The Mystery and the Passion* (Minneapolis: Fortress Press, 1992), pp. 58-60.

16. See Mircea Eliade, *Myth and Reality* (New York: Harper & Row, 1963), especially chapters 2 and 4.

17. I rather suppose that some neo-conservative theologians, notably George Lindbeck and the late Hans Frei, may embrace narrativity as a way of guarding Christian identity. For example, see H. Frei, "The 'Literal Reading' of Biblical Narrative in the Christian Tradition," in *The Bible and the Narrative Tradition,* ed. F. McConnell (Oxford: Oxford University Press, 1986); and George Lindbeck, *The Nature of Doctrine: Religion and Theology in a Postliberal Age* (Philadelphia: The Westminster Press, 1984), chapter 6.

18. Franklin L. Baumer, *Religion and the Rise of Scepticism* (New York: Harcourt, Brace & Co., 1960) traces the historical rise of secular culture with considerable insight.

19. Perhaps we should notice the emergence of horror films and fiction in which supernatural creatures seem to threaten our lives. They are melodramas designed to exorcise spooky otherworldliness. But melodrama can move toward tragedy and begin to reinstate the mystery of a transcendent reality once more.

20. Such a scheme is implicit in Craine Brinton's remarkable, *A History of Western Morals* (New York: Harcourt, Brace & Co. 1959).

21. See the argument in Randall Stewart, *American Literature and Christian Doctrine* (Baton Rouge: Louisiana State University, 1958), chapters 2 and 3; see also, Peter Gray, *The Enlightenment: An Interpretation* (New York: Alfred A. Knopf, 1966), chapters 6 and 7.

22. Langdon Gilkey notices both transcience and relativity in *Naming the Whirlwind: The Renewal of God-Language* (New York: Bobbs-Merrill, 1969), pp. 31-71.

23. For example, see the essays in *The Bible and Liberation: Political and Social Hermeneutics*, ed. Norman K. Gottwald (Maryknoll, N.Y.: Orbis, 1989).

24. I am somewhat influenced here by Paul Tillich, "The World Situation," *The Christian Answer*, ed. H. P. Van Dusen (New York: Charles Scribner's Sons, 1945), pp. 1-44. But see also my *Homiletic* (Philadelphia: Fortress Press, 1987), chapter 4.

25. On "paradigmatic events," see Van A. Harvey, *The Historian and the Believer* (New York: Macmillan, 1966).

26. A phrase from W. Russell Bowie's splendid hymn. We urban children know that though the Bible begins in the garden, it is bound to end up in a city!

27. Note the structure of Paul's argument in I Corinthians 1:18–2:5. First he notes the foolish, impotence of the cross (1:18-25); then he describes the church as impotent and foolish (1:26-31); and finally, he remarks that, as a preacher, he himself was weak and foolish (2:1-5). But preachers who are weak and foolish, as indeed all we preachers are, permit congregations to realize that God is the power of the gospel word.

28. II Corinthians 2:16. Paul is well aware that the gospel is bad news to those who have over-invested in "this present age."

29. We suspect that an average "good" sermon registers around 45 percent of the language. As long as the main structural movement of thought forms in consciousness, we can afford to lose a percentage of spoken words. Research seems to suggest, however, that because of homiletic error whole blocks of language may be excised. Preaching is a delicate craft.

30. On recent liberation hermeneutics, see *Interpretation for Liberation* eds. K. Cannon and E. Schüssler Fiorenza (Atlanta: Scholars Press, 1989). On the matter of feminist hermeneutic, the recent anthology *Feminisms: An Anthology of Literary-theory and Criticism*, ed. R. R. Warhol and D. P. Herndl (New Brunswick: Rutgers University Press, 1991) offers over a thousand pages of essays that delineate a feminist approach; see also E. Schüssler Fiorenza, *In Memory of Her: A Feminist Reconstruction of Christian Origins* (New York: Crossroad, 1983) and fine examples of feminist reading in Phyllis Trible's, *God and the Rhetoric of Sexuality* (Philadelphia:

Fortress Press, 1978). For homiletics, Rebecca Chopp's *The Power to Speak: Feminism, Language, and God* (New York: Crossroad, 1989) is an important book. On the matter of an African-American hermeneutic, see W. H. Stewart, Sr. *Interpreting God's Word in Black Preaching* (Valley Forge: Judson Press, 1984); S. B. Reid, *Experience and Tradition: A Primer in Black Biblical Hermeneutics* (Nashville: Abingdon Press, 1990); D. T. Shannon and G. Wilmore, *Black Witness to the Apostolic Faith* (Grand Rapids: William B. Eerdmans, 1985); plus, of course, all the many books of theologian James H. Cone, but perhaps especially, *God of the Oppressed* (New York: Seabury Press, 1975).

31. For example, see the brilliant study by Chaim Perelman and L. Olbrechts-Tyteca, *The New Rhetoric* (Notre Dame, Ind.: University of Notre Dame Press, 1969) which should instruct contemporary preaching.

11. PREACHING THE BODY

1. Fred B. Craddock, *Overhearing the Gospel* (Nashville: Abingdon Press, 1978), p. 9.
2. James D. Whitehead, "The Religious Imagination," *Liturgy* 5 (1985): 54-59.
3. Phillips Brooks, *Lectures on Preaching* (Grand Rapids: Baker Book House, 1969), p. 126.
4. Urban T. Holmes, *Ministry and Imagination* (New York: The Seabury Press, 1976), p. 87.
5. Charles Wright, "HALFLIFE/A Commonplace Notebook" *Field* (Spring 1987): 22.
6. Dietrich Bonhoeffer, *Wordly Preaching*, ed. Clyde E. Fant (New York: Thomas Nelson, 1975), p. 16.
7. Gerard Manley Hopkins, *Poems and Prose of Gerard Manley Hopkins*, ed. W. H. Gardner (New York: Penguin Books, 1953), p. 106.
8. From "God's Grandeur," ibid., p. 27.
9. Holmes, *Ministry and Imagination*, p. 8.
10. Wright, "HALFLIFE," p. 31.
11. Eudora Welty, *One Writer's Beginnings* (Cambridge: Harvard University Press, 1984), p. 69.

12. THE HEARER'S EXPERIENCE OF THE WORD

1. Fred B. Craddock, *Overhearing the Gospel* (Nashville: Abingdon Press, 1978), p. 112.
2. Fred B. Craddock, *As One Without Authority* (Nashville: Abingdon Press, 1979), p. 78.
3. Ibid., p. 85.
4. Craddock, *Overhearing the Gospel*, p. 17.
5. Fred B. Craddock, *Preaching* (Nashville: Abingdon Press, 1985), p. 218.
6. Craddock, *Overhearing the Gospel*, p. 43.
7. Craddock, *Preaching*, p. 160.
8. Ibid.
9. Ibid., pp. 170-209.
10. Ibid., p. 173.
11. Ibid., p. 71.
12. Ibid., p. 218.
13. James Russell Lowell, from "The Present Crisis," stanza 5 in *The Hymnbook* (Philadelphia: The Presbyterian Church in the U.S.A., Presbyterian Church in the United States, Reformed Church in America, 1955), hymn #361.
14. Craddock, *Preaching*, pp. 172-73.